# BEYOND
# SHELTER

WITHDRAWN

EDITED BY MARIE J. AQUILINO

# BEYOND SHELTER

## ARCHITECTURE FOR CRISIS

 Thames & Hudson

-10 miles tijuana

# CONTENTS

# PREFACE
# BEYOND SHELTER: ARCHITECTURE AND HUMAN DIGNITY

MARIE J. AQUILINO
ÉCOLE SPÉCIALE
D'ARCHITECTURE, PARIS

Two hundred million people (that's two-thirds of the population of the United States) have been affected by natural disasters and hazards in the last decade. For every person who dies, some 3,000 are left facing terrible risks. Ninety-eight percent of these victims are in the developing world, where billions of dollars in aid are absorbed annually by climatic and geologic crises. Now we are learning that extreme temperatures, intense heat waves, increased flooding, and droughts due to climate change are expected to expose vast numbers of people to the status of eco refugee, a condition that poses a real threat to human security as people are forced to migrate. Twenty million people are currently on the move in Pakistan, where torrents of mud and water have forced them from their homes. Experts are also finding that as these natural hazards increase annually in frequency and severity, the ability to protect communities once thought safe will diminish, leading to ever-greater loss of life.

In 2008 over 100,000 people died in the Chinese province of Sichuan when buildings collapsed during an earthquake. Among them, 19,000 school children were buried in rubble when unsafe school buildings failed. Suddenly questions were raised about the role of architects. Looking to assign blame, officials turned on architects to account for what had happened, and in almost the same breath turned *to* architects and engineers from around the world for solutions that would calm outraged families. A few months later in Myanmar a storm surge in the low-lying, densely populated Irrawaddy River delta called Nargis left an estimated 140,000 people dead. In Haiti on January 12, 2010, an earthquake shook poor-quality materials and construction into twenty million cubic yards of boulders and dust, interring at least 220,570 people and leaving a million and a half homeless. The number of children who perished has not been published, though half the population of Port-au-Prince was underage. Yet in an even more powerful earthquake in Chile that same year about 500 people died. The Haiti earthquake, though severe, was not the only cause of so high a toll: the other culprit was unsafe buildings.

Urgent questions about the role and responsibility of architects have been circulating since the Indian Ocean tsunami killed more than 200,000 people in 2004. At that time the relief effort exposed troubling gaps between humanitarian aid that targets the short term and our ability to rebuild homes, infrastructure, and communities well. While aid agencies are willing, they do not have an architect's knowledge or insights; consequently, the buildings that replace destroyed communities are frequently unsafe.

Unfortunately, this is as true today as it was seven years ago. However corrupt or appalling the politics (and policies) behind the catastrophes in Sichuan and Haiti, professional architects—whether in the developing or developed world—are notably absent from efforts to protect people from disaster. Yet architects have recently been very active in other areas of public interest—for example, they have instigated a range of creative strategies to improve social, environmental, and economic equity, some of which have become books about how to alter the way we think about the design process. But in extreme circumstances, in crises, architects offer no coherent response. They play no sustained role in shaping policy and have had little active presence or voice in leading best practices in disaster prevention, mitigation, and recovery. There is still no career path that prepares students to work as *urgentistes*—design professionals who intervene at a crucial moment in the recovery process to produce enduring solutions.

Which is precisely why this book is about the architects who *are* helping save lives. Innovative, fascinating work is being done by small teams of outstanding professionals in Asia, Latin America, Africa, and the United States, who are proving to be critical, relevant partners helping communities recover from disaster and rebuild. The highly skilled architects and leaders in other fields who have so generously contributed to this book are providing resilient solutions that ensure the safety of new homes and bring coherence to land-use planning. These teams assess damage but also research innovative building technologies. They are at the forefront of the use of low-cost, energy-saving, environmentally sound materials and new methods of prefabrication. They have discovered ways to bring affordable high-tech solutions to vulnerable communities. These teams are experts in how best to bridge the gap that separates short-term emergency needs from long-term sustainable recovery. And they are experienced in helping reduce future risk, promote awareness, and protect relief investment. Admittedly, this level of expertise is rare, concentrated in the hands of far too few professionals working worldwide.

*Beyond Shelter* is a call to action. When I started writing this book and searched for practicing architects skilled at working with risk almost everyone asked me the same question: why architects? As if to say, what is it to us? At the conference Risques Majeurs 2008 (Major Risks 2008) sponsored by the European Union, two or three architects were present. The officials and ministers I spoke with reminded me that on average architects contribute to only 3 percent of the world's built environment. Their indifference—or worse, irrelevance—to the world's most vulnerable communities made them seem hardly worth talking about. Three percent is a terrible number.

But if not architects and planners, who is in charge of rebuilding towns and villages leveled by earthquakes and cyclones? The answer is disquieting: no one is in charge. Typically, a patchwork of nongovernmental charities, government agencies, and residents themselves cobble together solutions. In large-scale disasters, even when aid pours in, the expertise and planning infrastructure needed to make best use of the money are lacking.

Myriad organizations worldwide respond to catastrophic events, some providing emergency and transitional shelters, others building permanent homes for hundreds of thousands of displaced people. In the last ten years the major international NGOs (Oxfam, UN-Habitat, Care, Red Cross Societies, Caritas, and others) have taken on the responsibility of properly housing people after disasters. And their efforts have led to success stories. The International Federation of the Red Cross now offers oversight and assistance to less-experienced agencies, although only on a voluntary basis. There is still no coordinated response. No one is ultimately held responsible (beyond operations within individual agencies).

As a result thousands of smaller groups play a critical role in protecting the homeless, and these vary widely in scope, competence, approach, and effectiveness. Few among them specialize in building homes or infrastructure before disaster strikes, and rarely are they screened for expertise. Worse, many of these groups do not have the capacity to judge the quality of experts they employ. Ironically, the plethora of published guides and internationally accepted standards for good practice, intended to help professionalize the sector, can just as well empower individuals who do not have the operational or technical skills to work on the ground in reconstruction. Competing mandates and donor priorities, weak coordination, fragmented knowledge, and a blatant disregard for environmental health often characterize the failed practices that prevail after a disaster, and that lead to new dangers as well as intolerable waste. More than ever there is a crucial and immediate need for architects (along with other built-environment professionals) to bring their training, competence, and ingenuity to disaster-risk prevention, mitigation, response, and recovery.

Here are just three of the many ways in which architectural know-how is critical in post-crisis situations. The first has to do with capacity. Well-trained architects who are actively building have wide-ranging experience. In addition to their ability to erect secure, durable structures, they are expert contract managers capable of calculating needs, resources, and budgets through the arc of a program. All of this helps save money and improve humanitarian action.

Representation is the second area: architects working in close collaboration with communities can help them act on their own behalf. Playing the roles of designer, historian, negotiator, and advocate, architects develop site alternatives that help secure land tenure, reblock overcrowded slums, afford better access to water, sanitation, air, and light, introduce public spaces, and improve the relationship with the local ecology. They can then represent community consensus on viable projects to intransigent or indifferent governments, and this, in turn, promotes local independence. It is terribly difficult for communities to successfully represent their own best interests in the face of intractable politics.

The third function is vision. Recovery extends well beyond the need for shelter. In a state of emergency it is difficult for desperate individuals to imagine a better future. Architectural expertise can promote public health, encourage investing in new skills and environmental awareness, and advocate for mitigating risk, which together help ensure a sustainable and safe way of life.

But for these qualities to take hold after crises, architects and planners must engage in a broader conversation, among the experts in humanitarian aid, anthropologists, conservation ecologists, bankers and economists, structural engineers, public-health officials, surveyors, and within the context of policy makers and communities. These groups also need to know whom to turn to and where to put their confidence. And practitioners—including architects—must guard against the tendency to fall into rote responses and convenient solutions. Industry-wide, good ideas and know-how succumb to habit and the need for efficiency, which may stifle the opportunity for invention. Yet architects are not only skilled technicians; they are also creative artists, and those talents are needed in such circumstances. Fresh approaches that lessen the vulnerability of fragile populations and strengthen their resilience and potential will only come from the combined resources and experience of these groups working collaboratively. Simply put, we must start speaking with others.

Open and sustained debate is also needed to hold everyone involved accountable—to produce credible solutions and coherent strategies that address the myriad problems: spatial and environmental planning, the need for vernacular and appropriate housing, the overwhelming scale of today's disasters, preservation of cultural integrity, funding streams, and how best to function on the ground. There has been a tendency in the aid community to accept massive waste as a corollary of speed; they play down the abandoned projects, the systematic demolition of undamaged homes, poor land choices, and environmental degradation that routinely accompany the recovery process. Homes have failed before anyone had a chance to live in them, and some post-disaster settlements have led to serious physical and mental-health problems for their new residents. The absence of expertise is a trespass that leaves communities more vulnerable than before. The best intentions are rarely good enough, especially if they are not scrutinized in light of their outcomes.

*Beyond Shelter* is intended to help this diverse group of decision makers understand, value, and engage architects—*as partners*—in shaping principles that respond to the growing threat of disaster risk in urban and rural settings around the world. We cannot wait. To help re-create a decent quality of life at scale is an enormous challenge. To meet it we must reinvest architecture with the capacity to be a powerful, disruptive force, a source of discovery and change.

So this is also a book for students in the design fields—to inspire and stir a passion for reform. The urgent need to afford the next generation of architects new relevance has compelled a handful of professionals to change the way we think about architectural education. At Columbia and MIT, at schools in Portland, San Diego, New Orleans, Montreal, Paris, Caracas, São Paolo, and Santiago, and at new universities being established in Japan and India, students are working on projects that revolutionize social housing, tackle poverty, segregation, and violence in cities and rethink our response to risk. These innovative programs are providing alternatives to the traditional design studios that promote self-interest and flights of fantasy—though these qualities are not in themselves bad. Rather, when aspiring architects are confronted with the real world, when they test their mettle against social injustice, and especially when they are given the opportunity to work directly with communities in need, they draw upon honesty, life experience, and fear, which unleash fresh insights and lead to highly creative solutions.

All of this is in our best interests. We who live in wealthy nations are not immune from disasters, and we, too, struggle with our own disinvested communities, inequalities, and poverty. We have a lot to learn from our poorer neighbors about dealing with crisis at home. Learning from extreme conditions in the developing world is a powerful source of creativity. Evolving risk requires new ways of thinking. For instance, the emerging use of microfinance and microinsurance, which helps increase resilience in poor communities, is bringing new business models to affluent markets at a time when the business climate is otherwise not favorable. Citizen-led reconstruction, an empowering and collaborative process that supports socially equitable development, is teaching us how to value and forge collaborations and synergistic partnerships rooted in local priorities. Streamlining costly, complex innovations has led to the development of such clever devices as portable ultrasound readers, LED lights, and point-of-origin water purifiers, as well as strategies for a low-carbon future and greater biodiversity. The strides being made to address poverty and scarcity are already improving our use of technology. Similar *trickle-up* approaches are being tested in education. And make no mistake, among the richer nations risk mitigation remains woefully neglected and underfunded. Japan stands out as a world leader in risk prevention, yet the combined impact of the 2011 earthquake, tsunami, fires, and small nuclear explosions overwhelmed preparation, leaving us dumbfounded by the troubling reality that we still ignore the need to address risks as multiple and simultaneous, and that true resilience requires an integrated system of response. Certainly, new ways of solving the ingrained problems that put us at risk will come from an array of cultures, economies, and geographies that share our desire for greater security.

What does it mean to be safe? Safety, I have learned, is not only anchored in better technologies or better buildings. Safety lies somewhere beyond shelter, in the freedom of being secure enough to relax, play, aspire, and dream for generations.

A school in Pétionville, Haiti, after the earth-quake of 2010. Nearly 5,000 schools were destroyed or severely damaged.

# INTRODUCTION
# THE ARCHITECTURE OF RISK

VICTORIA L. HARRIS
ARTICLE 25, LONDON

After a conflict or disaster are the risks people face addressed poorly by the sprawling community of disaster-relief and development specialists? Can the humanitarian sector improve the way it responds? I believe the answer is *yes,* and that better architecture and construction are crucial to tempering people's vulnerability after disasters. By *better* I mean more durable, more sound, more fit-for-purpose: buildings that serve their occupants in comfort and safety. I also mean built better, in the sense that a better process of building is followed. The building process can be improved to include training local builders, engaging local markets, and ensuring that every structure functions within a larger development scheme. Further, there are not enough good *long-term* building projects spearheaded by NGOs and donors, a situation that perpetuates vulnerability in developing communities and leads to catastrophe when natural calamities strike. Simply put: there is not enough architectural and design expertise within most organizations and agencies to address and solve this problem.

This means that architects (alongside other built-environment professionals) are vital to creating significant change in how disaster relief and development are practiced. In March 2006 Hilary Benn, then the UK Secretary of State for International Development, declared, "Rarely do disasters just happen—they often result from failures of development which increase vulnerability."[1] One of the most significant failures of the aid and development process is, quite frankly, in the unintended results of our interventions in the name of recovery.

## THE ROLE OF THE ARCHITECT

The specific skills that architects bring to post-disaster reconstruction include the ability to do more with less. The best NGOs persevere to make the greatest difference for the people they serve. During reconstruction NGOs often find themselves responsible for deploying significant funding without necessarily knowing much about construction: they are neither designers nor builders; they have no experience managing contracts; they are not sure what to expect from professionals; and they may not have the capacity to evaluate expertise.

Article 25 is a charity based in the United Kingdom that offers a design consultancy service to nongovernmental organizations, or NGOs. The staff members are built-environment professionals from all disciplines. It is a part of our mission to provide NGOs with design and construction expertise. Many NGOs come to us because construction projects have gone wrong—contractors have walked off the site, structures are inadequate or crumbling, they are over budget or past their deadline, and communities are divided over the outcome. The architect is the professional whose role it is to manage all the parties on a project. Architects are designers and builders, certainly, but they are also expert contract managers, able to see the arc of a project. Architects are the party responsible for taking the budget and resources available to a credible, pertinent, long-term built solution, along an optimal path.

This, of course, is not the popular view of an architect. At best the public sees architects as artists, at worst as superfluous—profligate spenders charged with executing the whims and fancies of a client's vision. And heaven knows the press and media outlets have not helped change this perception. If the online reader comments on an article published in *CNN Opinion* after the massive Haiti earthquake in 2010 are any indication, many people think that architects exist to "make things look pretty."[2] But now more than ever architects whom we rarely hear about are using their skills to solve problems and improve building in developing countries. This includes erecting schools and sustainable housing as well as participating in post-disaster reconstruction projects around the world.

→ When disaster does not meet development: Gujarat after the flood of 2008

→→ Micro tiles being molded locally, in Nepal

↓ Children participate in a design workshop as part of the planning process for a school built by Article 25 in Goa, India.

Architects can find solutions that make structures more efficient, cheaper, more resilient, and better suited to their purpose. They steward the hopes, needs, and funding of a client through to project completion. So, if architects are active in many NGO and government-sponsored projects, what is going wrong in disaster relief?

The answer is complex. We started Article 25 specifically to help build safer buildings in the context of development and disaster relief. If we are to take people's vulnerability seriously, we must deploy—and insist on—much greater technical expertise in architecture and construction. Architects can provide some of this expertise, but their skills are not being effectively transmitted to the workers who execute projects on-site—that is, to the permanent residents of the community who will build there in the future. George Ofori of the University of Singapore has studied the factors affecting resilience in communities after a disaster; he advocates developing "the construction industries of the poorer nations in order to equip them to manage disasters" and concludes, "It is important to enhance knowledge on the linkage between good planning, design and construction, and disaster prevention and management. A key missing element is awareness among practitioners."[3] There is significant awareness of this deficiency among the best organizations, but it has not yet led to consistent industry-wide action on the ground. We are failing to transmit expertise to the lowest practical level. This may be because there is a gap between what architects are perceived to do and what they actually can do.

If architects are much more than design experts, good design is much more than aesthetics. In the NGO sector the skilled architect can coordinate the roles of project participants, which allows members of the community—the clients or beneficiaries—to get involved in line with their abilities. The process of construction can include training, skill sharing, and creating economic benefits for local suppliers and markets.

This last is crucial: relief and reconstruction offer an opportunity to stimulate and support local businesses. Unfortunately, through lack of expertise, vision, or staff, many NGOs take the path of least resistance and use a single contractor, which often means that the economic benefit to the local economy leaves town when he does. NGOs should not miss the opportunity to bring informal markets and local labor forces into a project; this leads to reduced vulnerability by increasing future capacity, providing a more cohesive and coherent project, and affording the community a greater sense of ownership. Good community consultation and planning can be a powerful engine for change. Architects are adept at such planning methods.

These interactions need not be elaborate or fraught. In our first project at Article 25 we designed a school for street children in Goa, India. During the design process we consulted the children and teachers who would be using the facility and discovered that what they most wanted was a theater. We made a simple, cost-free change to the plan, shaping the double step at the front of the building to curve outward to form a stage. Two years after the building was completed I received a flyer advertising a performance by the children to entertain the local community and tourists in the area.

## THE EXPERTS

Before the 2004 tsunami in the Indian Ocean, architects had hardly figured in the task of post-disaster aid. But when the enormous waves destroyed homes, property, and infrastructure over vast coastal areas in eight countries, the need for shelter became an emergency on an unprecedented scale. Suddenly, reconstruction entered the disaster-relief agenda. It quickly became clear that the skills of architects were not being employed in this effort; worse, they were being neither offered nor sought. We were all caught flat-footed. Since then the profession has recognized that it has skills of critical value to long-term recovery.

Still, the number of competent architects involved in non-profit work remains small. All too frequently lip service is paid to the need for real expertise in construction and architecture while at the same time, on the ground, NGOs are putting most of their efforts into training novices to execute only basic skills. There is a plethora of booklets produced by NGOs, targeted at those with no experience or professional expertise. This serves only to promote the use of unskilled, barely trained, well-intentioned volunteers, who arrive from all corners of the globe in the wake of a disaster, at the expense of putting truly skilled best practices in play. Thus, lack of expert staffs is common in NGOs. Meanwhile, after a disaster local experts may have died or, if they are present, may be preoccupied with personal crises or in need of retraining to respond to the structural problems raised by the event.

The use of expertise should not be confused with imposing top-down solutions. On the contrary: expertise is a key tool to integrate an NGO project with a community. It genuinely brings capacity, not prescription. It also brings credibility that is vital to persuading local and national governments to act, as well as innovative ideas that communities need to better steward donor funds. Yet at conferences around the world we continue to talk about plastic sheets and lean-to structures—temporary fixes—while NGOs plow ahead without the professional skills they need to rebuild properly.

## THE DONORS

Large donors have a role to play here. Donors rarely fund the placement of innovative construction expertise in the field.

They do sometimes provide funding for basic training, but this is rarely a good idea.

It does not help that most shelter groups define themselves solely in terms of humanitarian or emergency work. They have no truck with the long-term, complex matter of building sustainable, resilient systems. Emergency funding and disaster relief are their domain. Shelter provision in these silos of practice is basic, temporary, inadequate for security, and does nothing to help restore people's livelihoods. This sort of practice, fueled by competition among agencies, impairs the human rights of those suffering after a disaster. Further, emergency humanitarian funding stops abruptly at the transitional-shelter stage, precluding long-term solutions and effectively condemning people for years to inadequate shelter.

Donors have been called on to increase funding time-scales and link disaster response to long-term development. This is wise but not easy. For example, one experienced NGO initiated a policy in 2006 that allows funding to be used over three years, where only 30 percent can be spent in the first six months. Unfortunately, in practice, the unintended result is that the emergency-shelter phase gets dragged out, while relief is still not linked to long-term reconstruction. Indeed, in practice, emergency-relief shelter groups go out of their way to exclude, even ignore, the goals of longer-term development and recovery. The three-year window, adopted by many NGOs, has become a means to extend their territory, prolonging basic emergency-shelter response long past the immediate moment of crisis and condemning communities to a protracted state of provisional shelter.

For the larger, well-known agencies emergency funding is easy to come by. The outpouring of sympathy that developed nations muster after natural disasters is usually immense; it has even sometimes forced international aid agencies to turn down donations because they lacked the capacity to deploy the huge sums available. The responsibility to resolve this quandary lies with donor nations and governments, who must take the lead in demanding that organizations seek high-value solutions, and matching their offers of funds to much longer time frames. At present, unfortunately, the opposite is common practice: donors often insist upon a term limit to a redevelopment project. They want a clear end date to be established in advance and may require that millions of dollars be spent in just a year or two. As a result money may go unspent or be returned; medical supplies are thrown out, supplies bottleneck, and resources are wasted. This is inexcusable.

An obvious way to use money wisely after disasters is to build better, safer buildings that embrace long-term infrastructural and environmental planning. It is an old truism that earthquakes don't kill people; buildings do. In a disaster the death toll is compounded by the loss of infrastructure. This is nowhere more evident than in the heartbreaking reality of the earthquake in Haiti, where critical buildings such as hospitals were lost. Donor agencies must promote safe built solutions, and this requires that they allow funds to be spent gradually, across tenacious programs overseen by international as well as local NGOs. Disaster relief and long-term development must be inextricably linked, and development opportunities assessed and insisted upon in every aspect of the reconstruction process.

## ARTICLE 25: WHAT WE DO

Article 25 is a group of architects, engineers, surveyors, development professionals, planners, communication experts, and financial analysts. For us the process of development and the process of building are seamlessly intertwined. The opportunity to use a building as a catalyst for lasting change is not to be missed in the design and construction phases. Project design is imbedded not only in building design but in how the whole construction process is coordinated. This is where architects become not only relevant, but vital.

In Sierra Leone we are developing schools. The country is extremely poor, with heavily damaged infrastructure following a civil war. Our brief was to design a new model school that would drastically improve the quality of the buildings and, therefore, education. Article 25's designs match or improve on the costs of the Plan, Care, and UNICEF models per square foot. And we go considerably further, improving cooling and ventilation systems, using space more intelligently, and addressing child safety. We also accommodate structural variables, such as allowing for the interchangeable use of either sawn timber or bush-poles collected locally during construction. As these features suggest, our designs enable community-based solutions rather than relying solely on a prescriptive, contractor-oriented approach.

Experts on the ground can leverage funding and design parameters. In Pakistan an Article 25 team member was charged with ensuring safe building practices while training the local labor force to construct the seismically resistant homes that we had designed. He had limited funding but his presence made all the difference. While the design had worked well on paper, he introduced changes that saved the budget: for example, a more-than-adequate 6 mm-gauge rebar was used instead of the proposed 8 mm rebar, reducing both transport and material costs. In a project of this nature, in remote, mountainous villages, transport can be two-thirds of the cost of materials. Having saved money on transportation, he was able to construct retaining walls on the mountain where the houses were being built. Being flexible and able to adapt to the terrain saves lives at no additional cost, and shows the leverage architectural expertise brings to a project.

Even one-off funding of a building in post-disaster development has great potential for the community. Good processes reverberate long after the cameras are gone. A recent study for the World Bank concludes that "school construction programs are irreplaceable opportunities to improve the skills of the informal sector, if they are given the opportunity to compete for local small contracts and receive *adequate site supervision.*"[4]

Maintenance is a central issue that is often overlooked by development organizations with a short-term remit. The same study also points out that the durability of school buildings in developing countries "not only results from design and quality construction, but also relies heavily on maintenance." Embedding skills and a sense of ownership in the beneficiary group can guarantee that maintenance will be managed by the local community, which thus is able to safeguard the initial investment and maximize the building's long-term utility. All too often we hear of brand-new homes, built by well-intentioned NGOs, whose upkeep was too expensive, so that they are abandoned by their residents, leaving crumbling white elephants. The opportunity to involve local small contractors and labor—and supervise them well—is another asset that the architecturally adept NGO brings to the project cycle.

## POVERTY

Despite vigorous recent arguments that development opportunities should go hand in hand with post-disaster reconstruction, little has changed in practice. We need to ask whether our task should be undertaken without addressing the root problems that contribute to the scope of a catastrophe. Root causes revolve around poverty, in many cases abject poverty, which grossly increases people's vulnerability to catastrophic events. Peoples living in countries low on the United Nations Human Development Index are far more likely to live in unsafe, poorly built, poorly located accommodations, and are far less likely to have the resources to cope with or recover from catastrophic pressure.

Poverty is every bit as much a disaster as an earthquake or tsunami. But it is long, slow, and drawn-out, an emergency missing the initial precipitating event. Antipoverty development should be higher on the global agenda, but it makes for poor media copy compared to a sudden and horrifying single event such as a natural disaster. The "CNN Effect," in which relentless news coverage of an immediate and vivid event stimulates mass interest in it, affects the perception of a need for action. For example, by February 2005, one month after the Indian Ocean tsunami, the international community had donated $500 per person affected by the tsunami, compared to the $0.50 received for each person affected by Uganda's eighteen-year war.

Further, not taking *anthropic* risk into account leaves people in harm's way. Countries recovering from human-created disasters fall into a game of Russian roulette, to use the phrase of the economist Paul Collier of Oxford University. After a civil war ends, he explains, in the poorest countries there is a one in six chance that a nation will return to war within ten years, because a critical demographic, young men, are left out of recovery planning.[5] Effective post-conflict reconstruction can address this directly. Reconstruction is a programmatic, systemic task, not a surgical intervention; it is labor-intensive and as such can generate livelihoods. Building builds capacity builds security. Building fundamentally reduces vulnerability.

## PAYING THE WAY

Collier is able to comment effectively on this because he is well-equipped to assess incentives, risk-and-reward scenarios, and market forces. We measure the development of the poorest countries—the bottom billion—with the UN's Millennium Development Goals, eight rules of thumb that remind us of

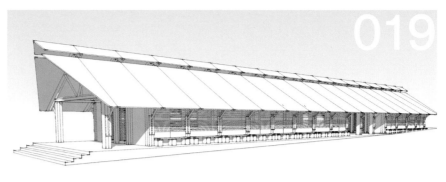

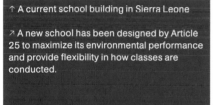

↑ A current school building in Sierra Leone

↗ A new school has been designed by Article 25 to maximize its environmental performance and provide flexibility in how classes are conducted.

← An earthquake-safe house with a reinforced timber frame and corrugated galvanized iron roof under construction in Jareed, Pakistan, 2008

↙ / ↓ A house in Bagh, Pakistan, using the same construction techniques and shown at later stages. The walls are of timber, mud, and stone. A roof-truss ridge and wall-plate column, features designed to withstand earthquakes, were added by the architect on-site.

↑ The courtyard of the Nkoranza Children's Home and School, in Nkoranza, Ghana

→ The Children's Home and School, built by Article 25, replaced a dilapidated area school.

→→ Schoolboys in Nkoranza working on their own design for the school. Article 25 developed the final design with community input.

what we would like to achieve as a global society by 2015.[6] Every goal implicitly depends on a building: schools are required for education and hospitals and clinics for health care. Alternative proposals—for instance, those that favor open-air education or street-corner schooling—are a vain and idealistic hope. A UNESCO report found that "outdoor learning may have been a viable emergency expedient in India when it was a newly emerging country [but] the 'no building' solution is unsatisfactory. . . . schools without their own building . . . tend to have low attendance and those who do attend are inclined to have a poor academic performance."[7] A World Bank study in Ghana showed that simply improving the physical quality of school buildings—mending leaky roofs, for example—improved math and literacy scores by over 2 standard deviations, or more than 97 percent. This improvement is greater than what was achieved by providing basic teaching equipment such as blackboards. The report argues, "A cost-benefit analysis . . . shows that repairing classrooms (a policy option ignored in most education studies) is a cost-effective investment in Ghana, relative to providing more instructional materials and improving teacher quality."[8]

At present the way emergencies are handled and funded militates against mitigation and sustained recovery. It is in the interest of the global economy to get disaster relief and development right, yet we do not assess the risks correctly; changes in the way donors fund post-disaster recovery and in the way organizations allocate the funds received are critical if we want to increase the investment in expertise over time. Currently, risks associated with short emergencies—precipitating events— are usually prioritized over long emergencies such as endemic poverty. Consequently, we do a poor job of assessing risk in relation to ongoing issues such as livelihoods. We prefer to respond to sudden emergencies; we attend to them psychologically and so are drawn to overreact to event-driven disasters, while overlooking long-term crises like HIV/AIDS and other diseases, poverty, or ongoing civil unrest. Donors focus too exclusively on emergency relief precisely because they are only human, but our indifference to the larger and longer emergencies perpetuates them. As a matter of principle, the project cycle of any development or relief effort should include capacity building.

So, if we are not good at evaluating risk, should it be done impartially, using a formula? Financial managers use a simple option-pricing equation, Risk = Hazard x Vulnerability, to analyze ventures. This equation has been adopted by researchers in other disciplines, but development and shelter practitioners usually see it as an analogy and not a strict mathematical relation to be applied directly to their work. They are mistaken. $R = H \times V$ can be illustrated in the simple act of buying a lottery ticket. The Hazard (in this case a good hazard) is winning the lottery. The Vulnerability is the chance of winning—one in fourteen million in the UK National Lottery, for instance. This means that multiplying Hazard by Vulnerability shows us that a fair purchase price for a ticket, if the jackpot is £7 million, would be 50 pence (i.e., £7 million x 1/14). On a rollover week, if the jackpot is £14 million it would be fair to price the risk at £1 per ticket and it would be reasonable to risk £1 in this case. This example shows that risk assessment can be a fairly precise calculation if the Hazard and Vulnerability can be well-quantified. Development specialists can benefit enormously from bringing in skills that are not part of their core set. These may well come from economists, who can optimize the costs and benefits of interventions, as well as from built-environment professionals.

Article 25 was founded on the premise that development, and construction in particular, should be brought to the fore as an integral part of disaster-risk reduction and emergency relief because decreased vulnerability to disaster depends on resilience—on having a long-term solution. One of the keys to resilience is a lasting physical fabric. As natural and man-made disasters increase—and they are on the rise—it is our responsibility to provide the means of mitigating vulnerability.

It seems so obvious. But I still find myself asking, will we be lucky *and* smart? Will we be able to look back, for example, on our current work in Haiti and say, for the first time, yes, we have taken the ethos of resilience truly to heart? At the time of the earthquake, former president Bill Clinton was appointed UN special envoy for the island; on January 14, two days after the event, he wrote in the *Washington Post,* "As we clear the rubble, we will create better tomorrows by building Haiti back better: with stronger buildings, better schools and health care."[9] This is not a trivial responsibility; taking "better" to heart means that NGOs must require that the expertise of built-environment professionals be at the forefront of rebuilding efforts. We must change our approach to building to consider *how* as well as *what* we build. If we intend truly to build back better and leave safer communities there needs to be a sea change in the way humanitarian work is carried out. It would be terrible if the billions of dollars in disaster-relief funding that are going to Haiti only leave people at greater risk.

Notes

1   "Reducing the Risk of Disasters—Helping to Achieve Sustainable Poverty Reduction in a Vulnerable World: A DFID Policy Paper" (London: Department for International Development), March 2006, 1.

2   "Building Houses to Resist Earthquakes," posted online on February 3, 2010, at www.cnn.com/2010/OPINION/02/03/cross.quake.resistant.housing/index.html?hpt=C2, accessed July 12, 2010. The article, an interview with Robin Cross of Article 25, describes the work of the organization in Pakistan and its plans to assist in rebuilding Haiti.

3   George Ofori, "Construction Industry Development for Disaster Prevention and Response," paper delivered at the 2nd International Conference on Post-Disaster Reconstruction: Planning for Reconstruction, Coventry, UK, April 22–23, 2004, online at www.grif.umontreal.ca/pages/i-rec%20papers/ofori.pdf, accessed July 12, 2010.

4   Emphasis added; see Serge Theunynck, "School Construction Strategies for Universal Primary Education in Africa: Should Communities Be Empowered to Build Their Schools?" (Washington, DC: International Bank for Reconstruction and Development/World Bank, 2009), 32, 125.

5   See Paul Collier et al., *Breaking the Conflict Trap: Civil War and Development Policy* (Oxford, UK: Oxford University Press, 2003); and Paul Collier, *The Bottom Billion* (Oxford, UK: Oxford University Press, 2007) and further bibliography cited there.

6   See www.undp.org/mdg/basics.shtml.

7   John Beynon, *Physical Facilities for Education: What Planners Need to Know,* Fundamentals of Education Planning series 57 (Paris: UNESCO, 1997), 18.

8   Paul Glewwe and Hanan Jacoby, "Student Achievement and Schooling Choice in Low Income Countries: Evidence from Ghana," *Journal of Human Resources* 29, no. 3 (1994): 843–64.

9   Bill Clinton, "What We Can Do to Help Haiti, Now and Beyond," *Washington Post,* January 14, 2010, online at www.washingtonpost.com/wp-dyn/content/article/2010/01/13/AR2010011304604.html, accessed July 12, 2010.

Community brick-making in Gujarat, India

# PART 1

# ARCHITECTURE AFTER DISASTER

"We presented an alternative plan that underscored the wisdom of allowing residents to rebuild where they lived."

# LEARNING FROM ACEH

ANDREA FITRIANTO
UPLINK, JAKARTA

## THE BACKGROUND

On Sunday, December 26, 2004, at 8:45 in the morning, a powerful earthquake, measuring 9.2 Mw, struck Banda Aceh and other coastal cities in the Aceh province of Indonesia.[1] The massive tectonic shift at the bottom of the Indian Ocean displaced a body of water that traveled at the speed of a jet airliner to the coasts of Thailand, Bangladesh, India, Sri Lanka, Somalia, and elsewhere in east Africa. The city of Banda Aceh, some 6 miles (9.7 km) from the quake's epicenter, was hit the hardest, weakened first by the earthquake and then washed away by a wall of water 65 feet (20 m) high. There was nothing left of the original coastline for 3 miles (5 km) inland. The tsunami devastated one third of the city, took 128,000 lives, and displaced a half million people.

I arrived in Banda Aceh, just out of architecture school, three days after the catastrophe, as a member of an emergency-response team sent by the aid organization Uplink.[2] We joined the largest humanitarian effort in history. Initially, our team delivered food and medicine to refugee camps and organized stress-relief activities for adults and children. Later, we worked on housing reconstruction and advocacy.

The scale of destruction in Aceh shocked the world. Media coverage galvanized global sympathy and support for the affected communities. Money started pouring in. This was both good and bad. In a very short period of time there was so much money that the process of recovery quickly became complicated, competitive, and suspect.

Further, it led the Indonesian government to begin very large-scale planning. As early as February 2005 the National Development Planning Agency banned all construction within a mile and a half (2.4 km) of the coastline. Initially, the government intended to relocate the mass of affected populations to a new, modern city to be built inland, southeast of Banda Aceh. The plan amounted to a statutory eviction that would seize the coast for future development. Uplink campaigned intensely in Jakarta against the forced relocation. We presented an alternative plan that underscored the wisdom of allowing residents to rebuild where they lived. The government's plan was so unpopular that it was dismissed outright after two months of debate

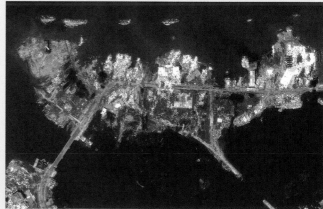

1.1
LEARNING FROM ACEH

ORGANIZATION
UPLINK

PROJECT LOCALE
BANDA ACEH, INDONESIA

and no new city was built. A replacement policy was developed, addressing the main urban population but not the smaller, difficult-to-reach villages in remote areas on the urban periphery. As a result in April 2007 Misereor, our donor partner in Germany, asked us to stay on and gave us a grant to carry out a comprehensive, people-driven reconstruction program in those villages.

## EARLY MEASURES, BACK TO THE KAMPUNG

The Indonesian government called on military personnel to construct 190 temporary barracks throughout Aceh and Nias to replace the provisional, short-lived tents that had been supplied in the first weeks of the emergency. The army was fast and efficient but paid little attention to individual or community needs. Site selection, for example, was based on fear of new tsunamis or quakes, and on keeping people away from the coast. The barracks were so remote that refugees could not return to work or help reconstitute their villages. Aceh is rich in

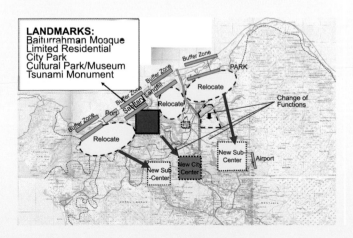

(previous spread) Banda Aceh, Indonesia, after the tsunami of 2004

←← Banda Aceh, before and after the tsunami

↑ Residents returned to Asoenanggroe village, near Banda Aceh, in February 2005. Little remained at the site but debris.

← The Indonesian government's original 2005 relocation policy for the displaced coastal residents of Banda Aceh required them to move inland.
Yellow = high-density urban populations
Red square = existing city center
Pink square = proposed new city center

Reconciling these two opposing logics—building back better and working quickly, with the rhythm of the people—is the most important challenge architects and planners face in post-disaster reconstruction.

natural resources but had been ravaged by twenty-five years of civil war that had pitted the government's army against GAM, the Free Aceh Movement.[3] There was a long history of civilian abuses by the military, so the local people distrusted the army and had little faith in its ability to oversee aid or rebuild fairly.

Moreover, humanitarian aid was delivered literally to the front door of victims, an act of misguided kindness that exaggerated the people's sense of dependency and lack of self-confidence. In fact the majority of tsunami survivors in Aceh were adult males who were working and therefore not in the *kampungs* (villages) when the tsunami struck.[4] Very few aid initiatives recognized their potential. In the first year these men were systematically excluded from the reconstruction process; their knowledge of community life and their physical capacity to rebuild their villages were largely ignored. This was terribly unfortunate, as one of the most productive ways to temper psychological trauma is to engage people in positive collective action. What's more, cash-for-work programs were adopted by some of the larger agencies, including Oxfam: villagers were paid in cash for clearing the land of debris and preparing it for reconstruction. But there was no viable monitoring system, so fraud and corruption were widespread. As soon as villagers learned to speak the language of money there was no reason to actually do the work. It was as if a second tsunami had hit the communities. The careless aid delivery and misused funds undermined the survivors' confidence, initiatives, and self-reliance—nonphysical assets that had been spared by the waves.

Uplink's approach to the reconstruction effort was significantly different from that of the government or the larger international aid agencies. We worked with disadvantaged communities along the city's western periphery, toward the hills of Ujung Pancu. Initially, the zone comprised fourteen communities in adjacent villages. The site had served as the base camp for GAM before the tsunami, and although the

insurgents were gone it became a sort of ground zero for those left out of the formal aid program. The first step was to return people to their kampungs and protect their land from appropriation, whether by the government or by other residents from the area. We provided tents and food and set up a communal kitchen. The majority of official supplies were distributed only to the authorized camps, so we delivered basic necessities on-site and encouraged survivors to focus on rebuilding.

## BUILDING BACK BETTER

Planners and policy makers like to talk about "building back better," but long into the process at Aceh this phrase remained more a slogan than a practice. Delays in planning, especially at the government level, inhibited the sort of spontaneous initiatives that can emerge from real need. Planners following a conventional approach failed to consider that tsunami survivors wanted to reconstitute their lives as they had been before. Reconciling these two opposing logics—building back better and working quickly, with the rhythm of the people—is the most important challenge architects and planners face in post-disaster reconstruction.

To overcome this contradiction we moved the Uplink planning desk into the field and joined the villagers. (We continued to maintain an office in Banda Aceh as well.) We were looking for a solution on-site. The first facility we built that spring was in the middle of an empty landscape, a temporary *meunasah*, or traditional community center. In 2006 we replaced it with the first major new permanent building. The open inside space served as a headquarters for further planning by the community.

The community center was intended first and foremost to help manage the intake of aid from donor and government agencies and forge a sense of common ground among the various communities in the area. Using the center as our base, on March 7, 2005, we assisted in the formation of an organization called Jaringan Udeep Beusaree, or JUB, a "network for living together." The JUB, which later grew to include twenty-six affected communities, played an indispensable role. Not only did members animate and coordinate the reconstruction process, but they acted as a counterpart to our presence as an external (albeit Indonesian), aid organization. JUB administrators were elected locally, and weekly meetings served as a forum where problems and solutions were shared and collective decisions taken. The entire experience was new to the participants, who had barely known one another prior to the tsunami. The JUB also helped restore the social infrastructure by establishing other community organizations. We quickly learned from the JUB that "building back better" means much more than building better facilities; it is fundamentally about building better relationships. For a local community to take such a strong leadership role is still rare in disaster recovery.

## TEMPORARY SHELTER

Together with the provisional community center, Uplink installed temporary shelters, made out of recycled materials, to replace the tents. These served as reliable protection and helped survivors move quickly from emergency aid to recovery. Their form and placement were chosen with community participation.

Many of the larger international organizations, such as the International Organization for Migration, provided prefabricated shelter units made outside the country. These were not only expensive, but prevented aid from being rooted in local investment. The prefabricated designs were ad hoc, and the units were time-consuming to assemble. It took the International Red Cross and Red Crescent societies six months to start distributing shelters. These prefabs were of two types: one, made from imported light steel frames and wood panels, cost $4,500 each. The other, prefabricated concrete modules, were too brittle to be earthquake-safe. And neither model included instructions for post-emergency use or disposal. As a result abandoned temporary shelters all over Banda Aceh became common, sad reminders of how easy it is to waste money and resources.

Community labor provided by the JUB collected tsunami debris timber and recovered and straightened nails, which Uplink recycled for new construction. Recycling encourages efficiency. We also distributed corrugated metal sheeting and additional nails. In five months we built 450 temporary shelters in twenty-three kampungs with almost no external help. Our goal was to provide temporary shelters that addressed a range of urgent needs—environmental, economic, psychological, and social.

## COMMUNITY SURVEY AND MAPPING

The first step in the reconstruction process is a community survey. Community surveys and maps form the basis of a reliable database. Base maps are not only crucial for planning; they also help avoid future land disputes, unjust land distribution, and, in the worse cases, inadvertent exclusion of the most vulnerable survivors. Accountable, equitable surveys, based on community participation and created with transparency, serve as the basis for reconstruction. A typical community survey identifies and describes all residents of the area. At the Uplink site listing the status of each individual was slow because some families had been scattered into barracks, away from their homes. But once the list was complete and signed by a kampung representative it became the reference for the next step: the needs assessment.

Making maps is also a key early task. Kampung maps formed a bridge from the community's past to its post-tsunami future. Collective memory of the kampungs as they had been before the disaster becomes part of the document. Individual kampung members used their map to assert their assets in the village. Using the kampung maps we made a scaled map and then a digital topographic survey of each kampung that recorded, among other details, the traces of floors and foundations of buildings largely erased by the tsunami. Survivors then marked out plot boundaries, using these traces as guides. The land survey also identified plots that had been deformed or lost to the sea or that had become part of a new coastline. People who had lost plots were given land from the common holdings of the community.

## KAMPUNG PLANNING AND MITIGATION

Post-tsunami spatial planning was developed with the JUB. Our spatial plans involved providing better access to roads and escape routes as well as clear vistas toward the sea and hillside. We wanted to bring the beauty of the natural setting back into kampung daily life. The concept for a kampung master plan was based on the traditional principle of *gampong loen sayang,* or "my beloved kampung," a philosophy that emphasizes the need to balance environmental, cultural, and spiritual life by minimizing the impact of human presence. The program therefore incorporated tree planting, eco-farming, green architecture, green energy, and a sound sanitation system. A mitigation plan was put in place to raise awareness of the risk of natural hazards, which required that we sometimes modify the disposition of the kampung slightly. For example, culs-de-sac were removed but the road networks, which help maintain a strong sense of place, were preserved. We paid particular attention to agricultural lands. Houses were placed according to the reconstructed pre-tsunami village plan but owners, while required to respect the rules for easements and offsets, were free to decide their actual position.

## HOUSE DESIGN

We started designing houses with individual owners four months after the tsunami. The sessions were particularly well attended by women, who were very enthusiastic about participating in the designs and worked closely with Uplink's architects. This did not happen by accident. From the outset we had been especially concerned to represent women's needs and priorities. But in the beginning only men had attended community meetings; women were excluded, and looked on from outside the meunasah. Uplink then insisted that women be present at all community gatherings. The men resisted but soon accepted the idea.

Since Indonesia is prone to tremors, earthquake safety was the main focus of house design. With Misereor we brought in architects and engineers from Hunnarshaala, a technical-assistance NGO based in Bhuj, Gujarat, India. The Indian team had helped with the recovery there after a big earthquake in 2001, leading owner-driven reconstruction. The size of each house was fixed at 388 square feet (36 sq. m), the standard set by the Aceh reconstruction authority. In the first stage two landed houses (that is, not raised on stilts) with different options for the orientation of the roof were approved. At this point residents were adamantly opposed to traditional stilt houses. As it happens, the traditional wooden-stilt Acehnese house, with its thatched roof, is well-adapted to local conditions: it is not only climatically efficient, but earthquake-safe. The light construction and the flexible footing allow the house to sway freely,

↖ The temporary community center in Cot Lam Kue village was an open-walled shelter with an elevated floor. We held our early planning sessions here.

← The new community center was built in an Acehnese style on raised pylons and with a steeply pitched roof.

↑↑ Prefab temporary houses provided in 2005 by the International Organization for Migration continue to litter the Aceh landscape.

↑ Maps and models reconstructing destroyed villages gave residents the chance to establish where their houses had been.

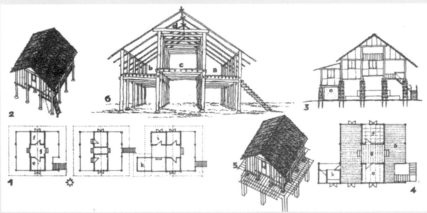

↑ A landed (ground-level) house under construction

← A traditional Acehnese house, raised on stilts and with a steep peaked roof of thatch

→ The five house designs included reinforcement to resist earthquakes, such as wind braces and concrete footings. They were publicized with plans, drawings, models, and descriptions posted at the community center.

→→ Villagers making stabilized soil-cement blocks

absorbing shocks. However, most people no longer build traditional homes. The modern house, with its masonry walls, concrete columns and beams, ceramic-tile floor, and earthen-tile roof, is a creature of urban design, unfortunately often fatal during an earthquake or tsunami.

Working with community members Uplink's architects developed five models of earthquake-safe modern homes (with different floor plans) that would suit people's daily needs. Despite resistance we felt strongly that raised houses on stilts were the best basic form. In addition to their capacity to withstand earthquakes, stilt houses respond well to the local climate: air seeps up from under the floor, lowering the indoor temperature. Raised houses are as well-suited to fisherman as to farmers—the two principle professions of the region. The ground level can be used for storage, as a work area, or as a playground for children. It provides a semiprivate space where members of the kampung can gather and reinforce their sense of neighborhood. We raised our houses 6 ½ feet (2 m) off the ground to keep the floor dry during monsoons and protect coastal homes from high seasonal tides.

Still, stilt houses were a hard sell. We constructed pilot homes in several kampungs and promoted them with printed T-shirts. We invited community members to visit the model homes and talked about their advantages. Owners quickly realized that although 344 square feet (32 sq. m) was slightly smaller than the promised landed house (a cost-saving measure), the raised design meant that each family would effectively get double the floor space.

## BUILDING MATERIALS

The most difficult problem we faced was how to acquire building materials. In the aftermath of the disaster there was a high demand for brick, cement, steel, and wood. The market for wood risked putting terrible pressure on the forests in Aceh, potentially causing a secondary environmental disaster. Clay, sand, gravel, and stone were harvested at rates that will take two generations to replace. Uplink purchased wood from a certified workshop in Kalimantan, in Indonesian Borneo. We also

bought everything we thought we might need in bulk early in the process. This was critical. The construction boom doubled the unit cost of homes in one year (from $3,000 in 2005 to $6,000 in 2006). As a result many projects were forced to radically decrease the number of houses they had promised.

We were largely able to avoid the price hikes and keep the cost of each house under control. We avoided contractors, who often use subcontractors, which adds expense to the process. Instead we asked owners to find the best deals for building materials and accessories. The JUB provided storage and set up a distribution system within each community, making kampung members responsible for keeping materials secure and in good condition. Conventional red bricks take a lot of time to prepare and must be baked, which uses considerable energy. As an alternative Hunnarshaala taught our communities to produce a stabilized soil-cement block using a simple press. Pressurized blocks take fourteen days to make, use a small amount of cement, and are environmentally sound. To operate a press requires five people (often women), which assured temporary employment within the kampungs. Uplink also established community-based workshops where owners received training in steel rebar construction and rehabilitated salvaged steel for reuse.

## CONSTRUCTION MANAGEMENT

Home owners were responsible for managing the construction of their houses. Each kampung formed a committee for housing construction and infrastructure. The grant from Misereor was allocated to families and paid in two parts. Labor costs were granted at 10 million rupiahs (about $1,100) and materials rated at 26 million rupiahs (about $2,900). Labor costs were reimbursed at the end of each of four stages of building: substructure,

wall, roof, and finishing. Building materials were distributed using a voucher system. A set of cards was given to each home owner; each card represented a particular building material and defined the quality and quantity needed, as determined by Uplink experts. Home owners gave the card to the selected material supplier at the time of delivery. Local suppliers were used, a practice that increased accountability and reinvested aid in the community.

In the first round we constructed one house in each village. We used the pilot house as a sort of classroom for villagers. In the second round the kampungs each took on construction of twenty to forty houses, depending on local capabilities and managerial skills. We found that although participatory reconstruction, tied to community development, is slow in the beginning, it picks up speed with experience, becomes efficient through training, and is sustainable precisely because time is invested in developing experience and skills within the community.[5]

Technical assistance was essential. To ensure that the new houses would meet higher safety and quality standards, Uplink's young engineers lived in the community. Each engineer was responsible for two or three villages. We also sent architects to supervise construction. We trained home owners to assess the quantity and quality of building materials and act as monitors and building inspectors. To further ensure a good minimum standard of skill and knowledge, we offered training sessions for builders.

## WHAT WE LEARNED

Uplink turned the project over to the individual communities in February 2007. We finished 3,500 houses, twelve community centers, and one mosque in two years. Because we had involved the community from the beginning there was no need for an

← Uplink's owner-constructed houses on the Aceh coast

↓ New stilt houses in the village of Lam Isek

exit strategy. For example, management of brick and rebar factories was transferred to the JUB.

Housing in Indonesia had traditionally been the responsibility of the community until, after the tsunami, the government and private sector took over the role of building homes. Unlike so many of the international aid agencies that swept in after the disaster, we asked the tsunami survivors to help design and build their homes with our assistance, shifting the process of post-disaster reconstruction back to the people.

This decision may seem trivial but it was crucial to being accepted and respected by the community. Our offices in Banda Aceh were open to villagers twenty-four hours a day, seven days a week. They were modest structures, without air-conditioning, that doubled as our home. We never drove SUVs into the kampungs. Our personnel used road motorcycles and bicycles. Community groups often view aid agencies with a good deal of suspicion. To overcome this, successful reconstruction involves the survivors from the outset and a well-coordinated strategy includes local institutions. In spite of civil war Aceh has maintained its traditional institutions and has numerous associations (religious and secular)—such as fishermen's groups and savings groups—with whom we formed productive relationships.[6]

In reality master plans are cumbersome; typically, they are too slow and rarely keep pace with the work accomplished on the ground. We find that it is more productive to disseminate a very short list of principles than to design a master plan. We used community meetings, popular media, T-shirts, posters, and leaflets to communicate and reiterate Uplink's principles of advocacy, organization, and networking. In the end, together we re-created infrastructure, revived the local economy, reinforced social relations and cultural cohesion, enacted policy change, and helped regenerate the environment by replanting mangroves and training villagers in eco-farming. Our experience in Aceh demonstrates that trust in the people's resilience and wisdom—even in extreme crisis—is crucial to any successful intervention.

## LOCAL WISDOM

We are the sea people born at the sea, we live at the sea, so we will stay here as our ancestors did. They were born and buried here.
—Mr. Baharuddin, age 45, resident of Lam Teungoh village, Aceh, 2005

A tsunami had struck Aceh once before, in 1907, inundating the small island of Simeulue, off Sumatra. So in 2004 the people of Simeulue knew that they should run into the hills when they saw the sea withdraw suddenly and flocks of birds flee toward land. Unfortunately, the people of the town of Lhok Seumaweh, on Aceh's northeast coast, hurried to the beaches to collect the fish stranded by the receding waters, unaware of the danger, and were drowned. The oral traditions of an isolated and ancient people are lost to urban communities like Lhok Seumaweh. Indigenous Acehnese knew the warning signs of a tsunami, as certain as people in rural Vietnam recognize a coming typhoon in the motions of the bamboo tree.

As we enter a new and uncertain world, in which nature is less predictable and climate change threatens more frequent and severe natural crises, we should afford these ancient ways of understanding nature more respect in the processes and practice of disaster mitigation. For local wisdom is indispensable.

Notes

1   For further reading see Bruno Dercon and Marco Kusumawijaya, *Two Years of Settlement Recovery in Aceh and Nias: What Should the Planners Have Learned?* First Asia-Pacific Housing Forum: Social Practitioners Meet the Market on Habitat Matters, Singapore, September 24–26, 2007; and Abdul Jalil et al., *The World Bank–Financed Reconstruction of the Aceh Land Administration System (RALAS)*, International NGO Forum on Indonesian Development, 2008.

The Indo-Australian Plate collides with the Eurasian Plate at the Sunda Trench, to the south, off the shore of Sumatra. The accumulated energy occasionally erupts as an earthquake.

2   Founded in 2002 Urban Poor Linkage, or Uplink, is a network of nongovernmental and community-based advocacy and development organizations in thirteen Indonesian cities, dedicated to improving conditions for the urban poor through public policy and grassroots programs. Our strategy is based on advocacy, organization, and networking. In Aceh we deployed social-services and technical teams to assist in immediate relief efforts as well as longer-term reconstruction. We committed ourselves to a small territory within the area affected by the disaster and insisted on a holistic, integrated approach, from providing food and shelter to rehabilitating livelihoods. We have found that our approach saves precious time and resources typically allocated for intersector and interorganizational coordination. And we close the gap separating the aid organization from the community it assists. Uplink is affiliated with the Asian Coalition for Housing Rights, ACHR, and a member of the Habitat International Coalition, HIC, an independent, international nonprofit alliance of organizations working on shelter and housing issues. In 2008 our project in Aceh won the Dubai International Award for best practices to improve the living environment.

3   One of the few blessings of the tsunami was the peace agreement reached between the Indonesian government and GAM. The accord, which was signed in Helsinki on August 15, 2005, significantly helped facilitate aid delivery and other field activities.

4   The region where Uplink was working suffered a 23 percent mortality rate, the highest in the country: two women died for every man killed; children under nine and people over seventy were disproportionately victims.

5   A survey by UN-Habitat and Syah Kuala University in Banda Aceh found that Uplink's houses performed best in quality and owner satisfaction. See www.unhabitat-indonesia.org/newsletter/07/index.html, accessed August 21, 2010.

6   Savings groups, common in much of the developing world, act as informal banks and may be empowered to offer loans. Typically, the community's money is managed by designated trusted members.

"Our common efforts must serve to assure that…the world's most vulnerable people can access tools and techniques, ideas and innovations, strategies and solutions to build better futures."
—Judith Rodin

# BEYOND SHELTER IN THE SOLOMON ISLANDS

ANDREA NIELD
EMERGENCY ARCHITECTS AUSTRALIA,
SYDNEY

On April 1, 2007, a powerful earthquake hit the Western Province of the Solomon Islands; a tsunami followed. Thirty-six thousand people were displaced, 6,000 homes destroyed (8,000 damaged), and 165 schools were either leveled or left in need of extensive rebuilding. Fortunately, most people were outside, saw the tsunami coming, and took to higher ground. Only sixty-five people were killed, a number far too low to attract international media attention or much in the way of outside aid. The combined force of the flood and the quake also caused severe environmental damage. Closest to the quake, which measured 8.1 Mw, Ranongga Island was lifted up by some 13 feet (4 m). The reefs suffered major trauma; there were landslides and flooding; and subsistence farms and fish stocks were destroyed. Aftershocks were felt for months. When Emergency Architects Australia (EAA) arrived in April anxious residents were living in tents and settlements. In contrast to the tremendous response to the devastating Indian Ocean tsunami two years earlier, which had galvanized the world, it seemed that no one was going to help these remote communities recover.

In a state of emergency it is nearly impossible for desperate individuals and communities to imagine a better future or to carry out the detailed planning required to restore a sense of normality to life. Architects can be instrumental in helping them make the transition from the emergency phase to long-term redevelopment. They can promote comprehensive planning, safer building and habitation practices, and better access to clean water and sanitation, which in turn can lead to economic and ecological improvements.

The aim of Emergency Architects is to bring technical aid to victims of natural and human disasters, initially building for safety and securing the population but also assisting it in post-disaster reconstruction programs that focus on long-term recovery.[1] Our core principles are a fundamental respect for the values and needs of the communities we assist; accountability; and professional, well-researched advice. We also support, train, and guide volunteer professional architects, who work with us on-site. In our view it is imperative for architects to include post-construction conditions in their area of responsibility: to promote good health, recycling, and local skills; and to ensure manageable and cost-effective maintenance, material supply, and risk mitigation, which together ensure resiliency. Working in situations brought on by catastrophic events, architects must be more than technicians. We have the capacity and training to provide a coordinated vision if we are willing to develop projects collaboratively with those we intend to help.

In the Solomon Islands, Emergency Architects Australia developed an incremental response, working with the government and partner NGOs. Steps included mapmaking and surveys, damage assessment, and workshop demonstrations, all of which led up to designing building and constructing prototypes. We also seized the opportunity to initiate a school infrastructure program. We wanted to show villagers and government ministers alike that well-conceived remedies would make communities stronger—an approach that deepens and broadens as the process develops over time. Our architects and their technical assistants remained in the background, giving the islanders the know-how to rebuild for themselves. Our low profile allowed them to think beyond the world's neglect and take pleasure in acquiring self-sufficiency.

## PREPARATION

Based on a rapid assessment (completed in the first days), the EAA team produced a basic report, including satellite images and news feeds from various sources, outlining the location and extent of the damage. We then recruited aid professionals whom we knew in the disaster zone and Australian architects and engineers who had worked in the Solomon Islands. Since a typical new house cost about AU$2,000 and an islander's average annual income is around AU$200, fund-raisers were held to get us under way. Project funding also came from World Vision, Caritas, and the French Red Cross. Planning and design work were donated.[2]

For the first six months Gizo Island, the provincial capital, was our base camp and research center. From here we evaluated the level of destruction in neighboring villages and islands, reported on population security, and identified the actions to be taken by the follow-up team. During the assessment period we also taught workshops on why earthquakes happen, demonstrated how to set out and square up a salvaged building correctly, and how to pull and jack shaken structures that were habitable but leaning severely. Homes had failed because of poor foundations; there was no cross-bracing between the posts and the bearers were poorly tied. We wrote a manual with simple diagrams showing residents how to restore a building's bracing and fix its footing problems by pulling it back onto its piles—a particularly effective method for restoring buildings in earthquake zones. Residents also learned how to remove and safely bury damaged asbestos sheeting.

Three local carpenters acted as community teachers for the workshops. They were given EAA backup teaching materials and assisted by three EAA architects, who fielded questions. Construction tools, donated by partner agencies, were taken to each site. In some cases, where feasible, we brought lumber (taken from sustainable forestry projects) to islands whose timber trees had been decimated. To reach small villages scattered over many islands is a logistical challenge; nevertheless, in the first two months we were able to reach some seventy village clusters on twenty-two islands with one or more of these services.

1.2
BEYOND SHELTER
IN THE SOLOMON
ISLANDS

043

ORGANIZATION
EMERGENCY ARCHITECTS AUSTRALIA

PROJECT LOCALE
SOLOMON ISLANDS

(previous spread) / ↑ The 2007 earthquake and tsunami leveled traditional homes as well as concrete structures.

↓ House designs were developed with the community, combining specific cultural requirements with sustainable materials.

↓↓ Members of a community collaborate on rebuilding.

→ / ↘ Traditional houses in the Solomons are raised on piles and have steep thatched roofs and curved eaves. They are constructed of tied posts and locally grown thatch. Sago palm or bamboo is used for the roof and walls.

## BEYOND SURVIVAL

For the new houses an EAA architect, David Kaunitz, worked closely with communities to design a type that combines specific cultural requirements, such as roof-ridge details, with sustainable materials. These homes had to be affordable not only to build but to maintain. He drew up simplified construction drawings with attached cutting lists. The lists allowed home owners either to go into the bush, buy trees, and cut them to size with a chainsaw or to order the lot from the local lumberyard. Women were also given training in basic construction techniques and how to read drawings. During construction women carried most of the tools and materials, including timber. Therefore, timber sizes had to be adjusted to their strength. We also paid women to make lunch at the site, which encouraged their husbands to assist with the construction and gave families a little extra income.

Together with local carpenters we built demonstration homes on the two islands that had suffered the worst damage. The design was a simple elevated, extendable house with an outside bush kitchen that local people could build under any site conditions. Prototypes are important, as they allow us to confirm whether people have adequate cutting and building skills and if they can easily obtain and transport basic supplies such as nails and screws. Prototypes also help us assess the level of the community's determination to rebuild. For example, in Keigold, on Gizo Island, the community built a fine house that they now use as a community clinic; a similar structure on nearby Tappari had still not been completed three years later. Commitment and good organizational structure in a community are important to a successful reconstruction process.

There was an environmental advantage in reusing all the buildings, or salvaged materials from buildings, that we could safely save, and this was a priority. The Solomons are timber country and protecting their trees is essential, so it's better to salvage wood than to use new stock. Unfortunately, the plantation timber grown in the Islands is mainly for export; moreover, these are nonindigenous, fast-growing softwoods. The majority of footing and piling timbers for homes had to be termite-resistant hardwood, but hardwoods have become scarce. After the earthquake the situation was worse. In addition to lack of wood, several communities did not have enough roofing leaf (sago palm fronds are used for thatching) or none at all. Leaf thatch is more sustainable, easier to maintain, and much cooler than the inferior imported corrugated-iron roofs. In the Solomon Islands every tree is owned by a member of the community, who sells it for general use. It is then in the seller's interest to replace that tree, so we made every effort to encourage the replanting of indigenous hardwood and leaf trees.

## REBUILDING SCHOOLS

This initial housing demonstration program was a success. Once we had provided training and architectural advice, other NGOs with a focus on construction distributed materials for about 6,000 homes. As a result communities asked the Ministry of Education and Human Resources Development (MEHRD) to allow us to establish a process that would help them replace 165 schools that had been damaged or destroyed. The ministry established the Reconstruction and Rehabilitation Program to determine the extent of damage and cost of additional supplies. The program permitted any community whose school had been destroyed to ask for drawings for a similar or appropriate building type; rebuilding was to be carried out communally. One hundred and ten schools were identified for replacement or renovation.

With approval from the ministry we selected Ngari, on Gizo Island, as a site for prototype school buildings. The residents there were planning to transform their primary school into a community high school, so it was a good moment to build a new structure. The school had an excellent headmistress, a well organized Parents and Citizens Association, an actively involved community, and an excellent site for expansion.

To begin with, a demonstration school was built by four EAA architects with the local community. They finished it in twelve weeks, in December 2008. In 2009 two more EAA architects were added to the team and dormitories, a dining hall, and teachers' houses were built over the course of six months. Local carpenters, trained by the team, became project managers for subsequent construction.

Subsequently, classrooms have been built in over 100 schools and more than fifty dormitories are in progress or slated for construction; new schools continue to be erected.

We were well aware that these communities might again face extreme events on their own, so the prototypes were designed to withstand earthquakes and other natural disasters. The designs accommodated traditional building techniques, local culture, and available materials. As part of the design process, we held workshops with stakeholders, including local engineers in Honiara (the national capital) and in the Western Province regional office. A volunteer design team in Brisbane sketched up the recommendations made in these meetings and added master-planning best practices. The sketch designs were then reassessed in workshops with the directors of the schools.

The Solomons comprise 922 islands (one-third uninhabited) scattered over 460,000 square miles (nearly 750,000 sq. km) of ocean, and with a combined land area of 11,200 square miles (29,000 sq. km). The archipelago is 1,200 miles (nearly 2,000 km) from the coast of Australia. In short 60 percent of the cost of materials is in transportation. Our designs had to use as few imported materials as possible. The imported louvered glass windows that had previously been utilized in schools had

shattered during the earthquake, cutting the children's feet as they escaped. So instead of glass, the new classroom windows were woven of palm leaf using traditional patterns and techniques normally found in mats. The weave is strong and flexible in high winds and provides a mellow light and good cross-ventilation. For school dormitories we employed wooden shutters instead of woven windows to make the rooms somewhat more secure. Room walls in dorms were woven to allow both airflow and privacy. Families in the villages have now adopted shutters as part of their local vernacular style.

In Tatiana, on Gizo Island, brightly colored houses were built for teachers, and these, too, used wooden-slat shutters, woven-mat windows, and steep woven-leaf or metal roofs, and were raised on stilts. The village had completely disappeared in the tsunami, so residents were reluctant to return until they understood that their new homes would be built on higher ground.

Planning for the school program was completed in early 2010. The Ministry of Education is now prepared to roll out 800 new schools throughout the archipelago. This is a remarkable example of how disaster response can generate a resilient program for an entire country. Under normal circumstances there would not have been the impetus or the international funding to go forward with such a large project.

## LATRINES

Moving villagers to higher ground meant they could no longer use the beach as a public lavatory. Safe and sanitary toilets had to be built and accepted in the new villages. For instance, on Ranongga Island the earthquake had sent the village of Mondo into the ocean, so the replacement village of Keigold was sited in the center of the island, where residents no longer had access to the sea for washing. In June 2009 EAA began

↖ A team of community members pulls a new thatched roof into place on a boys' dormitory in Ngari.

↑ / ←← Weaving the roof for a dormitory takes many hands.

← / ↙ Dormitories feature reinforced bracing for stability in an earthquake, and louvered windows with wooden slats.

↓ In Tatiana roof leaf had been destroyed, so corrugated metal was used for a teachers' house.

→ / →→ One of the latrines built for the new village of Keigold. These are simple structures, placed at a short distance from housing.

↓ Students celebrate their new school with new uniforms, hand-sewn by their mothers.

a village latrine-building program at the request of Keigold's particularly proactive community. The construction, which we funded with an Australian engineering nonprofit called Partnership Housing, took three weeks and involved fifteen students from the University of Queensland and two from Lae, Papua New Guinea. The students helped build fourteen back-vented latrines. Ranongga Island communities have since taken over the program; to date fifty-four latrines have been built and the designs have been made available. The importance of the hygiene program should not be underestimated: something as simple as hand washing radically improves local health. A paid project manager, the local alderman, was given an e-mail account to keep us updated on the project's success and any problems. We have found that access to modern means of communication (the Internet, mobile phones) is essential for independent local action.

## MONITORING AND EVALUATION

It is EAA field practice to keep a team working continuously in a community during a program to ensure that best building practices are learned and maintained. We also want to be sure that the community has a reference point for questions and can make changes to the prototypes we have designed that are pertinent to their lifestyles, while still being safe. This practice also maintains momentum. Each team evaluates its completed project before leaving. A formal evaluation answers a set of questions: are the buildings suitable for their use? Have they survived weather, insect attack, and seismic events? Are they well built? Are they cost-effective? Is the community motivated to continue the reconstruction process? Are all the materials used sustainable? Can we make the timber sizes smaller or reduce the amount of timber needed? Is maintenance being done? Are there improvements that the community now feels should be incorporated into the designs?

A program is not considered ready to hand off to the local community until these questions have been answered satisfactorily. If some components call for improvement, the process for addressing them is handled by EAA staff with a local manager. For example, the communities preferred that schools not have large verandas, so that pupils would not loiter there after classes.

EAA works in many post-disaster sites worldwide. Our project in the Solomons offers a particularly clear example of how a collaboration with local people can take hold and evolve. Melanesians still endure a subsistence economy, with few amenities and no electricity. But despite the depredations of storms and logging, trees are still abundant there. The people, who have the skills and desire to be self-sufficient, were willing, engaged partners in every aspect of the reconstruction process. They came, with firm opinions, from all sectors of community life. In Ngari, for instance, mothers thought their children should take pride in their new school, so they designed and sewed new uniforms. As we worked we saw the Parents and Citizens Association becoming stronger and more active as a result of the collaborative process.

## GRASSROOTS PARTICIPATION

Aid is only as effective as the extent of grassroots participation. No reconstruction process should be undertaken without consulting and working locally with communities—not only at the outset but throughout a project. Working this way we learned a tremendous amount about local building practices and traditions, and about the rich association and sense of ownership Solomon Islanders have with their environment. We also

A great percentage of the world's population, particularly in remote locations, builds without guidance or access to specialized expertise and then fends for itself in an emergency.

uncovered widespread use of dangerous building materials such as asbestos, left behind by colonial powers and grossly promoted by religious organizations, aid agencies, and commercial companies. Before the colonial period there had been good building traditions that involved bracing and tying homes with bush rope to resist earthquakes, but the tradition had been lost. To successfully complete a reconstruction project, one must tease out all of this information, and take it into account in building design and execution. The history of building in the Solomon Islands explains why recent structures fail so often in an area prone to natural disasters.

A strong civil society is also critical to a successful program. More and more, empowered communities in the Asia-Pacific are demanding the right to take responsibility for and participate in the reconstruction process, with support from their government. Emergency Architects Australia has an important role to play in this movement to self-sufficiency, beyond simply helping work up designs or assisting in rebuilding. We must also be advocates, experts assisting these communities to find viable, safe, pertinent solutions that improve their quality of life—just as we would for paying clients.

## REBUILDING

For agencies like ours, which work to reconstruct the built environment in disaster zones as well as to encourage long-term recovery and development, the world is split in two: there are countries with disaster insurance and those without it. Historically, insurance is only available, even possible, in countries with planning laws, legalized land-ownership systems, and minimum building standards, which are not only well-established but implemented and enforced with inspections. Without these prerequisites most insurance companies consider insuring any

building too risky. Obviously, subsistence communities cannot pay premiums, let alone conform to building standards, many of which are incompatible with their building methods and use of materials. What's more, quality materials are often either unavailable or far too costly. In general, standards are written for a modern supply chain and standardized environments.

The communities of the Solomon Islands use tried-and-tested historical methods; sometimes these are reliable and well adapted to the environment, but sometimes they are corrupted by inappropriate colonialist materials and practices or lead to environmental degradation, such as rampant deforestation. Introduced materials such as asbestos have been used widely, with no recognition of the health risks they pose. The widespread use of concrete is also problematic. Concrete is a difficult material that requires adequate curing and correctly placed reinforcement. It is very easy, too easy, to use in ways that make it weak, unreliable, and dangerous, yet it has the appearance of great durability. In this region it is popular because it is cheap and associated with western standards of living, but most builders lack the education and training to build safely with it, let alone to an earthquake-resistant standard.

This problem is not confined to the Solomon Islands, of course. A great percentage of the world's population, particularly in remote locations, builds without guidance or access to specialized expertise and then fends for itself in an emergency. In a large-scale catastrophe national and even international support is often short-lived and the solutions offered short-term. In responding to disasters we constantly face a difficult question: when is it critical to assist affected peoples and when can the community recover on its own? The issue of dependency is vexing: outside aid may itself retard the growth of self-sufficiency and be an underlying cause of failure to develop. In my view risk prevention and mitigation are the sole means to enable communities to overcome cycles of fierce weather and disaster risk. So we work toward these goals. But Emergency Architects is itself dependent on the willingness of a state or national government to ask for external professional assistance. Countries such as India and China are internally self-sufficient and generally able to manage disasters without outside assistance. But smaller, poorer nations require help, especially in zones where catastrophic weather is frequent but insurance virtually unheard of. Our experience has taught us that the only way to help promote safety is to reinforce the capacity of these communities to rebuild independently.

## MAKING PREVENTION WORK

The most notable challenge we face in our work is, surprisingly, not a question of materials or techniques, but the fundamental lack of collective memory. The magnitude and devastation of even a large-scale natural disaster is forgotten within a generation or two. To counteract this forgetfulness, building skills and construction methods can be ritualized to keep memory alive. In highly seismic Japan, the Shikinen Sengu (Reconstruction) Festival, in which the Ise Shrine is rebuilt completely, is held every twenty years. The shrine is thus rebuilt, using the same methods employed since the seventh century, in every generation. Repeatedly rebuilding an earthquake-resistant structure, in this case an important religious artifact, ensures that these essential skills remain in the community. In Haiti, where few severe earthquakes have occurred in the past 200 years, most people had forgotten the toll they can take. Earthquake-resistant building techniques, particularly in timber, were replaced with reinforced concrete. In January 2010 the powerful earthquake that struck the island was rendered far more lethal by poor construction and corrupt practices that ignored earthquake loads; a lack of

schools to teach good engineering and construction practices compounded the problem. As many as 300,000 people died and much of the built environment in and around the city of Port-au-Prince was destroyed. Notably, many of the timber buildings survived.

## CONSTRUCTIVE AID

Our work in the Solomon Islands has taught us that evolving, collaborative efforts to rebuild communities after disaster can lead to sustained change. For this to happen we must remember that communities are living systems that may shift direction. One of the advantages of architects working as volunteers and advocates in the context of emergencies—rather than as a commercial enterprise—is that we can act independently and transparently, without our own or in-country governments coercing us into politically expedient results. Our role as architects is to advocate for people, to develop alternatives that promote safety and health, and to push for collective political action. As long as international assistance remains episodic, with external teams rolling in when there is a crisis, there will be little money and even less political will to invest in mitigating potential hazards before they happen. Greater emphasis must be placed on self-management, independence, and local ability.

Our experience in the Solomons has forced us to leave behind earlier models and principles that we had thought would always guide our work. As a result EAA has a new relationship with our neighbors. We, too, have evolved with those communities with whom we have had the opportunity and pleasure to work.

Notes

The quotation on p. 41 is from Judith Rodin, President's Letter, in *Smart Globalization: Benefiting More People, More Fully, in More Places* (New York: The Rockefeller Foundation, 2008), and online at www.rockefellerfoundation. org/uploads/files/03a6dd2d-2292-466e-9a21-8e92af518d58.pdf, accessed December 28, 2010.

1   Founded in 2005 Emergency Architects Australia is an accredited nonprofit agency and a signatory to the Australian Council for International Development (ACFID) Code of Conduct, with tax-deductible status as an international organization. We respond to disasters in the Asia-Pacific region and are part of a larger network of Emergency Architects, together with Architectes de l'Urgence, France, and Emergency Architects Canada. We provide humanitarian assistance in times of disaster, armed conflict, population displacement, and protracted crisis according to internationally agreed-upon standards and principles for ethical practice.

2   I would like to thank my colleagues on the EAA architectural team in the Solomon Islands: for rapid assessment, Patrick Coulombel (Architectes de l'Urgence) and Nielsen Warren; for early school design (MEHRD–EU Stabex), Peter Braun and Antoinette Wickham (program directors) and Guy Luscombe (EAA); David Kaunitz, in-country project director and workshop architect; workshop architects Jon Crothers and Tricia Helyar; workshop partner agencies World Vision, the French Red Cross, and Caritas; and for the school drawing teams, James Davidson (Brisbane) and David Rapaport, Nicolas Ewald, Simpson Associates (Sydney).

"Getting the affected
families involved in
creative work had a
positive effect on
their mental health after
the loss and grief they
had experienced."

# NEWS FROM THE TEARDROP ISLAND

SANDRA D'URZO
ARCHITECT AND POST-DISASTER
SHELTER ADVISOR, PARIS

After the tsunami of December 2004 I spent nearly three years, from February 2005 through December 2007, on the so-called Teardrop Island, Sri Lanka, off the southern tip of India. My eyes have randomly recorded moments and changes that occurred during this dramatic period of destruction and rebuilding. Now, in 2010, the mud-color ocean of the early days has turned again into a turquoise sea, tons of bricks and mortar have become new schools and homes, governments have changed, and most of the aid agencies have left town.

My mission started in Tangalle, a small village nestled into the south coast of the island, where the tsunami had struck hard. As a shelter advisor for Oxfam Great Britain, a large NGO with a long-term presence in the country, I was asked to develop a shelter strategy in the immediate aftermath of the tsunami's vast destruction, which affected some 900,000 Sri Lankans. At that point families were living under plastic sheets or in tents; our task was to offer them more comfortable and lasting alternatives—not only in Tangalle but throughout the southern coastal region. We knew that we faced an unprecedented collective effort. To provide longer-term housing we needed to identify suitable available land on which to build, but there were complex property-ownership issues, the scale of destruction was terrible, and the government had imposed a no-build buffer zone extending as much as 650 feet (200 m) inland from the sea. It was necessary, therefore, to establish a transitional shelter phase that would bridge the gap between the emergency relief provided in the first days and weeks and permanent housing and settlement reconstruction, which we could expect would take years to complete.

The strategy was to work alongside communities, prioritize their needs and aspirations, and identify the most vulnerable groups to assist in the first phase. This meant working hand in hand with providers of other technical aspects of relief, such as water, sanitation, and health care. Responding to social concerns, respecting cultural values, and strengthening indigenous and local skills were no less important to the process.

The Oxfam team onsite included architects and engineers. We started a pilot project in Tangalle in winter 2005, constructing seventeen transitional shelters for families considered the poorest of the poor—people with no friends or relatives to stay with immediately after the disaster. The pilot homes were built in the main public park of the village, which enabled the community to maintain ties with the neighborhood and access services and support. The site was prominently visible, the perfect showcase for a replicable model. Over the course of the first two months community meetings with residents and local authorities gave rise to the final design and the initial group of houses. We opted for a mix of timber, corrugated-metal sheet roofing, cement blocks, and other materials, keeping in mind that all elements were meant to be dismantled and reused in the future for permanent housing. Timber joints were bolted and floor tiles could be easily removed. The government's shelter policy had also established that no solid foundation could be excavated, and that the costs of materials and labor should not exceed $600 per unit. In addition to the shelters, families were given solar-powered lanterns and smokeless stoves (designed to reduce fuel use and the health hazards of cooking smoke).

Although professional engineers and site supervisors ensured quality control, a large part of the construction work was carried out by the families themselves. Additional skilled labor came from members of the community. We offered on-the-job training, especially to women, so that they could develop new skills. Training not only helps provide future income but gives people a sense of pride and control, which is desperately needed after a disaster. We also established incentives that encouraged families to transform the shelters into homes. For example, we provided a toolbox and training sessions to assist residents to produce their own rough

ORGANIZATIONS
OXFAM GREAT BRITAIN AND GTZ TSUNAMI
HOUSING SUPPORT PROJECT

PROJECT LOCALE
SRI LANKA

furniture. An image surfaces in my memory: Sumangali, a young Sinhala woman, at first quite shy during these hands-on construction sessions, telling me excitedly, "Before, I didn't know how to hold a saw; now I can build my own house!" I soon realized that getting the affected families involved in creative work like this had a positive effect on their mental health after the loss and grief they had experienced.

During the construction of the pilot shelters, we produced a video in partnership with a local Sri Lankan training agency. In it ordinary people tell their stories while they lay the foundation of their new lives. Once families were installed in their shelters we showed the documentary so that they could see what they had gone through, what they had achieved, how they were collectively healing. I was worried that our film would disappoint them, but it was a real success.

In a second phase, from March through July 2005, Oxfam built almost 2,000 transitional shelter units in various locations along the east and south coasts of the island. A key to the project was to avoid a one-size-fits-all approach; we developed tailored designs for families of different sizes that responded to varying climates and to urban and rural environments; designs also adapted to the particular skills, expertise, and materials available in each community. It made sense, for instance, to use thatched roofs where people knew how to work with *cadjon* (coconut leaves). In some places cement bricks were very expensive, while fired-clay bricks were locally produced and cheaper. Changing the construction typologies had little impact on the delivery schedule as long as everyone—Oxfam, the local authorities, and the beneficiary communities—agreed to these choices in advance. Overall, we were able to diversify the approach, be flexible, and reduce costs.

But the real key was to listen to the displaced families and empower them to make the choices they preferred. We were

(previous spread) A man looks out of his destroyed house on the south coast of Sri Lanka, soon after the tsunami of December 2004.

↑ A woman places a solar panel on the roof of her transitional shelter on the rural east coast of Sri Lanka, near Tagalle. All families received solar-powered lanterns to improve lighting.

Many resettlement houses were abandoned because they were too far from the coastline.

# Why do we reinvent the wheel at each disaster, when shelter needs are so predictable?

there to provide technical guidance and specific advice. Village development committees played an important role in mobilizing communities and bringing their vision forward. Community involvement in site planning reduced the risk that new villages would be abandoned as unusable, while care was taken that site orientation would respect the crucial rules of Vastu Shastra (traditional Hindu principles of design and architectural alignment). Although only temporary solutions, these shelters housed people for almost two years. Thus, some of the choices we made in the early days had an impact on the long-term quality of their lives.

Despite encouraging results, questions were raised concerning the overall program: if Oxfam's approach was correct, why did we build only 2,000 transitional homes out of the total 50,000 needed in the country? Could we have built faster? Were there no preexisting models of timber houses that we could have adapted to gain precious time during the emergency, rather than devoting extensive time to design and planning? In short, why do we reinvent the wheel at each disaster, when shelter needs are so predictable?

In September 2007, hoping to find some concrete answers, I returned with a team from Oxfam to Tangalle and other locations where we—and many other organizations—had built transitional shelters.[1] We were asked to do a survey of housing schemes that would give a broad overview of the building technologies used by the various suppliers of housing and analyze them from environmental, financial, social, and cultural perspectives.

The village park had been cleared of the temporary homes and I was heartened to know that the residents had moved on to more permanent houses. The entire coastline in the south had changed shape. Not only in the designated zones, but everywhere, small and large relocation sites had sprung up haphazardly, with endless rows of houses—some intended to be temporary, others more permanent. These were for people who had lived inside the buffer zone before the tsunami and were not permitted to return. Those who lived farther from the sea had rebuilt their own homes, incorporating the shapes and colors that distinguish the architecture of this island.

Unfortunately, many of the resettlement houses in the approved areas looked empty and abandoned in one manner or another. Families forced to move beyond the buffer zone had ignored the ban and returned to their shacks along the coast, where they could keep an eye on their boats and nets, instead of living far from the sea. The nicely built houses that we had struggled to put in place were kept as a dowry for daughters or treated as an asset that could be rented out, but they were not for living in.

Life in the region was back again. The papaya vendors displayed their fruit, the restless *tuc tuc* drivers strolled up and down the Galle Road that hugs the coast, the pungent scents of ginger curries and dried fish drifted in the air, and young couples met to walk along the shore. It surprised me to see groups of boys peeling off their school uniforms to head for a swim in the ocean—something they would not have dared to do the year before.

My return coincided with the work that GTZ, a German aid and development organization, was doing to support the Sri Lankan national and local authorities.[2] Its objective was to assist relevant agencies and officials to become more effective managers of the reconstruction process, raise the level of their expertise, and ensure that they would be better prepared for future disasters. From the outset local government agents had been overwhelmed by the hundreds of NGOs that had poured into the country from all over the world with little coordination or oversight. These had enthusiastically begun building all along the coast, each according to its own standards or no standard at all. The local authorities had no idea what was going on; nor did the various aid groups coordinate.

In order to avoid conflict within a community, it is essential to balance the assistance given those directly affected by the crisis with assistance for their neighbors, who are perhaps affected only indirectly but in most instances suffer, nonetheless, from poor living conditions.

Settlements named after donors sprang up everywhere: the Irish Village and the Turkish Village became brand names rather than new neighborhoods.

Not only the principal international aid agencies, but also well-meaning bankers from Europe and the US, Sri Lankan manufacturers, religious foundations, and other groups with no expertise or experience in development work were pouring money into the country by way of the flourishing reconstruction industry. Of course, they provided tsunami survivors with new homes, but it became crucial to establish common standards that would also ensure equity among the haves and have-nots. To assure an equitable response within an existing population in a disaster-affected region is the constant dilemma of post-disaster work. In order to avoid conflict within a community, it is essential to balance the assistance given those directly affected by the crisis with assistance for their neighbors, who are perhaps affected only indirectly but in most instances suffer, nonetheless, from poor living conditions. Our survey was intended to assess the quality of the wide range of housing stock now in place. The team included a Sri Lankan architect, a German engineer, and Sri Lankan architecture students. We reviewed twenty-five examples in depth and produced a catalogue that mapped houses built with conventional construction techniques, others that had introduced earth-based materials, those with metal-frame structures, and those that combined prefabricated elements with whatever materials were available. The survey was intended to assist Sri Lanka's national authorities to judge what was working well and what was not, advocate appropriate building technologies for specific regions, and encourage their use beyond the immediate post-tsunami rebuilding efforts.

Our analysis was informed by visual checks, desktop reviews of technical drawings, and direct interviews with engineers, site supervisors, contractors, and program managers.

This allowed us to cross-check information and garner the support of the responsible agencies, who were keen to share their approaches and willing to acknowledge weaknesses. For example, houses built by a famous Asian architect, which combined a timber frame structure with good-quality stabilized soil-cement block as infill, were technically fantastic but culturally alien; they were rejected by their residents and immediately sold or rented. When some recipients of such aid are able to turn their donated homes into financial assets, this can create unforeseen tensions and conflicts within a community. The design had an open, flexible plan—a closed core for kitchen and sanitation with rooms divided by several sliding panels, which improved natural ventilation. But the families the houses were built for come from a Muslim fishing community, and these houses were wholly inappropriate—"Too open, madam!" a home owner frankly admitted to me. The beauty and benefits of the solution were doomed quickly to disappear behind the confined masonry walls that each family would almost certainly add to make the design suitable to their lifestyle.

Another agency had chosen to use reinforced prefabricated polystyrene panels assembled on site, a Canadian technology that is rapid to build, well-insulated, and cost-effective when compared with more labor-intensive techniques. Here, the problems started when sand and cement mortar were applied to the panels—a normal step in the construction process. It would have been easiest to spray the panels using a special machine, but the pebbles and chips that constituted the locally available mixture were too big for the imported machinery to handle. The technology was new and no one could yet guarantee its performance, so repair, care, and maintenance were real concerns. In the end people who wished to add a room or cut a new window had to do it by using a traditional infill system. The capacity of the design to convert from transitional to permanent housing was therefore very limited.

← "Microwave ovens": transitional shelters in Batticaloa, built with climatically inappropriate materials and on flood-prone land

↓ Studying the plans of a safer permanent home under construction in Sri Lanka

As we surveyed the area it was clear that a lot had been accomplished in two years: the commitments to international solidarity by a plethora of agencies and NGOs had produced concrete, visible results. At the same time a close look at twenty-five different projects revealed that the reconstruction process brought unequal assistance to beneficiaries, provided failed structures that collapsed before being handed over, and raised myriad serious social and technical concerns.

In July, two months before my return, GTZ had been asked to help improve building practices. The challenge was to ensure the same standards of quality for all, in line with existing rules and guidelines for coastal reconstruction established by the National Housing Development Authority and Urban Development Authority, the relevant agencies of the Sri Lankan government. These standards had been fixed soon after the tsunami, but in the chaos and urgency of first response a great deal of construction had gone forward without attempting to meet them, and the volume of work was such that they could not police all the activity.

Our catalogue did not rely on subjective criteria for the quality of houses, but provided a definition of *quality* as a common denominator that expressed and met minimum requirements. Some agencies have their own methods for quality control but others, with less technical expertise, face problems with contractors and unskilled laborers that may jeopardize the quality of projects. A set of standards and measurable indicators was established through a holistic approach that assessed much more than mere construction.

For instance, properly executed foundations, structures, and roofs were considered essential to the durability of a house. But now sustainable water sources, sewage systems, and solid-waste disposal were no less relevant. Cost-effective housing schemes, social well-being, and environmental choices also contributed to the final quality rating. In a second survey we assessed a much larger number of houses and settlements. The team agreed on a scoring method for each component and subcomponent. Data management was eased by a partnership with the IT department of the University of Ruhuna, which set up a database to elaborate scores and provide feedback with visual tools and diagrams. Once the criteria and measured scores were entered for a house or settlement, a sustainability graph was generated by the database program that depicted each project in clear visual terms. The larger and more centric the graphic, the more sustainable the housing project.

The database and its associated software, called the Quality Assessment Tool, had a dual outcome: on the one hand, it enabled technical offices, field managers, and beneficiaries to identify poorly designed settlements and underperforming buildings; on the other hand, it highlighted good practices in housing technology, energy efficiency, and sustainable development. Thus, in addition to identifying good and bad structures, it was useful in building construction capacity.

A testing phase was launched in the Matara District, where the survey assessed some 3,000 houses. The same survey was conducted in Galle and then, in late 2007, the software was adopted nationwide. Reconstruction was still far from over, especially in the north and east, which made it all the more imperative to push through the newly established quality controls and build capacity. There, regions such as Batticaloa and Ampara also benefited from the approach, although political unrest, deteriorating security, and regular *hartals* (strikes called by the insurgent Liberation Tigers of Tamil Eelam) slowed down the construction process in the east. Many tsunami-affected families survived the monsoons and dry seasons of the first two years in poorly built transitional shelters, some of these rightly renamed "chicken boxes" and "microwave ovens" because they were made entirely out of corrugated-metal sheets. Housing schemes were progressing but at the rhythm of a war zone, in which nothing was predictable.

As I was getting ready to wrap up the survey and leave the country in late 2007, I was asked to set up emergency shelters in camps up north, where internally displaced persons were again on the move, caught in the crossfire between the Sri Lankan army and the Tamil Tiger rebels. The process felt like some sort of terrible game in which you start building during an emergency, advance to temporary shelters that afford some semblance of normalcy, and gain the winning points if and when you finally get to construct permanent housing before—and for reasons beyond your control—being sent back to step one again. I found it sad and ironic that my colleagues were repairing newly completed houses now scarred with bullet holes and damaged by grenades. As an architect and social worker I could only ask, why such waste? Solidarity is quickly eroded by egoism and revenge. And the social justice that many hoped and fought for after the tsunami was quickly squandered. Peace eventually came in 2009, but at a terribly high human cost.

I left the country on a Poya Day, the day of the full moon, dressed in white like most Sri Lankans. I prepared my bag, keeping some space for a homemade dal curry and a couple of temple flowers. They say that you need to leave an island to see an island, that when you're too close you miss the multifaceted shape of things. From disaster to disaster, unless we are prepared to assess, analyze, and correct our errors, we will repeatedly reinvent the wheel, while the people whose needs we aim to meet continue to suffer.

Notes

1   Transitional homes are those intended to last at least two or three years. However, "transitional" may be a misnomer, since many people never leave these homes, nor are the homes upgraded. This was not the case with the housing built by Oxfam, but was quite common in housing constructed by less-experienced NGOs, particularly in the buffer zone.

2   GTZ (Gesellschaft für Technische Zusammenarbeit) is an organization of the German government that supports projects in international development. Its focus is on cooperation and capacity building for sustainable political, economic, ecological, and social development worldwide. Its Tsunami Housing Support Project (2006–7) aimed to build the capacity of government agencies in Sri Lanka during the reconstruction process.

# FROM TRANSITIONAL TO PERMANENT SHELTER: INVALUABLE PARTNERSHIPS IN PERU

INTERNATIONAL FEDERATION OF RED CROSS AND RED CRESCENT SOCIETIES, GENEVA

The departments of Canete, Chincha, Pisco, and Ica were hit hardest in the punishing earthquake that struck the Peruvian coast on August 15, 2007. Seventy-five thousand houses were leveled in the urban center of Pisco; but the rural areas, where 90 percent of the houses were in various states of collapse, suffered the worst losses. In all, 593 people died and 131,393 families were affected.

In response several National Societies of the Red Cross, together with the International Federation of Red Cross and Red Crescent Societies (IFRC), provided immediate relief that enabled residents to return to work quickly while instigating a program to restore permanent homes. The unique partnership, which also included the Pontificia Universidad Católica del Perú, Architectes de l'Urgence, and PREDES (a national NGO), moved residents swiftly from temporary shelters to permanent houses and led the way in testing and implementing new building technologies and construction techniques, which are now being studied. Recovery efforts focused initially on Bernales, an agricultural village off the coast and to the north of Pisco. There, the core of the village is densely populated, but the most vulnerable people live in the countryside in houses whose bricks, made of sand from the nearby desert, are loosely piled together into walls. Their precarious lives were made all the worse by the fact that most families lacked legal land title. In Peru land tenure is an alarming challenge. Illegal settlements include illegal occupation of land in high-risk areas, where self-settled migrants from the rural areas build makeshift homes on terrain that is prone to floods and mudslides.

## TEMPORARY SHELTER AS DIGNIFIED LIVING SPACE

Temporary shelters were introduced to replace tents and better protect people against the radical temperature shifts common along the coast. The frames were made of eucalyptus timber and exterior wall panels were thatched from local plant fronds; the panels were lined with sturdy plastic sheets, which helped keep out the sand during windstorms. The poles and the panels were purchased from the local market, which kept the funds within the community's economy. Plastic sheeting and hardware elements (nails, hinges, etc.) were purchased in bulk elsewhere. Building with these materials cost 25 percent less than the amounts other local organizations spent on provisional shelters made of timber or low-grade galvanized sheets. During the first phase of recovery family members built 500 shelters in Bernales. More than 6,000 shelters were built across the region.

There is a long tradition in Peru of starting out with semipermanent materials, which allows families to construct more formal homes over time. Here, the 20-by-10-foot (6-by-3-meter) modules were designed to be dismantled and reassembled, enabling families to move or reuse them. Portability was also a means of permitting individuals without land tenure to participate in the program. Within two years the shelters had become a reliable source of income for many families, who converted them into rental properties, turned them into small shops, or held onto them as storage spaces.

After the earthquake in 2007 Red Cross and Red Crescent Societies acted quickly to move residents first into sturdy temporary shelters and then into sound permanent homes that met the structural needs of each region:

↑ / ↗ Temporary shelter

→ / →→ / ↓ / ↘ Improved adobe construction

↘↘ A garden planted in front of a new home

## A MOVE TOWARD PERMANENCE

As early as February 2008 IFRC partners had initiated a series of social and environmental studies in the affected areas that would lead to rebuilding secure, earthquake-resistant permanent homes. Each family designated two members to work in an intensive training program. Communities led the building process, providing stones and sand for foundations, clearing the land, unloading materials, and making straw mats. The IFRC provided the logistic, financial, and technical support. The designs were based on intelligent use of local materials and indigenous knowledge that improved construction techniques and respected local culture while keeping costs under control and an eye on using less energy and minimizing waste.

Civil engineers, construction workers, local government personnel, and architects contributed to the process. Materials and designs were tested at the Pontificia Universidad Católica del Perú laboratories to guarantee their seismic resistance. In all cases the basic building component was soil. Improved adobe (adobe that is stabilized with a geo-grid) was used by the British Red Cross in the district of Independencia, in Pisco, and by the Peruvian and Spanish branches of the Red Cross in the districts of El Carmen and Chincha Baja, in Chincha. Improved *quincha* (in which a grid of woven bamboo panels is covered with a mud plaster), lighter than adobe and more consistent since it is made with sandy soil, was utilized in Independencia and Humay, in Pisco, and in San José de los Molinos, in Ica. Blocks made from a stable, durable compound of earth and cement were used in the district of San Clemente, in Pisco. All of the houses are equipped with water, electricity, toilets, and an energy efficient kitchen, and their thick, earthen walls insulate the homes against the extreme temperatures.

## COMMUNITY LIFE

Communities were also taught to manage the land regulation process and to use job training in reconstruction as an opportunity to address local priorities, such as the need for better public hygiene. Members cleaned up plots, built foundations, transported gravel, and managed a materials warehouse. The earthquake had left the region littered with millions of cubic meters of debris, and the local authorities were hard pressed to cope with the scale of this solid waste. Citizens consolidated the inconsistent sandy slopes by reinforcing roads with the earthquake debris and creating new pedestrian paths. Knowledge sharing and problem solving among community members created a domino effect. Today, vibrant public spaces and vegetable gardens are enjoyed by everyone.

Also in the affected region the Red Cross and Red Crescent Societies introduced small-scale business management, assisting women's groups and individuals to establish businesses based on local crafts and services; helped build new schools and community centers; and equipped health facilities. The Peace Corps, also a project partner, trained communities in local ecology and solid waste management. Strong social commitment, teamwork, and mutual support across a range of activities—when built into the reconstruction process—have encouraged communities to think holistically and lead their own development, which in turn ensures greater resilience in the future.

# PART 2

# WHAT SHOULD GOVERNMENTS DO?

"A house is probably the largest asset owned by most families, whether in developing or developed countries."

# WHEN PEOPLE ARE INVOLVED

THIRUPPUGAZH VENKATACHALAM
RESEARCH SCHOOL OF PACIFIC ASIA
STUDIES, AUSTRALIAN NATIONAL
UNIVERSITY–CANBERRA

There is a tendency to privilege a practice known among professionals as ODR, owner-driven reconstruction, a post-disaster method of recovery that involves people in rebuilding their own homes. The method is perhaps the only way to work at scale, making it possible, for example, to rebuild 630,000 homes in record time in rural Kashmir after the Pakistan earthquake in 2005. The World Bank supports this approach, encouraging governments and NGOs worldwide to set policies that favor ODR in the aftermath of a crisis.

Despite all the attention and support, does owner-driven reconstruction lead to building back better, safer communities? What are the issues and challenges for governments that choose ODR following a catastrophic disaster? Why does it seem so promising? Housing reconstruction is one of the most challenging aspects of recovery, particularly when people are in a hurry to return to their lives. In Gujarat, India, I was the joint chief executive officer of the Gujarat State Disaster Management Authority (GSDMA) following a devastating earthquake there in 2001, and I returned in 2008 to review the successes and failures of the project in the field. Lessons taken from this experience can guide future actions.

A house is probably the largest asset owned by most families, whether in developing or developed countries. Ownership confers self-esteem and privacy, builds wealth, reduces migrancy, and enhances the scope of active involvement of individuals in a society. After a disaster, policy decisions—on the location of housing resettlements, the nature and extent of assistance, and criteria for eligible beneficiaries—as well as the processes that make funds available and the quickness with which decisions can be taken determine the outcome of the housing programs, regardless of the recovery model. How well we respond to these interrelated questions determines the speed, quality, and sustainability of housing programs. At the same time a critical question is always: *who* will build the houses?

Following the earthquake in 2001, Gujarat undertook one of the largest recovery programs in India's modern history. The Kutch district became a huge laboratory where several agencies experimented with diverse housing types, technologies, materials, and approaches, creating numerous permutations and combinations of housing-recovery initiatives. This provided an ideal framework to evaluate the relative merits of ODR compared with other recovery strategies. The analysis is particularly pertinent now, as we attempt to understand and manage the damage caused by large-scale earthquakes in Haiti and Chile and floods in Pakistan in 2010.[1] Based on what I learned in Gujarat, I believe the success of ODR—or, perhaps better, *people-centered* reconstruction (as not everyone owns a home)—depends not only on empowering residents to rebuild their houses but also on enabling them to undertake reconstruction through a truly participatory approach.

## HOUSING RECOVERY: POLICY, PACKAGES, AND PERFORMANCE

On January 26, 2001, as India was about to celebrate its 52nd Republic Day, one of the most destructive earthquakes ever measured in the region struck the Kutch district of Gujarat state in western India at 8:46 am. It measured 7.7 Mw and affected more than 7,600 villages and 14 towns. About 1.2 million houses were damaged, of which around 220,000 fully collapsed and about 917,000 were partially damaged. At the epicenter more than 70 percent of the built environment was destroyed.

The government of Gujarat launched a comprehensive reconstruction program with loans from the World Bank and the Asian Development Bank and assistance from the government of India. The program was divided into two phases. The first phase focused on repair, reconstruction, and rehabilitation to bring people's lives back to normal. The second phase aimed to create additional infrastructure that laid the foundations for long-term disaster management and mitigation. Today, all the major projects have been completed.

Housing recovery posed a major challenge. The enormous area affected had different types of houses with varying degrees of damage. In addition a single standard house model could not be used, as seismic risk is different within various zones of the affected area and housing requirements were different in rural and urban areas. In order to cater to real needs the government announced six housing-reconstruction packages, extending a range of options from complete relocation to in situ reconstruction.[2] A private/public partnership program was set up through which NGOs could be involved in constructing houses and villages, sharing costs equally with the government by adopting a village for 50 percent of the total project cost. NGOs could also construct houses and one-room kitchen facilities without government funds, allowing construction to be completed by individual beneficiaries with government assistance. The degree of financial assistance to owners and residents depended on the seismic zone, type of house, and local cost of construction.[3]

Though the government was willing to involve the private sector and NGOs in housing reconstruction, it preferred ODR. This preference was clearly spelled out in a policy document that stipulated a range of options and enabled communities to choose the place and mode of reconstruction through a participatory decision-making process. In each village a resolution by the village council was mandated; the entire voting population of the village voted on whether to relocate or support in situ reconstruction. If they relocated, communities could choose the site that best suited their specific needs from available land, as proposed by the government in relocation zones. The choice of owner-driven or NGO-driven reconstruction was also

INSTITUTION
RESEARCH SCHOOL OF PACIFIC ASIA
STUDIES, AUSTRALIAN NATIONAL
UNIVERSITY–CANBERRA

PROJECT LOCALE
GUJARAT, INDIA

(previous spread) / ↑ A single-family and a multifamily dwelling in Gujarat built with owner-driven reconstruction, using approved earthquake-resistant methods. The styles of owner-driven reconstruction in Gujarat varied within the earthquake-resistant models.

left up to the families and communities. Overall, people preferred to reconstruct the houses themselves rather than secure a house built by an external agency.

Since the earthquake some 200,000 houses have been rebuilt and over 900,000 repaired. Of the total number of rebuilt houses, nearly 160,000 were constructed by owners who received financial assistance from the government. (The policy to help renters was less comprehensive.) The remaining 42,000 were built by NGOs and donors. There are important reasons why the owner-driven approach to post-disaster housing worked in Gujarat.

First, owner-driven houses provide greater satisfaction. Owners speak of feeling safer in them and express confidence that they are of better quality and will protect against future earthquakes—presumably because they have themselves overseen the construction. (People have no way to judge the quality or safety of contractor-built homes.[4]) Whether in situ or at relocated sites, owners report that the houses they built are better suited to their lifestyles and more satisfying. The owner-driven approach also helps build local skills, as people share knowledge and technology. It also offers a perfect opportunity to communicate the reasons behind earthquake-resistant construction methods. This last point is particularly revealing. A survey of the worst-affected area, Bhachau Taluka, found that while 45 percent of the extensions or additions in the owner-driven houses had earthquake-resistant features, only 8 percent of the people whose houses were constructed by NGOs incorporated safety measures when they later built their own additions to their homes.

We have also found that when owners rebuild their homes the designs are more culturally appropriate. Most of the NGOs hired architects from outside the affected region, who adopted uniform housing designs tied to a gridiron village pattern. Ostensibly, these met minimum safety standards. Toilets were put inside the house, which is considered unhygienic and unacceptable. In Kutch, where firewood is used as fuel, kitchens are traditionally constructed outside the main living area to keep smoke away and prevent blackening of the walls. But the NGOs put the kitchen indoors, so residents simply used the space for storage and built another kitchen outside. The indoor toilets remain unused. These sorts of cultural misunderstandings are not benign, as unused kitchens can cause expensive maintenance problems (leaks, corrosion of pipes and fixtures) down the road.

The people-centered approach has the further advantage of incorporating residents into the process of reconstruction. Women in particular get involved in every aspect of decision making, material and site selection, design, quality control, and construction, from the foundation to the choice of color. In Kutch men rarely decide questions related to house construction without consulting the women. In sharp contrast to this tradition, people were largely left out of the process when the house was built by an NGO, which sometimes promised designs that did not match the finished result. NGOs often handed designs over to contractors, who came from all over India and who took little interest in involving the future residents in the reconstruction process. In large part problems arose because the residents did not know which house they would live in; even those who may have wanted to participate saw little reason to build someone else's home.

Finally, ODR enables people to get back to work early, which in turn puts the economy back on track. Gujarat is the first earthquake disaster recorded in post-independence India in which a significant amount of outside aid contributed to the local economy. Of course, money also went to airlines, hotels, consultants, and invited companies, but on the whole, when people build their own homes, using local material and local labor, the local economy benefits. It is also worth pointing out

↑ Women at a planning session in Mandvi Surat

→ / ↓ Culturally appropriate owner-driven reconstruction includes traditional materials and styles. The circular house is a traditional type called a bunga that developed in Kutch after an 1819 earthquake but was gradually abandoned as people turned to modern construction. Some architects and NGOs have recently revived the form because of its earthquake-resistant features.

↘ The unfortunate result of contractor-built homes in Gujarat

that when people build their own homes, they stay in them, in part out of pride and a sense of community, but also because the particular home—its size, number of rooms, amenities—meets the owner's real needs.

## OWNER-DRIVEN RECONSTRUCTION: PRACTICALITIES

Though an owner- or people-centered approach to post-disaster reconstruction is better than other options, it is not easy to carry out. There are significant challenges that are rarely acknowledged or discussed. The owner-driven approach is not simply a matter of giving cash to affected individuals. And it is wrong to label ODR a self-build solution, as it is closely monitored and supervised. It requires many stakeholders coordinated in a comprehensive process to build back better. The mode of distributing cash assistance is the key. A one-time payment to residents after a disaster is nothing more than an extension of first-response relief. There is a good chance that the money will be diverted to other needs, urgent or otherwise. In Gujarat assistance was disbursed in three installments. The first payment was made before work commenced but the second and third were disbursed after two built stages had been inspected. This ensured that everyone collecting payments was adhering to the prescribed safety standards—including, in the case of some restored houses, retrofitting. In order to make the payments, the government opened 660,000 bank accounts in four months, so that individuals could be paid by check without middlemen (a common practice in India, where many people with low incomes do not manage their money through a bank). Villagers enthusiastically agreed that the government should make the payments in installments; as one resident commented, "If all the money had been given at one go—that is 90,000 rupees, which is a lot of money for many families here—they would have spent it on something else and wasted it. They would not have built houses."[5] However, the system was not perfect. Sixteen thousand houses in Gujarat (less than 2 percent of the damaged housing stock) remain incomplete because the beneficiary either did not start rebuilding after having received the initial installment or stopped construction at the plinth level, that is, after receiving the second check. The lesson here is to disburse the money in installments *after* the necessary preconditions for each phase have been met.

It is also important to realize that citizens have their pre-disaster city or village in mind and may not wish to wait for a better city to be designed and constructed. In order to discourage hasty and haphazard rebuilding, a long-term, process-oriented reconstruction requires good temporary shelters. These structures should be fit to last at least three years and provide basic infrastructure—drinking water, sanitation, electricity, etc. Temporary resettlement sites must be placed thoughtfully, so that residents can carry on with work, school, and family without being forced into long commutes.

## INFORMATION, MONITORING, COST CONTROL

One of the biggest challenges in adopting ODR is in educating people about the importance of disaster-resistant construction, particularly when building codes are neither regulated nor enforced. Affected communities are in a hurry to return to normality. Unless people are informed and educated before a disaster, they will rebuild using the same old vulnerable methods, thus missing the opportunity to mitigate future risk. The GSDMA carried out a massive public-information campaign using pamphlets, films, folk dances, buses, street plays, posters, exhibitions, student competitions, radio jingles, and even jokes to convince people in some 3,000 villages to use earthquake-resistant reconstruction. We also conducted 1,800 literacy camps to educate people about their entitlements and legal remedies.

To be sure, these sorts of campaigns cannot alone guarantee safe construction. It is necessary to set technical and safety standards and to provide guidance in following them, particularly in the rural areas, where housing construction is undertaken by residents rather than professional builders. The GSDMA prepared and disseminated technical guidelines for using local materials in hazard-resistant construction, including norms for seismic safety in low-cost reconstruction and retrofitting, cyclone-resistant building practices, walls of stabilized soil-cement block, and new technologies, as well as guidelines for how to repair, reconstruct, and retrofit masonry buildings. Shake-table demonstrations, cassettes, videos, and booklets helped carry the message. To be honest, without supervision and monitoring, such information campaigns and technical guidelines would be of little use. An independent third-party audit was put in place to check quality and safety. Fifteen hundred earthquake engineers were appointed to guide villagers through earthquake-resistant construction. Mobile material-testing vans were deployed to test the quality of the building materials used. To manage all this staff and activity, a special engineering division was created within the government and deputy engineers were required to certify each building before second and third payments were released. Though such an elaborate arrangement created time lags, the process proved invaluable in helping to reduce people's future vulnerability.

The success of the owner-driven process also depends on whether proper building materials are available and their costs controlled. Costs escalate dramatically after a disaster. Entire villages are constructed in the aftermath of a major event, so as infrastructure and building materials become scarce their cost

rises well beyond the means of the affected poor. In Gujarat we adopted a two-pronged strategy to keep building materials available. Cement was distributed at a subsidized price through 1,082 material banks established in rural areas and tax exemptions were provided to manufacturers working in Kutch. State-subsidized material banks help stabilize the prices of raw supplies during periods of high demand. The policy employed large numbers of people in industry, raised household incomes, increased the number of women in the workforce, and employed rural handicraft and trade workers. As a result, since the earthquake Kutch has experienced a fivefold increase in bank deposits. The loss of tax revenues was borne by the state and federal governments.

## TRAINING AND CAPACITY BUILDING

To overcome the shortage of skilled masons and engineers needed for this massive undertaking, the government trained some 29,000 masons, including women, and 6,500 practicing engineers. The masons underwent a crash course in earthquake-resistant construction and were provided with tool kits. The engineers, all new recruits, trained to meet the new standards. Both engineers and masons were asked to think in terms of long-term disaster management and the need to construct seismic-resistant buildings as a normal practice. This quickly created oversight in the workforce and enabled the construction of so many ODR houses to proceed speedily.

The Gujarat government quickly realized the advantage of institutionalizing these training programs to better ensure future safety and began certifying masons through third-party testing. Testing and certificates were also set for engineers by an autonomous council. Unfortunately, this initiative had only limited success. Stakeholders such as local officials and NGOs showed little interest in the certificate programs and did not adopt or

The GSDMA public-awareness campaign included buses displaying posters, tables laden with leaflets, and student competitions.

maintain them. Certifying masons never achieved the expected results despite initial success and the passage of a law in Gujarat requiring registration of professional engineers, which exists on paper. Failure to institutionalize training and standards underscores a harsh reality: unless all stakeholders are serious about disaster mitigation and see themselves as having a vested interest in it, political will alone does not suffice.

The merits and success of owner-driven reconstruction make it a good option in post-disaster reconstruction, but its limitations need to be discussed openly. People can (with aid and advice) rebuild their own homes, but only in the right context. The much-touted success of the program is limited to rural areas and small towns. There are no success stories in the megacities, where multistory dwellings and apartments were destroyed. In cities the obstacles are great: people have little experience in building houses; the land on which a building sits may be owned by another party or ownership may be in dispute; repairs to one building may depend on what building is next door and who lives there; the result is that, often, contractors end up doing the construction. All of this makes ODR nearly impossible in cities. For example, in the capital of Gujarat, Ahmadabad, a city of 3.5 million, 46,000 houses were damaged and 1,650 totally collapsed. There, practically all residents preferred to buy ready-built flats from builders, or else move in with relatives, instead of constructing their own apartments.

The second problem is that not all families have the same capacity to rebuild their own homes. Not every family has the manpower, resources, time, or knowledge to participate. In Gujarat large-scale farmers, big families, members of Forward Castes, and people above the poverty line preferred ODR, while small farmers, the landless, small families, and members of Backward Castes, Scheduled Castes, and Scheduled Tribes—above and below the poverty line—preferred NGO-built houses.[6] Put simply, landless laborers and agricultural workers who

earn their bread day to day did not have the time and resources for ODR. These gaps had to be filled by the state or NGOs. Owner-driven reconstruction cannot be promoted without offering the alternative of ready-built houses to those who cannot undertake construction on their own, which includes people with special requirements or, in India, without men in the home—the aged and handicapped, widows, single women, and households headed by a woman.

Third, ODR needs a huge establishment and expands the role of the state. We cannot pretend otherwise. In Gujarat government officials had to visit each house on average ten times during construction in connection with damage assessment, certification, and release of payments.[7] Delays and regulatory overload due to this necessary oversight cannot be avoided. Therefore the process takes longer than NGO-driven construction—although not necessarily by a great margin, depending on local conditions.

Fourth, the willingness and capacity of people in crisis to take the responsibility of reconstruction on their shoulders may vary. Many villages after the 1993 earthquake in Maharashtra preferred NGO-driven reconstruction, though government policy required ODR in villages constructed in situ. Similarly, villagers in Tamil Nadu preferred NGO-driven reconstruction after the Indian Ocean tsunami decimated the coastline in 2004. Many reasons shape this decision beyond being incapable or too busy. For example, frequently women expressed the view that if cash had been given instead of a ready-built house, men would have spent the money on alcohol instead of construction.

Last, the issue of political will—up and down the hierarchy from local to national—is important. Political culture and political determination play a major role in making policy choices. The selection of NGO and state-sponsored, contractor-built reconstruction adopted by Tamil Nadu after the tsunami and by Karnataka after floods in 2009 was mainly driven by political

> Make no mistake: it is the manifestation of political will, reflected in policies, that determines the reach and effectiveness of actions at the local level.

considerations. The political will to expand the role of the state, for the state to assume responsibility, must exist but the political culture must also embrace and promote the idea of making people partners rather than passive recipients of aid. In Gujarat we facilitated the choice of ODR by making full use of our political clout. We in government developed and implemented need-based approaches and took care to put in place appropriate safeguards to ensure that state sponsorship of ODR would not fail to involve the affected populations as much as possible. Make no mistake: it is the manifestation of political will, reflected in policies, that determines the reach and effectiveness of actions at the local level.

The Gujarat case underscores the need to redefine the role of the state in housing recovery. Yes, we can say that ODR delivers better results and that states and NGOs should facilitate the process by making use of an array of appropriate financial mechanisms, material support, technical help, and human resources. This is better than providing ready-built houses through contractors. But as we have seen, and contrary to general belief, the responsibility of the state increases when we adopt a posture of ODR. The state has to ensure and deliver a well-designed policy that integrates verifiable indicators of progress and quality and ensures availability of materials and trained manpower; it cannot leave the market to dictate the terms. Education and regulation play an important role in ensuring quality, safety, and long-term sustainability. And we need solutions for cities of all sizes, which is much more difficult to achieve with owner-driven initiatives.

But what if the state is weak or largely absent? Can ODR work without strong governmental presence, as in Haiti, where civil society is not strong and much of the government infrastructure was itself destroyed by the recent earthquake? International NGOS, external agencies, the United Nations relief and recovery system, and donor countries rush to fill this void. But these external organizations rarely favor ODR because they see houses as a product rather than a process.

If external organizations are to serve well in the role of an absent government, they must revise their practices. The first thing that needs to change is the timing of reconstruction. External organizations typically race to deliver aid and then disappear. Second, they must ensure that their construction funds enter the local economy and stay there; no longer should they take the opportunity of disaster to award contracts for mass housing to companies in their own countries—and they should absolutely stop providing ready-built houses. Third, one-time cash payments to victims should end. Cash is always more effective when it is paid in installments that are tied to specific goals or to designated purchases such as building materials.

To help people build their own homes, first and foremost external NGOs must have real expertise in reconstruction and be willing to stay on hand for an extended period of time. Part of their brief is to build the capacity of the affected people and to reinforce civil society. Large-scale training of engineers and masons, educating residents about safe construction, formulating proper technical guidelines for seismic-resistant construction, and instituting building codes all take time. It is equally important—and this is especially true in Haiti—to build capacities within the state, without which long-term risk mitigation will fail. This can be done by working with whatever state infrastructure has survived to carry out some of the tasks it normally would perform itself. These include circulating manuals on multihazard-resistant construction; identifying and training technical experts (masons and engineers); setting up material banks to stabilize the prices of building materials; erecting demonstration houses that are low-cost and hazard-resistant; conducting technical audits to ensure quality control (and establishing the culture of requiring audits); launching a massive public-awareness campaign; and providing cash assistance in installments directly to residents. To facilitate ODR in places as broadly devastated as Haiti, where a grave lack of infrastructure preceded the disaster, it is also essential to build human resources and systems *before* taking on a new urban plan or building permanent homes, difficult though this may be in the press of crisis. Otherwise, people will be left out of the process and the risk of recurrence increases greatly.

A strong commitment to people-centered reconstruction implicates time, money, and visibility in particular ways. When one is starting from scratch after a large-scale catastrophe like the one in Haiti, reconstruction should not be done in a hurry; hence the need for good solutions regarding temporary housing. This requires that more resources and money be committed to long-term planning to ensure future permanent housing—which may seem counterintuitive in the heat of the moment of crisis. ODR does not serve the visual success that donors and NGOs profit from—those rows of identical houses whose number and scale can so easily be counted and measured. In the owner-driven model, people typically reconstruct in situ, where their houses used to be, adding components over time, and the results are not uniform or picture-perfect.

So yes: ODR is possible in the absence of the state, but it is a far more challenging choice for NGOs and donors; it means spending more time and more money and being willing to sacrifice good publicity and visibility. Nevertheless, it is a worthwhile choice, for people-centered homes and communities are rebuilt with respect—not only to fulfill real needs but to restore ways of life that have been devastated.

Notes

1   For further reading see John Cosgrave, ALNAP (Active Learning Network for Accountability and Performance in Humanitarian Action), and ProVention Consortium, *Responding to Earthquakes 2008: Learning from Earthquake Relief and Recovery Operations*, policy paper (London: ALNAP, 2008), and online at www.alnap.org/pool/files/ALNAPLessonsEarthquakes.pdf, accessed March 6, 2010; Asian Development Bank, *India: Gujarat Earthquake Rehabilitation and Reconstruction Report; Completion Report* (Manila: Asian Development Bank, 2008), and online at www.adb.org/Documents/PCRs/IND/35068-IND-PCR.pdf, accessed July 10, 2010; Jennifer Duyne Barenstein, *From Gujarat to Tamilnadu: Owner-Driven vs. Contractor-Driven Housing Reconstruction in India*, paper presented at the 4th International i-Rec Conference: Building Resilience; and Achieving Effective Post-Disaster Reconstruction, Christchurch, New Zealand, April 30–May 2, 2008, and online at www.resorgs.org.nz/irec2008/Papers/Duyne.pdf, accessed May 7, 2009.

2   Full text of these packages is available at www.gsdma.org.

3   In rural areas a maximum of 90,000 rupees (about $2,000) and in urban towns a maximum of 125,000 rupees (about $2,700) was provided; in the megacity of Ahmadabad the maximum was 175,000 rupees (about $3,700). In the case of NGO-driven reconstruction government shared 50 percent of the construction cost subject to a maximum of 45,000 rupees ($970). In the third category NGOs constructed one room and a kitchen at a cost of 45,000 rupees, while the government provided 45,000 rupees directly to the beneficiaries to complete construction of the rest of the house.

4   To obtain these statistics I conducted a household survey of 500 houses in May 2008. The survey had a mix of owner-driven and NGO-driven houses from Bhachau town and the 71 villages of Bhachau Taluka.

5   Author interview with Rasikhbhai Chavda, Manfara, Kutch, May 19, 2008.

6   "Backward Castes," "Scheduled Castes,"and "Scheduled Tribes" are official demographic terms of the Indian government, referring to communities that suffer from extreme social and economic underdevelopment (typically including social ostracism, primitive agricultural practices, lack of infrastructural facilities, and geographical isolation). Such groups receive certain benefits and protections under the Indian Constitution.

7   These included visits to the affected house for initial and final damage assessment; to open the resident's bank account; to check construction quality after plinth, lintel, and completion stages; upon release of first, second, and third installments; and for technical guidance and quality audits.

"We introduced shake tables in 1995. These subject half-scale models to sideways shocks and crudely imitate earthquake forces."

# CITIZEN ARCHITECTS

RUPAL AND RAJENDRA DESAI
NATIONAL CENTRE FOR PEOPLES'
ACTION IN DISASTER PREPAREDNESS,
AHMEDABAD, INDIA

"We want houses on springs." A man was speaking from the crowd that had gathered on the outskirts of a village in the rural Latur region of central India. It was October 1993, three days after a devastating earthquake, the first of this magnitude in 500 years. Local people had had no sense of urgency, no active awareness that they were living in an area vulnerable to catastrophic seismic activity. For months afterward no one would speak of stone or timber, let alone consider using these materials to rebuild their homes. Stone and timber had snatched away their loved ones. The speaker had heard about the latest technologies, like those used in Japan. He was asking Sharad Pawar, the visiting chief minister of Maharashtra State, to use them in the upcoming government reconstruction program for the village.

In fact, at that time the Indian government was using technology—real and imaginary—as a symbol to reassure people that their new homes would be safer and more secure than those they had lost. Through advertising campaigns, appearances by official representatives, and word of mouth, the slogan "safety at any cost" made its way into the public imagination, associated with modern building technologies. Stone was out, brick was in; mud mortar was out, cement mortar was in; mud roofs were out, reinforced-concrete roofs were in; rural house plans were out, and plans resembling those for city dwellings were in.

The new homes, in the end, were more expensive, smaller, mimicked the look and functions of houses suited to more urban contexts, and offered little additional protection against earthquakes, as we discovered when we ran tests in the field. The government and the public associated modern, urban-style "houses on springs" with safety. We learned that they were not necessarily safer, and indeed raised a host of other problems. Both parties associated traditional Latur house construction with danger. We found that neither the traditional layout nor traditional building materials made a home vulnerable. Its square plan in fact affords the maximum safety in an earthquake; it was the structural assemblies—specifically, the absence of certain features—rather than the materials, that put people at risk.

Working as an independent design team on contract to the Indian government, in 1993 we launched a project to design and build appropriate new homes in Latur. We wanted to incorporate aspects of vernacular construction important to local culture and the environment with innovations in structural design that provided seismic reinforcement. Our six-year experience led us deep into the politics of disaster recovery, in a situation influenced by unprecedented amounts of aid from local and foreign sources. Here is how we turned our design theories into practice.

## HOUSE PLANS

When our team of architects and engineers first visited Latur, our brief from the government was to carry out post-earthquake damage assessment. We had been chosen because we already had a decade of experience in assisting rural artisans in the building trades—masons, brick makers, roofers, and the like—to gain expertise and training in safe and cost-efficient construction techniques. The damage assessment was the first phase of a multiyear housing-reconstruction program intended to provide long-term housing to the affected region. Some 220,000 homes, spread over a large area, needed to be repaired and retrofitted and about 50,000 houses had to be rebuilt, most of these at sites designated by the government. Government engineers were brought in to advise the home owners.

This first visit piqued our broader interest in the problem of post-disaster reconstruction in rural areas, and we eventually

2.2
CITIZEN ARCHITECTS
IN INDIA

085

ORGANIZATION
NATIONAL CENTRE FOR PEOPLES'
ACTION IN DISASTER PREPAREDNESS

PROJECT LOCALE
LATUR, INDIA

worked with local individuals, NGOs, and government agencies to carry out reconstruction projects in various regions throughout India.[1] However, what we remember about our first visit to Latur was that the traditional houses took us by surprise.

These houses are large and fortresslike, with an introverted quality. Massive rubble walls and ornamental timber doorways are trademark features. The walls and mud roofs insulate them extremely well; interior temperatures are more or less uniform year round. The inward-looking square plan opens onto a central courtyard; rooms follow the contour and a semicovered verandah at center extends the rooms into the courtyard. The verandah is the most versatile space in the house and serves a variety of cultural functions. Large grain storage bins are placed in one part; other areas are divided and used for sleeping, resting, cooking, socializing, and studying. Wooden pegs are fitted into the walls to hang utensils and clothing; niches function as storage spaces. On cool winter nights the entire family sleeps on these verandahs. On hot summer afternoons they are naturally cool. Newlyweds sleep here as part of a nuptial ritual. The central courtyard is a protected, private space but is open to the sky; it serves as a playground for children, a utility space for washing clothes and cooking vessels, and a place to dry foodstuffs.

The first official, state-recommended plans for earthquake-safe houses were drawn by city architects and engineers. They were designed for prefabricated concrete-panel construction and had a discrete living room, bedrooms, and kitchen on an urban model. These were adopted from village to village across the region: uniform, duplicated homes were built by the government with little owner input. They were initially attractive to a public reeling from the recent disaster and suspicious of traditional construction. Moreover, younger families sought modern homes. But as the plans were followed, the allure quickly faded and problems arose. Building materials had to be bought and transported to the site, increasing expense and time for

(previous spread) A shake table with a 1.5-ton pendulum: when the table sways on its rollers the well-built house on the left remains standing but the house on the right, which lacks seismic-resistant features, collapses.

↑ Massive stone walls of a typical traditional Latur house

↑↑ / ↑ Prefabricated houses made, according to state-recommended design, of precast concrete hollow-core panels

↗ In this earthquake-resistant house vernacular stone-wall construction is strengthened with bands of reinforced concrete. The roof is made of precast concrete panels overlaid with mud.

→ A traditional vernacular house with stone walls and stone-tile roof construction. Standardized room functions did not correlate to the necessities of rural life. The feeling of personal security and privacy created by the introverted style of the traditional house was lost. Women felt more exposed and at risk in a local culture that demands discretion. During the monsoons the reinforced-concrete roofs leaked and were not easily repaired. This compared poorly with a traditional mud roof: in a monsoon all its owner had to do was to climb up, pull out the weeds, and spread some new clay soil over the hole. The doors in the new houses were too small to allow large grain storage bins through. New metal containers replaced the old bins—at additional expense—but now insecticides had to be used to keep bugs away. The houses were cold in the winter and so hot in the summer that residents worried that their stored seeds would not survive the season. Unlike traditional houses they needed electric fans, which increased energy demand. The white-washed walls, unlike the mud plaster of vernacular dwellings, turned black from the smoke of traditional wood-burning stoves. Painters had to be called in, increasing maintenance expenses. Even hanging pictures—a significant gesture to personalize an otherwise generic home—was more difficult. The concrete walls required special electric drills and the power to drive them. Stone walls had not needed special power tools: one simply pushed a hook into a crevice.

By 1994 the fear had subsided and the infatuation with modern construction had given way to reality. Using steel and concrete was expensive and inconvenient, especially if you had to pay for supplies out of pocket. Consequently, people simply returned to cheaper, readily available, traditional materials and building methods. In Yelwat, one of the first villages to be rebuilt, a farmer had a stone addition put on his house just months after he moved in. He went back to the site where his previous home had collapsed, gathered up the stones left lying around, loaded his bullock cart, and asked a local mason to build the new wing. The stone walls of the extension were built in exactly the same manner as had been used before, with all the structural weaknesses that had brought down the walls the first time. When we pointed this out, the farmer told us that he would use the extension as a storage area and not for sleeping—ignoring the fact that an earthquake may strike during the workday.

Experiences like this led us to believe that instead of investing our architectural expertise in repairing single homes we should attempt to educate communities about safe rebuilding. We wanted to demonstrate to local populations from different villages that by following basic structural-design rules for stone-rubble construction they could build stronger houses—possibly even stronger than those marketed by the government. We eventually worked with communities and NGOs in villages across India to develop educational programs, practical lessons, and demonstration projects.

## OUR ROLE IN REHABILITATION

Often vernacular architecture and local materials are best suited to a particular climate and lifestyle, but in regions of seismic activity local construction methods must be adapted to achieve a heightened level of security. In Latur (and the other regions where we worked) there was, in fact, no need to avoid building with stone and mud. However, there are structurally sound ways to build masonry walls and apply clay roofs that help them overcome inherent weaknesses and render them safer and more earthquake-resistant. With stone these include integrating horizontal reinforced-concrete bands into the walls at various levels to help the masonry resist tension that could cause cracking. The roof can also act as a diaphragm, distributing the force of the earthquake over the walls, thus reducing its impact. Diagonal braces help increase the roof's stiffness and therefore its efficacy during the tremor. This allows the inherent strength of the walls to improve the overall seismic resistance of the structure. We struggled to convey these ideas to residents and local builders.

Our communication challenges stemmed in part from our own zeal to offer an alternative design practice. For example, we knew that deforestation had taken an enormous toll on the regional environment, and most of the trees were gone as a result of centuries of indiscriminate logging. We proposed using an alternative to traditional timber roofs that consisted of doubly curved precast-concrete panels supported on partially precast reinforced-concrete joists. We preserved the traditional modular nature of the roof in the new design, because it bore directly on the proportions of individual rooms. We eventually realized that by promoting the new technology we were telling people that their timber-and-mud roof was no good, whereas in reality it offered some environmentally sustainable techniques, particularly the possibility of adapting clay from the site as a building material. Originally, we had overlooked that aspect of the tradition. We needed to work much harder to resolve the balance between intelligent and safe building methods and environmental sustainability.

Some of our challenges were based in communities' lingering anxieties and an ingrained distrust of outside experts. Some residents refused to sleep in the houses that were still standing. Others came up with their own ideas about how best to address personal security. They removed the heavy mud-and-timber roofs and replaced them with light tin roofs supported on simple frameworks of wooden posts. They dismantled the upper part of the heavy stone walls, reducing their height to no more than 4 feet (1.25 m), and reasoned that stone falling from that height would not kill a person. They salvaged heavy timber beams from the ruins of their homes, cut them into planks, and used the pieces to fill in the gaps between roof and wall. Through word of mouth and improvisation people convinced one another that

it was safer to trade the comfort of living under a cool mud-slab roof for unbearable summer heat under a tin roof, and that inserted bits of cut timber could stand in for a real structural solution. Many replaced their stone walls completely with brick, thinking erroneously that brick is lighter than stone, and therefore less likely to kill someone if it falls. Clearly, such ad hoc modifications often did not increase safety at all. Conversely, knowing how to build safely and economically with local materials did not assuage people's fears.

Latur was the first post–natural disaster situation we faced. As architects we had little experience with how survivors would react to the reconstruction process. What we knew about building technology and construction techniques was wholly inadequate to the situation. We had to first understand and take seriously the fact that local people were psychologically stuck. They were fixated on what materials they thought they could and could not use to rebuild their homes and protect their families and heavily reliant on custom and rumor for that information. We wanted to demonstrate that safer walls and roofs could be built at least in part using traditional materials. At first, no one believed us.

We decided to build two demonstration houses in the village of Budhoda, an easy distance from Latur. The first challenge was to select the individuals who would benefit from the homes. We identified two widows and built houses for them with introverted plans following the vernacular pattern and proportions. One house had random-rubble walls (walls made of undressed angular stones of varying size that are fitted into each other) in mud mortar with mud roofing placed on a deck made of precast elements. The second house had part adobe, part random-rubble walls with mud roofing placed on a timber deck.

Aid-agency workers, government officials, and donor-agency representatives visited the finished houses and were happy with the results. Naively, what we didn't count on was a simple

← This house survived the earthquake, and with the aim of reducing risk its owner modified it by replacing the upper part of the stone walls with timber and adding a new, corrugated-tin roof.

↓ Installing a roof made of doubly curved precast-concrete panels on stone walls. These panels have stiffened edges that respond well to torsion and stress.

It is critical that what we teach be feasible in remote villages, where skilled workers may be few and access to materials limited. We also make a special effort to engage women in the community.

yet overlooked cultural reality: our beneficiaries were poor widows, so people identified our construction techniques with poor people. And who wants to go and see a poor person's house, much less live in one just like it? Unfortunately, these women would never be looked on by their community as spokespersons for new building technologies. For our ideas to become acceptable and widespread, the strategy had to be promoted by the right people. It may seem an obvious point, but our project called for a spokesperson whom people could identify with, someone they could trust and look up to.

We found our advocate in the ex-*sarpanch* (village head) of Almala village, some 6 miles (10 km) away. We met with him to talk about seismic retrofitting and discussed ways for individuals to reduce the vulnerability of their existing vernacular homes rather than demolishing them and starting over, which was what the government's engineers were promoting. At the end of the meeting the ex-sarpanch offered his house, along with his disaster-relief payment from the government, for our remodeling demonstration. He followed the process through every step. His two wives and four children also worked on the site to help speed things along. While we retrofitted his house he learned the basics of the design and convinced two of his friends to retrofit their houses, too. Once three houses were done, there was no turning back: in less than a year thirty-four homes were retrofitted on our model.

## WHAT WE HAVE LEARNED ABOUT LONG-TERM SAFETY

Our approach in Latur had limited success. It was time-consuming and labor-intensive. Large-scale reconstruction was under the sway of a government that promoted "houses on springs," and while we were talking about the use of load-bearing masonry,

the NGO we were working with was talking about reinforced concrete. Once we convinced the donor and the NGO that traditional materials would perform well, we had to convince the local masons and the residents from neighboring villages. The two houses we designed for the widows were built by twenty masons, who had to be followed and instructed at every stage. Three weeks later, standing in front of the finished homes, the masons unanimously claimed that their houses would hold against a future earthquake, but we were still not sure that they could talk about our methods with conviction. We were not even sure if they were fully persuaded that building with stone could be cheaper and safer. We were missing the communication tools that would help people relate their own safety to various technical measures with confidence and understanding.

Working with community groups, we finally hit upon the idea that objects from daily life could help explain important concepts in earthquake engineering. We used a stitch-through cotton mattress to convince people of the need for through-stones that hold the wythes (the exterior wall faces) together in a random-rubble wall. (In the absence of through-stones the wythes can separate, become unstable, and collapse.) A plastic bucket with bent rim demonstrated how a concrete band at eave level works to strengthen the walls. The stiffness of a canister with its lid tightly shut showed the importance of securely connecting the roof to the walls. We kept adding to the list. Even abstract concepts like inertia forces could be explained to people by holding a flexible twig with a lump of clay attached to its tip and shaking it gently. We also introduced shake tables in 1995. These subject half-scale models to sideways shocks and crudely imitate earthquake forces. Even laypersons went home convinced that they could improve their safety by adding concrete bands, through-stones, and vertical reinforcement embedded within the masonry to their homes. We made videos of the results in several languages, including Marathi (the Laturi dialect), and circulated them throughout affected areas of the country.

For years we have encountered people more or less willing to rely for their information on myth and fear, hearsay and peer pressure. Locally, technical expertise continues to be limited and when it comes from the outside it is not always trusted. After some twenty years of fieldwork we are convinced that the only way to break the cycle of ignorance and fear is to demonstrate appropriate building technologies capable of withstanding the forces of natural hazards.

Today, we train construction artisans, village architects, and local engineers in these technologies. To promote confidence among local people, training programs should be a collaborative affair; for example, we develop house designs together with masons. The training program for professionals always parallels work with the community: villagers are asked to observe their masons at work and residents are invited to visit the site. It is critical that what we teach be feasible in remote villages, where skilled workers may be few and access to materials limited. We also make a special effort to engage women in the community. As we are a husband-and-wife team, we are able to conduct meetings and training sessions for women and girls only. This allows women to interact freely.

Because we work mainly in response to disasters, after the training programs we rarely see any of our trainees again. As a result it is hard to judge how many new ideas they adopt, use consistently and with authority, and retain over time. (Funds for follow-up assessments are rarely available.) Our training program in Kashmir in 2006 was an exception. There, masons built hundreds of houses over several years, using our techniques, and trained three times as many masons as we were able to train personally. Seeing what these masters accomplished, we are confident that this hazard-resistant method of combining materials will take root in the region.

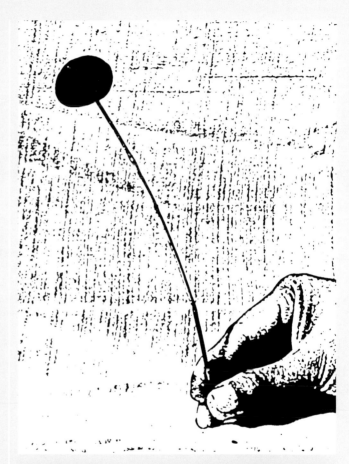

A twig with a lump of clay on the tip demonstrates inertia force: when the twig is shaken and then held still, the clay ball continues to sway, putting stress on the twig.

↑↑ A bucket with a folded rim, a tightly shut canister, and a stitched cotton mattress help villagers understand basic principles of safe construction.

↑ A traditional village landscape with stone roofs

→ A changed landscape: houses with earthquake-resistant reinforced-concrete roofs

## VERNACULAR ARCHITECTURE
## AND POOR COMMUNITIES

We stayed in Latur for six long years, and have since worked in post-disaster contexts throughout India. In the aftermath of the Kutch earthquake in Gujarat in 2001 we worked on an unusually ambitious project for the state of Gujarat. Our program offered technology demonstrations, training, and confidence-building exercises for a state government that encompassed nearly 500 villages with over a million inhabitants in five districts that span some 116 square miles (300 sq. km). Here the shake-table demonstrations were major public events. We invited artisans, villagers, NGO personnel, government engineers, and state officers to observe them. At one event 600 people showed up.

Our biggest challenge is to make sure local builders understand certain fundamental concepts, such as ductility of materials and the need to use concrete bands and single reinforcing bars within masonry walls (which help the masonry resist tension when the wall bends vertically). They need to be able to understand the concept and practice sufficiently to teach other masons and to defend their work in the face of market forces and misguided engineers. Today, videos of shake-table testing, pilot homes that demonstrate simple working models, and brochures make our task a great deal easier than it was in the early 1990s.

Vernacular architecture is the backbone of traditional housing, especially for the most vulnerable members of society. The post-disaster reconstruction phase is an unprecedented opportunity to usher in changes that have a significant impact on the long-term safety of people who are otherwise not in a position, financially, to reduce the vulnerability of their homes. Unless the right options are selected and the right strategy adopted, people will remain vulnerable in spite of unprecedented aid.

Note

1  In Gujarat State in 1987–88 we provided hands-on training to masons in tribal areas for adobe construction and in 1991–92 training in Gujarat in cost-efficient building technologies, including terra-cotta tile-clad adobe and terra-cotta tube vaulted roofing. We conducted training for skills upgrade in earthquake-resistant construction and retrofitting of existing vernacular buildings for earthquake vulnerability reduction in 1994–99 in Latur, in 2000 in Uttarakhand, in 2001–5 in Gujarat State, and in 2006–7 in Kashmir State. Since 2006 we have continued to conduct regular, ongoing training in Gujarat State to upgrade these skills. Training is mainly hands-on at a construction site, accompanied by lectures that use specially made working models and videos. All important points are based on the prevailing building codes.

"Living in a precipitous valley at the confluence of two rivers, residents had suffered floods and landslides before, but few people realized that their city is sandwiched between two major fault lines that run directly through the capital."

# WHAT ABOUT OUR CITIES? REBUILDING MUZAFFARABAD

MAGGIE STEPHENSON AND
SHEIKH AHSAN AHMED
UN-HABITAT PAKISTAN, ISLAMABAD

ZAHID AMIN
DEVELOPMENT AUTHORITY
OF MUZAFFARABAD, PAKISTAN
ADMINISTERED KASHMIR

Pakistan has suffered its share of recent crises. In 2005, after the Kashmir earthquake, 3.5 million people were left homeless; an additional 1 million lost their homes after floods in 2007; 100,000 needed shelter after the Baluchistan earthquake in 2008; in 2009 1.5 million residents were displaced by armed conflict. In 2010 flooding displaced or affected 20 million people (with 12 million needing humanitarian assistance) and destroyed or damaged 2 million homes. Apart from sustaining catastrophic events, Pakistan, with over 160 million people, is one of the fastest-growing countries in the world; its cities are expanding astronomically. Thus, energy, water, housing, and skills shortages constitute increasing challenges that compound the impact of each disaster.

Five years ago the world's sympathy focused on Kashmir. The earthquake's epicenter was only kilometers away from Muzaffarabad, the region's capital city, which suffered massive damage.[1] The United Nations Human Settlements Programme, known as UN-Habitat, is the United Nations agency for human settlements and was active in the recovery efforts from the start. We were members of a UN-Habitat team that has continued to track the progress of Muzaffarabad's recovery from those first chaotic days. We saw firsthand what happened to a city still struggling to get back on its feet. This is an opportunity to contribute to the debate on how best to respond to disaster when it strikes an urban area and to raise urgent questions about the relevance, capacities, and agendas of technical professionals such as architects and planners in urban post-disaster reconstruction.

In response to the scale of the Kashmir earthquake the government of Pakistan established the Earthquake Reconstruction and Rehabilitation Authority (ERRA) to manage recovery in all sectors. UN-Habitat worked closely with ERRA to plan and deliver programs, including the successful owner-driven reconstruction of over 630,000 rural houses. But Muzaffarabad is a different story.

## MUZAFFARABAD

Muzaffarabad is the political and administrative capital of Pakistan Administered Kashmir (PaK), the internationally recognized name for an area spread over nearly 8,100 square miles (13,000 sq. km). Before Pakistan's independence and partition from India in 1947, Muzaffarabad City was a transport stop between Rawalpindi and Srinagar, where in 1985 the population was still only 37,000. By 2005 the population had grown to nearly five times that figure. Today, the city is the administrative and service hub for some 4 million people. Winter is severe with heavy snow and below-zero temperatures. During the summer, for several months temperatures reach over 100°F (38°C) and are punctuated by monsoon rains. The majority of people are forced to build their homes on steep slopes.

Living in a precipitous valley at the confluence of two rivers, residents had suffered floods and landslides before, but few people realized that their city is sandwiched between two major fault lines that run directly through the capital. The intensity of the earthquake in Muzaffarabad averaged 6.9 Mw; in some areas the shaking was worse. More than 10,000 people were killed downtown; 34,284 people in the district died. An additional 13,143 were severely injured in the city proper. While this number is dwarfed by the figures from the 2010 earthquake in Haiti, it represents a sizable percentage of the population. Over 8,500 homes were destroyed and 6,600 seriously damaged. The only two hospitals were devastated. Eighty percent of government offices, universities, and schools were leveled. The heaviest damage was in the old center and areas north, where the collapse of a mountainside along the fault line resulted in the disappearance of whole villages. A cloud of limestone dust hung over the city for months.

ORGANIZATION
UN-HABITAT AND DEVELOPMENT
AUTHORITY OF MUZAFFARABAD

PROJECT LOCALE
MUZAFFARABAD, PAKISTAN
ADMINISTERED KASHMIR

## URGENT CALLS, EXPERTS, AND RELOCATION

In the immediate aftermath of the earthquake experts in engineering and earthquake mitigation arrived to help but made
little impression on the local authorities, who were busy dealing with their own families and responding to urgent issues;
they were inundated by politicians and media visits and
swamped by phone calls. While the authorities were grateful
for the concern and expertise, it was nearly impossible in the
early days for them to respond to complex and long-term
issues like vulnerability assessments, development of new construction codes, and reconstruction planning. They were
overwhelmed by competing demands, limited capacity, mandates, preconceptions, inexperience, and the outright
complexity of recovering from such a disaster. Still, the first
concern was simple, expressed again and again by citizens:
"Will the city be rebuilt in the same place or will we all have to
move? And what will that mean?" Neither they nor the government knew that many other cities, located in equally hazardous
zones, are able to manage the risk, nor had they been told that
attempts to resettle communities after similar disasters elsewhere had met with repeated failure. There was much talk of
satellite developments, though experienced technical experts
were sure that Muzaffarabad would be rebuilt in situ, whether
by design or default. For more than two years the city subsisted
in a state of seeming indecision, shaken by rumors and fears of
relocation, while an estimated 40,000 people with the means
to leave—businessmen, government officials, and professionals—uprooted their families and departed for more certain
employment in other cities. The drain of educated, active, qual-
ified persons further devastated the capital.

    As early as 2006 the government of Japan provided techni-
cal support in the form of an urgent development study,
intended to help rehabilitate and reconstruct Muzaffarabad.

(previous spread) A tent community for internally displaced persons in Muzaffarabad,
close to the Neelum River

↑ North of Muzaffarabad, a mountain collapsed
along a fault line, destroying this suburb.

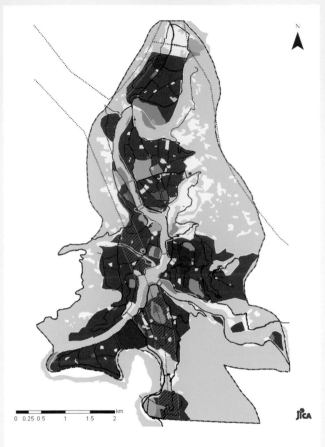

**Legend**

Urban Planning Area

• Heritage
••••••• Inferred Fault Line
▨ Potential Fault Zone
River

Circulation:
— Primary Road
— Secondary Road
— Tertiary Road
— Bridge
Development Promotion Area

Land Use:
Residential
Spontaneous Settlement
Government/ Governmental Housing/ Utility Facilities
Commercial & Business
Industrial
Army
Education
Hospital/ Medical Facilities
Mosque/ Shrine
▨ Grave Yard
Park
Forest/ Agriculture/ Cliff/ Riverbed/ Bareland
Bus/Truck Terminal & Parking Area
River

← The 2006 master plan prepared by Japanese experts for Muzaffarabad provided thoughtful and detailed analysis but was not implemented.

↑↑ Medina Market, in old Muzaffarabad, after the earthquake

↑ Shopkeepers and customers in Medina Market before the earthquake

The report said that the process would take ten years and targeted 2016 for completion. This master plan addressed the physical aspects of the city's reconstruction as well as social and institutional recovery. It emphasized the need for a common vision and offered feasible and succinct recommendations for development and mitigation. Sensitive to funding priorities, the report included proposals for a new bridge and bypass for through traffic, water-supply and sewerage works, wider roads, commercial plazas, and recreational spaces. It also recognized five distinct geographical areas with characteristic topographic, social, and economic conditions. The master plan had enormous potential to engage and mobilize communities, set local priorities, and harness local potential—had there been the will, capacity, and resources to implement it.

The consequences of ignoring these recommendations are nowhere more evident than in hazard mapping, where the information about risk was good, but management infrastructure to implement zoning controls was absent. The master plan recommended two categories of land use: promotion zones, considered safe to develop, and preservation zones, restricted lands where it was unsafe to build. But communicating this information, even in its simplest form, proved largely ineffective. The result is disturbing: the fastest-growing areas in the city are squarely in the designated preservation zones. Once the visiting experts had gone, the plan's precise and rigorous hazard mapping was largely wasted. We failed to grasp an essential reality: weak local authorities, left to explain, defend, and advocate for critical technical priorities, were unable to effect decisions on the ground. Turnover among key officials weakened their grasp of good disaster management, donor interest waned, and federal priorities shifted to other pressing concerns.

## PRIVATE VS. PUBLIC SPACE

Where the city's master plan was implemented, there, too, problems arose. The plan had been conceived by a strong but short-term external technical team collaborating with city officials, who were weak. Federal interests did not want strong municipalities to counter centralized decision making. As a result it was implemented in patches and with insufficient forethought. Scattered government offices were consolidated into a single complex, the main hospital was rebuilt, and a small number of other one-off set pieces were constructed. A new bridge for through traffic to bypass the city is under construction. The old city, its bazaar, and residential areas were devastated in the quake. Infrastructure was limited and congested. Thus the decision was made, driven by technical advice based on engineering standards, to reconstruct the city with wider roads that would improve access.

But widening the roads changed the ancient center irrevocably. A bazaar is largely a pedestrian area that encourages close relationships among traders and with passers-by; it is the life and soul of a city community and typically also serves a wide rural area. The master plan proposed to replace the physical and economic structure of the bazaar with a series of multistory shopping plazas at selected locations. The fundamental differences between the public space of a bazaar and the private space of a plaza, which is enclosed and depends on electricity, were not well understood. The shopkeepers and their customers did not challenge the premise, believing that the city was going to be rebuilt "like Tokyo," that is, earthquake-resistant. But no sustained technical support was available to recalibrate the plans according to real needs and local ways of life; still less were there funds.

## IN THE PUBLIC INTEREST

In Muzaffarabad neither the Municipal Corporation nor the Development Authority was strong before the earthquake. After the quake these agencies had fewer staff members, wrecked facilities, and missing records, all of which compounded their confusion. At no point since the earthquake has a single structural engineer been employed by city authorities. Only two people serve as building-control officers (surveyors and inspectors); this in the throes of repairing a city that is now home to over 150,000 residents. Government officials could not cooperate long enough to consolidate shared concerns and city priorities. And both federal and local authorities considered public works more important than houses and commercial development.

Cities are public space but primarily private property—residential and commercial. But governments tend to read the city as a series of public projects. In post-disaster contexts governments focus on public works rather than facilitating and guiding private-sector recovery, which would, in turn, privilege reconstruction and bolster the economy. Worse, urban priorities are often set by national politics, leaving local interests to flounder. Thus, the city hospital, government administration buildings, and other flagship projects were completed by donors and contractors promptly and offered as turnkey examples of effective recovery. These new (highly technical) public buildings are a source of pride, but are proving expensive to operate and maintain. Meanwhile, the city at large became invisible and fell silent. In Muzaffarabad there are twenty official wards; these coincide with community groups and physical limits that could have served as a basis for representing, consulting, and mobilizing local interests in reconstruction. Yet no city government elections based on ward boundaries have taken place since 1991. There was no channel through which to focus attention on issues of social infrastructure, such as regenerating key markets, invigorating civil society, and creating jobs. What's more, the disaster itself did not bring about political solidarity. In fact, instead of helping people forge common ground and consolidate their efforts, it escalated pre-existing power struggles.[2]

## LIVING IN LIMBO

More than 40,000 people lost their houses in Muzaffarabad. Another 30,000 were unable or unwilling to return home. Initially, people either moved away or onto open spaces and into tents and temporary shelters. Individual on-site shelters are an alternative to large camps, but in urban areas where land tenure is a problem and there is less material to recycle, they are a difficult option. The majority of families lived in one or the other of these temporary conditions for at least a year. People repaired or retrofitted their houses the best they could. Some families moved into rentals that were still intact, usually sharing exorbitant rents, and therefore living in crowded spaces. Where the master plan indicated high-risk red zones, appropriate only for certain infrastructure, property owners were promised they would be relocated to satellite towns. But in July 2010 these towns still existed only on paper. The land had not been developed and the designated families had not been relocated. Instead, the government of Pakistan requested that donors provide prefabricated shelters to be placed wherever space existed, including in the red zones, at an average cost of $5,000 per unit. Individual families paid for water and sewage connections, as well as the cost of boundary walls for privacy.

Before the government's shelter program got under way, UN-Habitat expressed concerns about large numbers of

Tariqabad, a fast-growing district of the city, is home to several thousand people and has no planning controls. It lies in an area identified by the 2006 master plan as among the most vulnerable to multiple risks, including landslides, erosion, and seismic damage.

people living for extensive periods in prefab units. When shelters are sited on valuable land, these units preempt or delay permanent construction and long-term recovery. Providing shelters also runs the risk of encouraging incremental construction that does not meet even minimum seismic standards. Ad hoc service provision and environmental deterioration, low density, and limited options for families also follow from decisions to use temporary shelters tied to a rigid package of short-term assistance. Unfortunately, these concerns went unheeded. As of January 2010, 3,074 shelters had been constructed. Some are owned by the original residents, some are rented out, and others have been sold.

These shelters now occupy the city. Installed on cleared and partially cleared sites, they elbow in on neighboring plots, drift onto roads, and interrupt rights of way. The prefabricated shells are utterly inflexible single-story boxes with 8-foot (2.4-m) unreinforced masonry walls that provide only a modicum of privacy in a culture where privacy is a social imperative. For the majority of families this is the only land they will ever own; but with the shelter on the site, they have nowhere to rebuild a permanent home. Moreover, plots that once accommodated a large, extended family in two or three stories can only provide a home for four to six family members; the others have no choice but to go elsewhere. Labor and material costs have skyrocketed and the price of land has escalated fourfold since the earthquake. Five years after the quake, over 35,000 people are still living in shelters or rented accommodations. Savings and assistance are exhausted and rents are so expensive that people are unable to save. This in turn cripples the economy and suppresses financial stimulus. It will take another ten years before these residents are resettled in permanent homes and rebuilding is likely to be piecemeal long after that.

## RURAL HOUSING RECONSTRUCTION: WHAT WENT RIGHT?

Over 90 percent of the population in Kashmir is rural. The quake left more than 3.5 million people homeless and 630,000 houses were destroyed or seriously damaged. The national government wanted to ensure that these distant communities would not be left behind. A massive air and road operation aided the heavily populated, steep, mountainous hinterlands, where people were facing a severe Himalayan winter. For ERRA rural housing was the largest sector, comprising over 40 percent of their total budget. As in most countries there are neither codes nor regulating authorities for rural construction. The rural housing reconstruction policy established by ERRA thus ensured that housing solutions were socially, culturally, economically, and environmentally acceptable and appropriate. Recovery was owner-driven and maximized the use of local and salvaged materials. Technical support gathered and promoted best practices, including vernacular building methods, endorsed solutions, and replaced bad habits with sound hybrid techniques.[3] Over 90 percent of the 463,000 new houses and 170,000 repaired houses were finished by 2009.

The government of Pakistan provided the same financial package (approximately $3,000) to rural and urban families who lost their homes. In rural areas this was disbursed in tranches correlated to progress and sound construction. But a payment that was adequate for a rural family was insufficient in the city. Further, urban residents received a single cash payment in 2008 because the federal government assumed that the authorities were already in place to provide technical guidance and enforcement—a dubious assumption even in normal times. Certainly people welcomed the money, but the bulk of it was not put into reconstruction. Urban housing is far more complex and expensive than its rural counterpart and would have required a system of loans to help ensure that homes were rebuilt.

↖ In the old city single-story prefab shelters took the place of three-story houses, leaving no land clear for rebuilding.

↑ A rubble-clogged street in the old city

← New construction in the old city has repeated bad habits; here, money was spent on an unsafe parapet and surface finishes.

↙ A demonstration model of confined masonry by UN-Habitat and the City Development Authority: correctly spaced, reinforced rebar that turns the corners, stabilizing them. Too much rebar can make a house rigid; not enough leaves it weak and vulnerable.

↓ UN-Habitat steel fixers at a reconstruction site demonstrate how to construct and place the metal frame that reinforces the concrete.

Illegal, uncontrolled construction on a waterway, where there is a high risk of floods and mudslides

## SITTING ON OUR HANDS IN MUZAFFARABAD

While ERRA strove to avoid the trap of leaving rural communities behind, it failed to notice that urban communities were struggling. Rural communities are more coherent, homogenous, and stable than those in cities. They generally find it easier to organize themselves after a disaster or conflict. Urban land is more valuable and there is more conflict about it. In rural areas private land is generally privately held, whereas in urban areas there are competing interests and priorities (e.g., owners, renters, and subletters) that set private rights against the public good, itself a highly malleable term.

Urban livelihoods are also likely to be disproportionately affected by disaster. Jobs in cities are tied to buildings, stock, and machinery, all of which can be wiped out and may prove prohibitively expensive to replace. In Muzaffarabad traders not only lost their shops but their stock, as well as the land taken from them to widen roads. Rubble blocked the streets for six months after the earthquake, paralyzing the city. Basic services and supply lines collapsed. Those who did not lose their shops outright could not reopen and shuttered their businesses indefinitely.

Many of the UN-Habitat staff who participated in the ERRA Rural Housing Program were from Muzaffarabad, so they, too, had lived in tents and shelters, moved during the early migration, or were trapped in rental and planning limbo. Despite this personal experience, earthquake-engineered design and construction and efforts at capacity building and getting good information out, successful in rural areas, were absent in Muzaffarabad, where damaged buildings were being cosmetically rehabilitated and new construction was indifferent to earthquake safety. UN-Habitat offered technical support to city authorities and communities but we were turned down by ERRA, even though funding was available. Public-sector infrastructure was the priority; there was simply no interest in helping individuals build back their homes and businesses.

The urgency and sense of abandonment felt within the city were never reflected at the state or federal level, where all decisions were made. So residents rebuilt anywhere they could, in any way possible. Three years after the earthquake the initial momentum that had led everyone in the city to pull together had drained away. Unity garnered during the emergency had been eroded by years of inaction and political divisions and replaced by an atmosphere of blame, frustrated expectations, disenfranchisement, and inertia. Professionals, teachers, and journalists never found their voice. So, in 2008, after we were again rejected by ERRA, UN-Habitat teams started a process of informal support.

## TOO LITTLE, TOO LATE?

Our Safer Cities, Safer Residents program focused on housing and ran on a minuscule budget that we shifted from the rural program. Our team—architects, engineers, and community-development professionals—stepped beyond institutional constraints to work in partnership with local, neighborhood, and city authorities. We got to know the city. We devoted evenings and weekends to training sessions for municipal authorities and public-awareness activities. We facilitated roundtable discussions for government stakeholders and civic leaders, constructed demonstration and model buildings, advised on materials selection and quality control, gave on-site training on building vulnerability and risk, and provided design advice through clinics. We brought support and information to the streets. We had a staff of thirty from UN-Habitat and brought in more than fifty additional people from government and universities. Teams went ward to ward, documenting construction practices, collecting questions, and identifying

Could not one of the world's many engineering firms have sponsored a structural engineer for Muzaffarabad?

community partners. Radio shows helped us reach a citywide audience. We wanted to demonstrate that the future safety of the city was in everyone's hands. We launched an initiative to involve schoolchildren, students, and teachers and did everything from providing fact sheets to holding essay and painting competitions and debates for the senior students. One hundred and twenty schools took part. Everyone we could rally with valuable information, knowledge, or skills contributed. Faculty from the university's geology department explained faults and landslide risks. We followed up with walking tours and talked about building materials and real dangers in places where residents could see and touch the fragile geology of their city. If nothing else the informal initiative allowed families to repair and partially rebuild their existing homes and apartments. It also helped create community awareness of safe building practice. Crucially, we learned that technical experts have a professional and moral responsibility to be proactive, to lead change.

Still, today in Muzaffarabad a worrying amount of development is taking place in high-risk zones. Assessments, while helpful, have little impact on practices. On one- to three-story houses, dangerous additions that rise to five or six stories are common, and very unsafe; some are toppling. Appalling workmanship and detailing characterize new buildings, particularly those in reinforced concrete, which is a complex technology that leaves a wide margin for error. Money is wasted on incompetent repairs that make people more vulnerable. In the event of another earthquake here, we will all have to ask ourselves why we abandoned a traumatized community whose institutions were so badly weakened. Professional architects and engineers need to reflect on why they missed so many opportunities to help. Donors need to ask themselves if the balance of financial and technical assistance addressed the right priorities. Such failures should not be tolerated.

At the very least we owe the citizens of Muzaffarabad an apology. But do we expect to do better next time? What will be different? We can start by recognizing that the purely technical exercises of hazard mapping and revising codes, while useful, will not alone bring about results on the ground. The greater challenge, particularly in our cities, is in *implementing* change. Technical professionals need to get beyond worrying about fees and become proactive: interfere, ask questions, advise, advocate, and be interested and available on the ground, on-site, in the community. We need to assume a professional moral responsibility and tirelessly promote safe construction as a life-or-death issue, first among colleagues and students and then within communities and to decision makers. We need to link professionals across disciplines and physical borders, enabling them to share resources and expertise that support intelligent, sustainable interventions. We need to tie the private and institutional sectors together under corporate social responsibility. Could not one of the world's many engineering firms have sponsored a structural engineer for Muzaffarabad?

## HOW MIGHT ARCHITECTS CONTRIBUTE?

At the city level most people are not equipped to envision a future different from the past or translate propositions into concrete proposals. Unfortunately, the common response is reactive. The more confident citizens ask questions, but they are often perceived as critics and malcontents. This is where the architect comes in. Architects and designers are particularly skilled at helping turn aspirations and ideas into viable proposals that can be discussed, considered, and priced. After a disaster it is invaluable to help promote diverse opinions, enable active participation, and harness the ingenuity and entrepreneurship latent in city communities.

Take reading maps, for example. Maps are a language that requires fluency. In developed countries we are familiar with reading all manner of maps, as well as the visual languages facilitated by computer literacy. There was, however, no commonly used or familiar map of Muzaffarabad before the earthquake. Even with the advances and accessibility of satellite images, maps and visual information are not self-evident for much of the world's population. Most people cannot pick out north and south, let alone recognize major landmarks, understand the Cartesian relationships between points, or identify abstract patterns. Planners assume that just because people know their city they can translate their on-the-ground knowledge into spatial experience. So when maps become the key

← Precarious stories added to a house, without recognition of the risk

↑ Expensive new construction goes forward without any understanding of seismic technology or earthquake-safe design.

tool in decision making, many people are excluded. It is unfortunate that although Muzaffarabad had a large university, there were no departments of engineering, architecture, or planning. Their presence might have provided an important and independent technical resource for the recovery and reconstruction process, as well as a partner to help different groups collaborate in certain projects of literacy and advocacy.

This, however, would require rethinking architectural education and practice in Pakistan, which focuses largely on aesthetics and favors elaborate forms that disregard concerns for structural integrity or environmental performance. Educated to serve the privileged classes, Pakistani architects have never acted collectively, nor have they said much of relevance about managing disasters. Is it any wonder the public does not see them as a resource? The disaster should have been a wake-up call. But five years after the Kashmir earthquake shocked the world, architects there still do not study earthquake-resistant design. There is still little sign that this or any other challenge—environmental sustainability, rapid growth—have had an impact on technical education or practice.

Meanwhile, as is often the case, the spotlight moved on quickly. Today, there is little interest in Muzaffarabad on the part of international donors or programs. In effect all the opportunities to learn from the process or consider what we might do better next time were squandered. Architects do not usually consider themselves complicit in the failures of public officials or responsible for promoting future safety. So we are left to ask: how do a city and community gain access to expertise and advice? How can they alert technical professionals to what is needed? How can professionals—both local and external—support the authorities' requests for technical capacity in the face of political intransigence?

## STAYING ON

In September 2009 the Shelter Inter Agency Standing Committee, a forum of UN and independent humanitarian organizations, identified urban recovery as a key global priority in humanitarian response. And yet after the 7.6 Mw earthquake in West Sumatra a month later, the heavily damaged city of Padang, with a population of over 750,000, received no shelter assistance for the first six months, while rural areas were given priority. Three months later the staggering scale of damage in the cities in Haiti has finally brought urban concerns and urban reconstruction to the forefront of disaster prevention and planning.

As we write, the Kashmiri government has at last taken notice of Muzaffarabad. The long-term negative impact of the temporary shelters is now recognized. The government has resolved to strengthen its support for reforms, lest the city continue to develop at ever greater risk. Officials and activists have finally been heard. But it is essential that technical support remain available. Attention and interest on the part of local authorities and international agencies are fleeting, and they are rarely patient or committed enough to insist on action or wait around until the time is right to help. UN-Habitat plans to stay on in Muzaffarabad, developing good practices and initiatives that can be replicated in other cities.

Notes

1  On October 8, 2005, at 8:50 am local time, a 7.6 Mw earthquake struck northern Pakistan; the epicenter was 7.4 miles (12 km) northeast of the city and 16 miles (26 km) below ground level.

2  Muzaffarabad had a highly politicized relationship with Islamabad (the capital of Pakistan) before the earthquake and with various political lobbies within PaK. Between 2005 and 2009 the government of PaK had four different prime ministers and cabinets, constantly reshuffling the political and technocratic landscape.

3  ERRA, supported by UN-Habitat, recognized a range of solutions addressed to various subcultures. Training was based on a cascade system that intensively prepared a corps of engineers and architects as master trainers to train a larger number of subengineers and NGO staff, who in turn trained larger numbers of master masons as mobile teams that could reach the vast numbers of artisans and households in need of information and practical advice. The same teams carried out building inspections. Of the homes built in this way 95 percent comply with ERRA guidelines. We gained unprecedented experience in addressing scale, speed, and urgency through the rural program.

# PART 3

# URBAN RISK AND RECOVERY

"The political dimension of the design of New Orleans is nowhere more evident than in the suburban settlements of New Orleans East, in the perceived conflict between sustainable communities and sustainable landscapes."

# BELOW THE SILL PLATE: NEW ORLEANS EAST STRUGGLES TO RECOVER

DEBORAH GANS WITH
DARCH, ARCHITECTS, NEW YORK

A full six months after Hurricane Katrina, New Orleans was still like a city the morning after, as if the revelers had all just gone home or the last fan had departed the Superdome after a game. Yet the detritus littering the streets was not the usual Mardi Gras bead-laced garbage, but streetlights blinking as they lay on their sides and houses unmoored from their stoops. We drove for miles past the wreckage along avenues named with insouciance in the face of previous historical troubles—Elysian Fields, Desire, Esplanade—then east across the Industrial Canal, another fault line in the present mishap, and on into a territory called New Orleans East. There, the blue cloudless sky set off the profiles of tidy ranch houses built side-by-side along gently curving streets. Gradually, we discerned the signs of an event and its aftermath—the broken windows and moldy sheetrock. In the absence of the neighbors, the writing on the walls told their stories in the emotion-laden language of graffiti scrawled on garage doors: "We Will Be Back," "House for Sale," "See You Soon!!!!" With a house on every block marked or under renovation, the people had placed a tactical hold on the neighborhood in hopes of saving it from demolition. Over the four years that followed we became advocates, planners, and architects for the *anywhere* suburbs of New Orleans East, in particular the neighborhood of Plum Orchard, and subsequently for portions of the Lower Ninth Ward. This is a story of our work from the ground up—of its rich range of consequences and, ultimately, of its limitations.

## PLUM ORCHARD

We began our involvement in post-Katrina New Orleans as participants in a Housing and Urban Development academic grant to aid particular citizens while developing strategies to prepare the city for future such events. Our local partners, Acorn (Association for the Community Organizations for Reform Now) and Acorn Housing, had strong constituencies in both New Orleans East and the Lower Ninth. After Katrina New Orleans East had received less attention than the historic and central Lower Ninth Ward, despite its equally dire circumstances and the significance of its location. The significance resides first of all in its ubiquity. New Orleans East is an extensive urban zone in low-lying, marshy land along Lake Pontchartrain. Not only is it large in itself but it represents the vast, increasingly vulnerable coastal suburban settlements of America. Second, it reveals the true demographics of such suburbs, which, contrary to popular assumption, house not just the middle classes but also lower-income populations—albeit on property that is the most flood-prone or otherwise marginal. We framed our efforts as no less than reenvisioning the coastal suburb in the age of global warming, in ways specifically beneficial to the lower-income populations.

The political dimension of the design of New Orleans as a whole is nowhere more evident than in the suburban settlements of New Orleans East, in the perceived conflict between sustainable communities and sustainable landscapes. The battle for New Orleans pits those who consider the entire city as a single flood plain, all of which is threatened by longstanding social dysfunction (as well as by global warming), against those who would shrink the city to high ground to save it from flooding. A now-infamous plan of the first recovery effort placed dots across a city map to indicate potential areas of prophylactic depopulation and house demolition in anticipation of future flooding; our site was included. The general assumption was that the residents of these areas, who had scattered during the crisis, would remain diasporic or move to other neighborhoods of the city. Yet our site is no lower in elevation than other damaged suburban developments, including the whiter Jefferson Parish, west of the city, so that to empty it of its residents took on undertones of ethnic cleansing. While the "dots" have now been officially discredited, the policy persists de facto in the lack of investment in these districts and as word on the street.

This territorial conflict emerges in part from the facts of the aftermath of the hurricane but also from habitual design thinking, which has long relied on extra-large infrastructure to control the environment, on the one hand, and on individual self-determination to structure the political process, on the other. The catalytic storm rendered this dialectical approach to planning ineffective. The call for the wholesale erasure of neighborhoods, presented as defending ecology, confronted the immobility of individuals, presented as asserting community. In our work with the residents of Plum Orchard we sought to overcome this standoff by accepting the existing suburban morphology of individual properties and then suggesting incremental adaptations to new environmental and social factors that could come to have the shape and impact of a master plan. Perhaps the clearest statement of our initial mindset was *Project Backyard*, a self-help brochure that we distributed to returning residents in the immediate aftermath of the storm. It offered charts of plants, trees, and ground covers suitable to the climate, accompanied by descriptions of how gardens act as easy, cheap, and cheerful ecological tools. It was a big hit in the neighborhood and at citywide rebuilding fairs. It explained that, according to the United States Department of Agriculture National Resource Conservation Service, the massing of many small plots of modified wetland can be an effective device of water management—perhaps as good as a major marsh. *Many*, in our thinking, was an alternative to *extra-large*. While we do not propose this as the only scale of approach to the problems of suburban resettlement, it represents a larger intent—to undo the overdetermined relation between an environmental problem and the social price to be paid.

FIRMS
DARCH AND GANS STUDIO WITH PRATT CENTER, NJIT INFRASTRUCTURE PLANNING, AND HOFFMAN BRANDT LANDSCAPE ARCHITECTS

PROJECT LOCALE
NEW ORLEANS EAST, LOUISIANA, USA

(previous spread) Plum Orchard: at the center of the neighborhood stands a venerable live oak that provides shade, uptakes water, and resists wind. The soft-paved street and the raised house are part of our design. The small house at right is a circa-1900 fishing shack. The blue line marks the level of a 100-year flood.

↑ Green Dot Plan: in 2006 the Bring New Orleans Back Commission unveiled a map with green dots designating areas where neighborhoods might be cleared and parks created. While the areas were low-lying, other equally vulnerable terrains were spared. The circles locate the green dots; one dot covers part of our site in Plum Orchard.

In the four years that we worked in Plum Orchard, we developed strategies that scale up, in time and territory, from the backyard and its retrofitted house to clustered settlements to an aggregation of twelve blocks called the Model Block, which in turn connects to citywide infrastructures.

## RETROFITS

The scattered site development that occurred in the wake of the storm secured the typical Plum Orchard block of houses separated with 3-foot- (1-m-) wide side yards but reduced the possibility for alternative settlement patterns and land use. In order to act fast—faster than architects and planners usually work—we came up with brochures addressed to those in the midst of rebuilding. Some listed available social resources and others described best building practices for flood-proof construction. *Retrofit the Rancher* went beyond specifying waterproof materials to visualize the environmental transformation of an entire neighborhood through devices that could

be implemented within an individual property, such as adding attic areas of refuge, solar roofs, cisterns, green walls and fences, and porches for shade and ventilation. As its moniker suggests, the brochure engaged the modest ranch typologies of the neighborhood and illustrated the proposed devices using actual homes and addresses so that residents could imagine such a transformation concretely and aspire to it— which they did.

## CLUSTERED SETTLEMENTS: REPOSITIONING IN PLACE

To move back onto an empty block in New Orleans East is to make oneself vulnerable to crime in the short term and water in the long term. There are neighborhood strategies to cope with this vulnerability that predate Katrina, however, and derive from informal social covenants far more powerful than any textbook principles such as "Eyes on the Block." These social covenants work well in part because they are rooted in the

Retrofit the Rancher: 4237 America Street, Plum Orchard. In this proposed renovation of a house in the neighborhood that survived the flood, a new lattice wall supports vegetation, provides shade, and screens an ADA ramp leading to an additional raised space of refuge.

Street Front

extended families that populate the neighborhood—for example, the Alexander family owns more than a dozen properties there. These families have historically formed strategic links between socioeconomic and physical infrastructure, using real-estate ploys like house swapping among family members according to need, a tactic that readily accepts an environmental logic of abandoning a flood-prone house for the safety of nearby higher ground. They have developed a land-use pattern different from the usual formulas of the suburbs, in that it mixes rental properties and double houses with single-family homeownership. Richer suburbs have resisted the introduction of exactly this economic mix, seeing these types as depreciating real-estate values. But our neighborhood understands that the mix allows families to move up rather than out when the floods come, and thus to remain housed whether young or old, wage earning or unemployed. Today, these networks and tactics sustain people physically and psychologically, in the absence of city investment.

The storm's destruction of the landscape created the need for a new kind of development covenant linked to the *right to return safely*. In its most succinct form, this covenant argues that no individual should reclaim a territory alone; that a neighborhood is the smallest sustainable unit socially, economically, and physically; and the smallest division of such a neighborhood is the housing cluster. We have made this implicit community understanding explicit in our proposal for clustered settlements. The housing cluster is the sustainable renovation of three or more preexisting contiguous houses. At its best this entails the rebuilding of a swathe at maximum density with a range of aspirational features, such as the aggregation of larger preserves of wetland and off-the-grid services. For several years Acorn Housing adopted this principle in their lending and development practices in that they encouraged and sought out for reconstruction contiguous building sites on higher ground within their areas of influence.

New Orleans is a landscape in which every inch of elevation counts. No enclave is categorically flat, including Plum Orchard, where the highest ground is 9 feet (3 m) above the low point. The covenant's seemingly small adjustments to where a family may rebuild within the neighborhood—to *repositioning in place*—can therefore have profound effects.

## TRUE BOUNDARIES: THE MODEL BLOCK, A PLANNING UNIT OF PROPER SIZE

In formulating a settlement scale larger than the cluster, we sought a planning unit that could support the possibility of safe return through some degree of infrastructural autonomy, both social and physical. To determine its reach we identified such standard community-based planning elements as the ten-minute walk to public transportation, schools, and markets, as well as the perimeters defined by family networks, natural drainage patterns in relation to existing sewer systems and pumps, routes of evacuation, and sites of refuge. A test "model block of proper size" emerged from this analysis, specifically as a group of about twelve blocks in Plum Orchard within a set of preexisting borders: three roads and a defined green space. The I-10 to the west is a major raised expressway and an evacuation route to Baton Rouge; Chef Menteur Highway to the south, on naturally high ground, is the old commercial artery that connects the east to the downtown; Dwyer Road on the north provides major drainage infrastructure at the lowest edge of the site; and the convent of the Sisters of the Holy Name to the east has an extensive campus. Most importantly, the inhabitants identified the area within these boundaries as a natural precinct they called "the Goose," for reasons no one can recall.

As we were documenting the implicit organizational structure of the Goose, the larger planning processes of New Orleans were

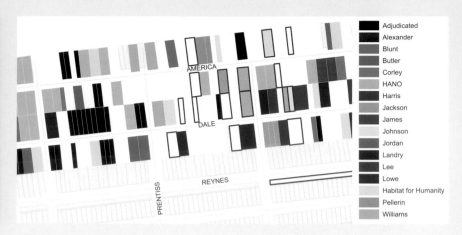

→ Each color in the Family Network represents the property holdings of a single family within the boundaries of our site. Habitat for Humanity and the Housing Authority of New Orleans (HANO) also own multiple lots.

↓ Zoning Diagram: the proposed rezoning is shown overlaid on the pre-Katrina plan of the Model Block. Densely zoned settlement and public infrastructures are proposed for the higher elevations toward Chef Menteur, while the lowest portion of the site, which included many destroyed HANO properties, is reserved for wetland. A pedestrian route runs past schools and recreational spaces. Bus and bike routes connect the Model Block to the city-at-large.

| | |
|---|---|
| ■ | Adjudicated |
| ▨ | Alexander |
| ▨ | Blunt |
| ▨ | Butler |
| ▨ | Corley |
| ▨ | HANO |
| ▨ | Harris |
| ▨ | Jackson |
| ▨ | James |
| ▨ | Johnson |
| ▨ | Jordan |
| ▨ | Landry |
| ▨ | Lee |
| ▨ | Lowe |
| ▨ | Habitat for Humanity |
| ▨ | Pellerin |
| ▨ | Williams |

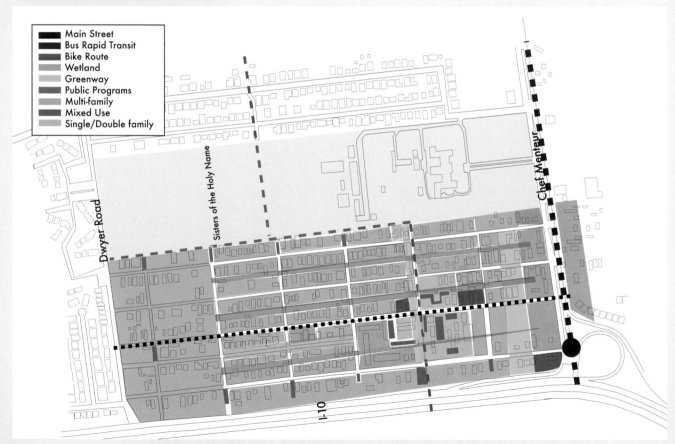

| | |
|---|---|
| ▨ | Main Street |
| ▨ | Bus Rapid Transit |
| ▨ | Bike Route |
| ▨ | Wetland |
| ▨ | Greenway |
| ▨ | Public Programs |
| ▨ | Multi-family |
| ▨ | Mixed Use |
| ▨ | Single/Double family |

under way. The Urban Land Institute Plan (2005) was replaced by Bring New Orleans Back (BNOB; 2006), which was in turn succeeded by the Lambert Plan (2006), itself succeeded by the Unified New Orleans Plan (2007). All of these plans called for determining the city footprint by the strength of community self-assertion. The BNOB process, for example, required that 50 percent of the local population declare they would return in order for the community to stake a claim to its future—a percentage that Plum Orchard had not yet met. Silence was tantamount to elimination. To stimulate community organization in a bedroom suburb was, therefore, to secure its immediate, short-term survival, as well as to germinate new civic structures for long-term environmental planning. Perhaps our greatest accomplishment was to hold church-basement community meetings and visioning sessions that helped create an educated and engaged citizenry capable of using the instruments of planning even if the City Planning Commission lacked the authority to transform community power into policy.[1]

The planning principles for the Model Block of the Goose begin with the consideration of the site as one continuous field rather than as a street map. A foundational principle for building in New Orleans is the Base Flood Elevation, or BFE, the elevation of a 100-year flood. It affects all aspects of life—from house insurance to zoning and ecosystems to livelihoods. We therefore chose to describe the landscape sectionally as a series of plans cut at different heights above sea level, in order to study the way in which floodplains might suggest new combinations of environment and behavior. Historically, the cultural landscapes of New Orleans have been linked by water and elevation to indigenous building types: saltwater wetland to fishing cottage; brackish marsh to raised Creole cottage; fresh water to house with a raised center hall; upland to shotgun house. Beginning at 2 feet (0.66 m) above the official BFE and descending northward to 8 feet (2.4 m) below, our site is an exemplar, in small,

of the total field of New Orleans, where myriad conditions coexist on a single hyperdifferentiated floodplain.

For instance, at BFE 0-0—that is, sea level—the Model Block is a continuous planted landscape, punctuated by the piles, porches, and stairs of raised houses, and features water-management tools such as bioswales and seasonal ponds. At the high southern edge of the site the plan cuts through an underground infrastructure of culverts and drywells. Using a numeric method to calculate runoff, our infrastructure team figured that this field can manage the 5 million gallons (1.89 billion l) per hour dumped by a storm once every ten years.

At BFE 20-0 one can see the scale and density of the neighborhood with a mix of clustered and traditionally sited houses in a multistory residential development. Along the high ground at the southern edge of the site the plan cuts through the lower level of a group of commercial buildings. The development houses and supports mixed demographics and can help pay for social infrastructures such as playgrounds. A hierarchy of ways designed to provide both social and flood infrastructures appears at this plan elevation. The first way is the major connection of the enclave to the city and its primary evacuation route, Chef Menteur Highway, for which we propose a rapid-transit bus system. Wide north-south streets running downhill from Chef Menteur are paved culverts that move water quickly to the bottom of the site; parallel to them run swales that also carry water. Narrower east-west side streets of gravel slow the water down and are selectively pedestrianized, planted, and regraded. Their culs-de-sac are captured as landscape or used as sites for collective off-the-grid services like solar panels, recycling stations, and cisterns for potable water. These can serve the Model Block in case of emergency and in the continued absence of city infrastructure investment. One cul-de-sac extends past a school and neighborhood commercial center into a greenway and bike path that connects to other communities farther east.

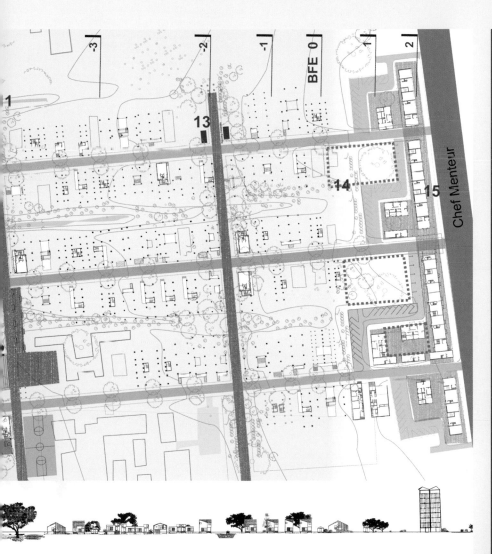

← Model Block Plan at 0-BFE: at 0 Base Flood Elevation, or sea level, the majority of the site appears as a continuous landscape of swales, water gardens, and plantings punctuated by the columns of raised houses. Above sea level at Chef Menteur, the plan cuts through ground-floor commercial property. Toward Dwyer Road, where the landscape is 8 feet (2.4 m) below sea level, the drawing reveals the house plans. This is a border zone of vulnerability between the neighborhood and the newly recuperated wetland.

1   Nature Trail Station
2   Backyard Swale
3   Wetland Park
4   Soft-Paved Side Street
5   Hard-Paved Thoroughfare
6   New Cluster-Housing
7   Bird Watch and Refuge Tower
8   Swimming Hole and Holding Pond
9   Pedestrian Route along Schools
    and Play Spaces
10  Solar Array and Picnic Shed
11  Foot and Bike Bridge
12  Bleachers across from Paved Court
13  Swap and Recycle Lagniappe
14  Underground Cisterns
15  Commercial Floor of High-Rise

↙ Model Block Elevation at 0-BFE: the red line marks 0-BFE, which is the level of the plan above. The mural depicts the zoning, infrastructure, and housing of the proposed Model Block with multifamily development on high ground at Chef Menteur, new housing types alongside the existing houses, new plantings, the soft-paved side street, and the connection to the city sewer at Dwyer Road.

Taken together the complete set of graded field conditions from BFE 0-0 to BFE 20-0 and their attendant water-management resources ensure that the neighborhood can be pumped out rapidly during almost any flood and help the community learn to live with water.

## THE PROJECT REALPOLITIK

At the conclusion of the grant many of the strategies and tactics that we developed for water management and some of the specific desires of the neighborhood that we communicated were incorporated in fall 2006 into the official Lambert/Danzey Neighborhood Rebuilding Plan for District Nine.[2] And while that plan has been superseded, our thinking, by virtue of its resonance with the infrastructural ideas of so many other community-based efforts, seems to have infiltrated the thinking of ongoing city planning.

Acorn Housing then hired James Dart of the firm DARCH and me as architects for a city-sponsored project slated to create as many as 400 prefabricated houses on adjudicated sites, some in New Orleans East but most in the Lower Ninth Ward. These properties were contested landscapes after the storm both because of their low elevations and because they had been condemned long before Katrina as blighted. The prognosis for the neighborhoods was therefore in question. To rebuild houses in these neighborhoods meant to rethink localities that had been troubled for many years. In short it required that we develop suitably raised and protected housing typologies while also looking *below the sill plate* at the social and economic ground on which these houses would stand.

In developing house types for Plum Orchard we always envisioned producing them in a factory. New Orleans seemed the perfect venue for prefabrication, given the immediacy of need, the scale of demand, and the dearth of local labor. Yet the most common prefabricated house in America, the ranch house, had been disproportionately vulnerable to water damage in the suburbs of New Orleans East. In the postwar years, as residents moved out from the Lower Ninth Ward across the Industrial Canal in pursuit of the American dream, they had torn down their old, environmentally sensitive elevated cottages and replaced them with standard suburban-style houses. But the generic American house is not well suited to New Orleans. It requires an elaborate foundation because the ground is not solid enough for the standard slab to rest on. Instead, the slab sits on edge beams that are, in turn, supported on subsurface piles. In Plum Orchard much of this modified ranch housing had been built by federal housing programs, designed for the poorest residents and sited on the lowest ground, and was consequently flooded out of existence during Katrina. This forensic analysis points to the great danger of pre-fabrication: the illusion of almost universal applicability—formally and socially. Thus far in the rebuilding of New Orleans assimilation to locale has often consisted of importing generic prefabricated homes produced in factories from Pennsylvania to Georgia and raising them to flood heights set by the Federal Emergency Management Agency (FEMA). Our ambition as the architects for Acorn Housing, as in our proposal for the Model Block, was to consider this industrial object, the prefab, together with its lot and landscape as a single entity.

The realities of the adjudicated properties tested our ambitions. The first 150 sites we were granted were scattered throughout the Lower Ninth Ward—recapitulating the problems of planning we had found in New Orleans East just after the storm. In order to remedy the isolation of the lots, Acorn attempted to acquire adjacent properties from neighbors willing to sell and reached out to others interested in rebuilding. We requested that they leave the lower sites fallow and begin

→ Maison Objet Trouvé (Found-Object House): much of the concern over rebuilding in New Orleans circles around the architectural and urban impact of raising houses. In fact there are many local solutions to this condition, as seen in this abandoned workshop with a generous roof.

To inform potential buyers, we prepared tear sheets on all five of our house types. The elevations at the bottom are variations of the basic plan. The back of each sheet described materials, environmental features, and costs.

↓ The Courtyard House is both a classic New Orleans and a modern type as a consequence of their shared concerns with light, air, and landscape. The kitchen is the bridge opening onto the court between the public and private wings.

↘ Mother-in-Law House: A rear residence is a full story above the ground; a street-level front unit is suitable as a studio apartment or for commercial use. The two units connect by an internal stair.

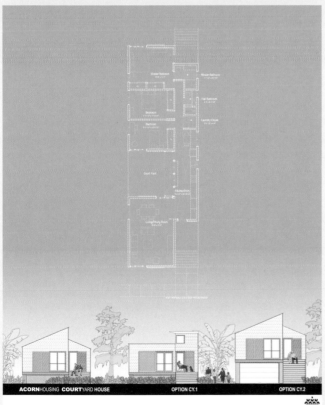

ACORNHOUSING COURTYARD HOUSE          OPTION CY.1          OPTION CY.2

ACORNHOUSING MOTHERINLAW HOUSE          OPTION ML.1          OPTION ML.2

> The lesson of our comparative cost analysis is that it is cheaper to build a neighborhood than a house—which is the financial corollary of our social claim: it is safer to build a neighborhood than a house.

building on higher ones that had the added benefit of proximity to Claiborne Avenue, a central city artery with commercial development potential. These gross tactics aimed to preserve the opportunity to reserve property near the levee in the Lower Ninth for wetlands and to establish a framework of graded development with higher density on higher ground. The test was to see if planting wetland landscapes on an ad hoc, site-by-site basis could create a latent field that could be stitched together over time. But legal complications impeded even this basic planning strategy. The problems of clearing title and establishing Acorn's ownership of the properties trumped the logic of base flood elevation. The first sites legally owned and marketed by Acorn were those with no claims on them, wherever they might be found—which was, not surprisingly, scattered about on low ground.

To develop basic prototypes for our prefabs we held focus groups with potential buyers, all of whom had connections to the neighborhood. From these we developed five designs that responded to the variety of family lifestyles presented to us. We dubbed our modified shotgun house the Best Shot, with a starter version called the First Shot. The Courtyard house brings the protected outdoor spaces of a New Orleans town-house to the suburban lot. The Mother-in-Law house has a front unit on the street for commercial, rental, or extended family use, while the rear is fully raised. The Central Stair house has a ventilated core that lends itself to coupling. The fifth is a Two-Story house for small lots. They all negotiate elevation through a series of thresholds that begin at the ground and end with the raised story. Each comes with several design variations for the street level, including stepped porches, garages, and enclosed patios. Several offer the potential for rental units or two-family situations and serve to increase density on the lots to be rebuilt on higher ground. Given the low price point of the neighborhood, the houses are cost efficient: they use passive technologies for

moving heat and air, such as orientation, ceiling height, heat chimneys, cross-ventilation, deep shading, and jalousie shutters.

In order to keep the houses as affordable as possible, we assessed cost according to four construction methods: traditional stick-built on-site; prefabricated as a complete unit with wood studs; prefabricated as panels of steel studs to be sheathed on-site; or prefabricated with Structural Insulated Panels. We produced three different sets of construction documents for each house and found that unless Acorn could build at least thirty of the 150 houses, prefabrication would have little impact on cost. Still, even a single house was far less costly than the heavily subsidized homes being built by high-profile developers like Global Green and the Make It Right Foundation. Our pricing increments came in at $140,000 for a 1,120-square-foot (104-sq.-m) Best Shot and $240,000 for a 1,780-square-foot (165-sq.-m) Mother-in-Law. The lesson of our comparative cost analysis is that it is cheaper to build a neighborhood than a house—which is, of course, the financial corollary of our social claim: it is safer to build a neighborhood than a house.

Because Acorn could not finance thirty houses up front, we were unable to begin development at the scale of a neighbor-hood. Instead, we took on the smallest sustainable unit, a housing cluster consisting of four lots on Caffin Avenue. But to date not a single house has been built. The organization was dragged into a media-enhanced political controversy, and although Congress eventually exonerated Acorn of any wrongdoing, it wasn't before they had withdrawn from the project. Even before those troubles Acorn Housing had been unable, or unwilling, to build an exhibition house that could stake a claim to the site and demonstrate the quality of the product they were offering. They lacked the financing and perhaps the experience to perform as developers for houses on spec. Nor would they entertain a rent-to-own alternative for those who could not afford a straight purchase, because they did not want to manage the ongoing maintenance and administration that rental properties require. They had hoped to spawn a community that was bottom-up and self-run, not one that would require top-down support for some time to come. Their increasing political difficulties made it difficult to secure loans, so the burden of financing these homes fell on prospective owners. Under the terms of the Road Home Program of the Louisiana Recovery Authority, returning residents are entitled to as much as $100,000 to rebuild, but they often receive much less and many have yet to see the money. None of the prospective buyers with whom we were working has been able to secure enough financing with Road Home grants, even in combination with local bank mortgages, for so much as a modestly priced home.

The current failure of this project is incidental within a much larger crisis in the rebuilding effort. It points to the limits of our approach when it is not supported by and coordinated with economic and physical plans at civic and larger scales. The city as a whole is rebounding, thankfully, but the neighborhoods that were at risk before the storm show only isolated pockets of redevelopment. The glamorous enclave of the Make It Right homes, funded by Brad Pitt, stands in the midst of a much larger area of devastation in the Lower Ninth Ward.

Within the miles of abandoned real estate in New Orleans East there lies a significant exception to this general condition. The tightly knit Vietnamese community of Village de l'Est has returned, as organized by Father Vien The Nguyen, the dynamic pastor of Mary Queen of Vietnam Church. He and his parishioners have lobbied City Hall and have even taken on FEMA directly in order to secure their return. Their first triumph was getting FEMA to lay out the infrastructure for temporary trailers in a plan that could later be used for permanent housing for the elderly. With a strong connection to the watery landscape reminiscent of their homeland, they have come back to fish the lake for a living and replant rice and vegetables in expanded community gardens and, eventually, on hydroponic farms. They have overcome the paralyzing conflict between ecology and community by convincing authorities, from the federal government to the city, to buy into their interpretation of what it means to be safe. Their answers are subtle scenarios in which safe haven includes new (or perhaps old) ways of living with water, climate, and landscape, of living in one's house and of evacuating it.

Compared with the linguistic, cultural, and economic specificity of the Vietnamese Village de l'Est, Plum Orchard and even the Lower Ninth Ward are in some regards typical of New Orleans—and of many American cities. Their refugee citizens, formerly regarded as banal suburbanites or marginal inner-city urbanites, are struggling to become decisive actors. They have asserted their right of return and thereby forced planners, politicians, and strangers to understand the difference between political and physical safety. In doing so these residents have inspired us to understand how design can help negotiate this difference.

Notes
The work described in this essay is a truly collaborative, interdisciplinary project of Professors Ronald Shiffman, Vicki Weiner, Brad Lander, Deborah Gans, and Larry Zeroth and their students at Pratt Institute; Professors James Dart, Robert Svetz, Darius Sollohub, and Robert Dresniak and their students at the New Jersey Institute of Technology; Professor Denise Hoffman Brandt and her students at City College of New York; David Bruner of the New York Botanical Garden; and Steve Handel of the Rutgers Center for Urban Restoration Ecology. The prototypes for Acorn Housing are the work of DARCH and Gans Studio.

1   Many other pro bono and academic community-planning efforts did the same, including those of Cornell University and Louisiana State University.

2   Much is owed for this to the infrastructure lead on our team, Darius Sollohub, who forged ties with various local planners, including St. Martin-Brown Associates.

"A slum is not merely an area of decrepit buildings. It is a social fact."
—Michael Harrington

# SLUMLIFTING: AN INFORMAL TOOLBOX FOR A NEW ARCHITECTURE

ALFREDO BRILLEMBOURG
AND HUBERT KLUMPNER
URBAN THINK TANK, CARACAS,
VENEZUELA

Today, more than a billion people worldwide live in slums situated largely on the physical, economic, social, and political fringe of the world's megacities. Thus far no large-scale reform or intervention has resulted in a more just and workable kind of city, nor have reforms been found that are broadly applicable. Instead, the practices and policies that have produced the asymmetries of today's cities persist. Approaches that involve large-scale, rapid change have razed slums, relocated populations, and infused poverty zones with cash through major public works, but have failed to eradicate the problem precisely because complex systems such as cities can only absorb so much change at one time. Moreover, success is less a function of available funds or technical expertise than of philosophical and cultural change. And we tend to forget that changes in lifestyle and expectations happen at very different rates than changes to the built environment.

The Sustainable Living Urban Model Laboratory (SlumLab) toolbox offers a working method for a supportive architecture that empowers people at the margins of emerging cities and promotes sustainable development in slum areas. It was devised by Urban Think Tank (UTT), an architecture and design practice based in Caracas, Venezuela, in collaboration with the Columbia University Graduate School of Architecture. Our agenda in creating the toolbox is twofold: to shift the emphasis of contemporary architecture and architectural education from form-driven to purpose-oriented and to eliminate the disconnect between design and its social impact. Rather than having a purely artistic objective, the architecture we call for creates buildings and infrastructure from more efficient, locally produced industrial materials and assembled in a kit of parts. This is slumlifting: the process of improving quality of life and infrastructure in underserved, dense, urban communities. We envision a viable, quick-fix urban architecture that functions as a life-support agent for the perpetually changing city that will benefit all cities in urgent need of solutions. Quick-fix is an emergency strategy to attend to people who are today living in inhuman conditions. It is, quite simply, activist architecture.

We focus our practical and applied efforts on the informal developments in the Latin American city, where we have strong roots. We aim to shift the city, with all its inequalities and potentials, to the center of a global discussion of the future role of architecture. The designation of Rio de Janeiro as the site of the 2016 summer Olympics gives our purpose new urgency. Perhaps the only truly global event that is not conflict-related, the Olympics will draw attention to Latin America as never before. And while there will be the inevitable feel-good coverage by the news media, there is also an opportunity for worldwide education about the potential of the southern megacity.

The informal city does not yield information or knowledge through traditional methods; satellite images are too broad and surveys cannot be conducted with any fidelity because slums are in a continuous process of transformation. So we make proposals and knock on doors. We take our students into a territory that they would otherwise never consider entering and work with them to creatively solve problems with the residents. The lessons we have taken from our work in South America can be implemented in the slums of Mumbai, Kibera, Lagos, and, for that matter, Caracas. By tackling problems at their roots and working with the public and private sectors, we devise and implement projects to solve real-world problems.

UTT's toolbox is a set of practical projects for structural intervention in a dense urban slum, shantytown, barrio, or favela. Our working method is to address each project through five themes: transportation infrastructure, water and sanitation, density and verticality, slum morphology, and local footprints/efficiency. Our solutions are tested, practical, widely applicable, and, above all, realizable here and now.

3.2
SLUMLIFTING

FIRM
URBAN THINK TANK

PROJECT LOCALES
CARACAS, VENEZUELA,
AND SÃO PAULO, BRAZIL

129

## TRANSPORTATION INFRASTRUCTURE

A defining characteristic of informal urban areas is lack of infrastructure. The small alleyways of the favela support diverse street life and pedestrian circulation but are often not wide enough to be used for public or private transportation. The resulting lack of access to interurban transit systems deprives the residents of basic services, including emergency response, and makes it difficult to network the slum into the greater city.

The traditional solution in cities—to insert new infrastructure on a large scale—is immensely costly and therefore routinely deferred. Decentralized infrastructure built on the favela's existing resourcefulness and alternative supply models is often more appropriate than typical centralized systems. In recent years Latin America has served as a testing ground for new systems of urban transportation such as Bogotá's Transmilenio bus rapid-transit (BRT) system or the Medellín and Caracas urban cable-car (Metrocable) systems.

Networks can be distributed loosely. Where existing bus routes only connect the city and the favela, reinforcing the division between the two and the city's fragmentation, a new bus line, bootstrapped onto the city system, can create a network of interconnections within the slum itself.[1]

Favelas are typically built on steep terrain. Modular stairs can be mass-produced and installed efficiently. Our modular-stair system is a replicable, cost-effective upgrade for pedestrian infrastructure that also creates construction-work opportunities for slum dwellers and provides training in metal fabrication. The stairs are prefabricated and easily installed using a minimum of two foundation points. On hilly terrain they are also built high above the surface walkways whose path they follow, which is especially useful when these passageways become rivers during heavy seasonal rains. The stair system is not yet available on an industrial scale, but UTT has

(previous spread) Informal urbanism: a favela in Caracas, Venezuela

↑ Modular stairs in a Caracas favela, built cheaply and swiftly by Urban Think Tank, improve access into and out of the neighborhood, reducing its social and economic isolation.

↑ / → UTT's Metrocable transit system for the favela of San Augustin in Caracas: the cable-car network is integrated with the city's metro system. It is 1.3 miles (2.1 km) long and moves 1,200 people per hour in each direction. Construction cost was low compared to the expense of laying rails—whether surface or elevated—or building roads for bus service. The cable system is ideally suited to the steep terrain of the favela, minimally invasive of the existing fabric, energy-efficient, and produces less air pollution.

→→ Developing transportation infrastructure is the first key to improving life in the favelas without radical and invasive clearance.

built one modular-stair system near a school in Caracas, and individual groups of people in Caracas have produced and assembled others. This underscores the advantage of a system that has only four elements: a carrying tube, step, counter step, and handrail. The stair is as well-suited to one-off construction as to a factory production chain. We call this a building recipe: you get yourself a plan (UTT creates such plans as a service) and use the resourcefulness of your community to execute it. The dimensions and structural calculations are part of the recipe, so it is easy to carry out.

An urban cable-car system can link topographically distant points with minimal disturbance to the existing fabric. The Metrocable in Caracas links three hillsides, not only connecting them to the existing metro line in the valley but, more important, linking parts of the barrio internally and making its upper reaches, previously difficult to access, newly desirable. The system has a small footprint and is minimally invasive, but significantly improves mobility.

## WATER AND SANITATION

Potable water is a luxury in slum areas. Where water mains exist, the supply is often interrupted and expensive. Where there are no mains, water is sold from trucks by distributors. The poor pay the highest prices. In Caracas water costs more than gasoline. Sewage systems present problems with respect to their inclination and diameter and are difficult to install in an existing, densely built environment, especially on steep slopes. Though rainfall may be abundant, it is usually concentrated over six months, so means are needed to store water for use during the dry season. Many cities with a rainy season (including Caracas) have a problem with surface and stormwater runoff during that period. Rainwater is wasted and black water (sewage) seeping down the hills of the slums causes erosion and destabilizes the hillsides, as well as creating health risks.

Individual rainwater harvesting may prove to be a cheap, easy solution to water woes. Dedicated small-scale units can collect and retain water for use by each household as gray

water during the dry season. Common water tanks for storage are preferable to draining water haphazardly into large area basins or pools.[2] Rooftops can be linked to a common cistern, surrounded by porous paving. These cisterns function like urban wells, collecting, filtering, and distributing gray water for uses not requiring potable, treated water (such as laundry, bathing, garden irrigation) to reduce household water costs. The paving mitigates runoff. (Solar panels can be used to power drinking-water treatment.)

Dry toilets are another viable alternative to traditional sewage systems, as they bypass the need for segregated black-water pipes and sewage-treatment plants and manage waste locally. We have installed several double-vault dry toilets in the Caracas slums and hope that the system will be approved by the Venezuelan Ministry of Natural Resources and replicated citywide throughout the barrios.

## DENSITY AND VERTICALITY

Apart from sports courts, favelas notoriously lack secure, well-lighted, and properly maintained public spaces. Perpetual growth, the absence of real streets, and low-rise high density are the culprits. Caracas has a density of 760 people per 2.5 acres (1 ha), compared, for example, to Manhattan's 550. Light is a particular challenge in the barrios. In many areas we have found that only 7 percent of the ground-floor level receives direct daylight. Delivering light to areas that are permanently dark requires an enormous amount of energy. Ventilation is no less challenging.

LED lights can run on solar panels and are very easy to install. During the day light can be delivered without storing electricity in batteries, since daylight is harvested and transported directly into dark areas. This system reflects our commitment to individual, noncentralized infrastructure, in which each household is responsible for finding a viable solution. We are currently experimenting with using sections of a corrugated-metal roof as solar panels. About 80 percent of the total surface of the

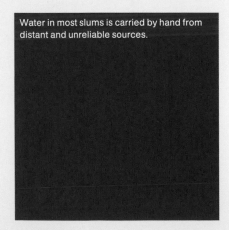

Water in most slums is carried by hand from distant and unreliable sources.

← Rendering of UTT's Vertical Gymnasium, Caracas, 2001–4. Located in Bello Campo in the poor and populous barrio of La Cruz, this 8,200-square-foot (2,500-sq.-m) complex houses a medical module of the city health department and sports facilities on the site of a former soccer field. It is the first installation of its kind in a favela and is full of activity day and night.

↓ Vertical Gym, Chacao, Caracas. Facilities include the largest public sports and training center in Chacao, basketball courts, a dance studio, weightlifting, an elevated running track, a rock-climbing wall, and a soccer field. The structure, funded by the city, is used for cultural, entertainment, and conference events as well, and includes the offices of the municipal sports director.

The daily life of the favela lends itself to an interconnected web of activities: housing may exist alongside work, commerce, sport, and even farming; together these can create a dense, economically self-sustaining hub for a healthy community.

Barrio Santa Cruz in Caracas is covered by corrugated metal-sheet roofs, making them de facto solar panels. In tropical climates corrugated roofs may prove to be the most efficient means of providing solar energy in poor neighborhoods. But we need many more solutions like this one, solutions that are accepted easily and can be incorporated into existing construction methods.

An open mind and close examination of existing practices reveal new spatial opportunities throughout the favelas. Investing these found spaces with activities and purpose requires new stimulus: connections, amenities, rehabilitated surfaces. For instance, we identified available space for a service building under an elevated highway where street children slept. So we built a soccer field between the underbelly of the highway and the roof of the children's "home."

Roofscapes and vertical surfaces are underused. The fabric of the slum already lends itself to rooftop greening at a local level, but as upgrading and other new construction take place there are opportunities to create large-scale gardens and urban agriculture, even for a continuous track of planting, bike paths, and pedestrian circulation built on top of new housing. Connected roof gardens would also help limit growth beyond structurally safe heights.

Public parks can fill risk areas to prevent future building in seismic, flood, or mudslide zones. The park can provide much-needed public space, reinforce the soil, and absorb runoff, as well as act as a placeholder to stop the favela from infiltrating unstable land. With productive parks the community gains precious open space while avoiding future calamity. Equally important, public gardens cultivate an appreciation for nature and pride of place, as communities willingly maintain their local parks.

Since the barrio has no space for horizontal expansion, we designed a vertical sports center in the Santa Cruz del Este barrio of Caracas. The Gimnasio Vertical is a multistory venue with a running track, volleyball court, basketball court, indoor soccer field, weight-training facility, and studios for martial arts, gymnastics, and dance, all with ramp access for disabled athletes. The facility is a magnet; it fosters community, fitness, and culture, thus creating a dense social nexus. Following the opening of the vertical gym, crime in the area dropped by 30 percent. A second one was built in Chacao, Caracas, and others are planned.

## SLUM MORPHOLOGY

The dense footprint of the favela follows a topographically based logic significantly different from that of nineteenth- and twentieth-century top-down urban planning. Slum morphologies thus require a completely new approach to development and improvement.

Slope is crucial to designing in informal settlements. Satellite maps and slope-intensity diagrams illustrate the dependence of the built fabric on the terrain, which drives development in particular directions, giving the settlement a grain of depressions, peaks, and ridge lines. Because each builder faces the same challenges and can access the same materials, subsequent responses to a site tend to be uniform and follow the local grain. The resulting fabric is composed of thousands of individual structures arrayed in linear clusters along topographic contours.

Not apparent in a satellite image are the large tracts situated in areas of geological risk. Favelas are often built in areas that challenge formal development, on undesirable land. In particular, land with extreme slopes and weak soil integrity is at risk of catastrophic and unpredictable events—landslides and washouts, for example—and their sites, density, and frail construction make them more than usually vulnerable to fires and earthquakes. Entire complexes of buildings are lost during rainstorms. These risk areas must be identified and redesigned, or reused, in ways that prevent future construction.

Informal morphologies are complex but consistent. The shape of buildings and blocks emerges from a bottom-up process. Houses are gradually built up with rectangular units, using available construction materials such as reinforced masonry, blocks, and scrap metal. Overhangs cantilevered over passageways, multiple levels, and bridging are common features. Slum morphology results from numerous small, individual decisions rather than from planning.

Houses are knit together or built wall-to-wall, creating residential quarters that swallow street space and convert it into private-access corridors. The prevailing culture privileges personal, qualitative space over anonymous, quantitative space. Thoroughfares are deliberately interrupted to reduce direct access and privatize street space. We have found gated communities and private roads in slum areas, an urban typology common to both formal and informal development and enabled throughout South America by the absence of institutional control (police, zoning regulations), lack of established formal layouts, the autonomy of individual units, and the supremacy of privately initiated arrangements over publicly regulated interventions. The result is the reduction of civic spaces and circulation networks.

The cellular structure of the informal city grows naturally and incrementally over time. The outcome is typically a multifocal pattern defined by countless subcenters of individual groups of buildings, rather than by the rationale of a dominating street grid. The morphological homogeneity of the pattern allows for multiplicities, distinctive variations that merge together to form an architectural unity. To shape a new slum morphology, we need geographic information system (GIS) maps that describe and classify natural features of a site, pinpoint the location of environmental problems, and identify and visualize the relationship between environmental problems and social networks inside and outside the settlement.

## LOCAL FOOTPRINTS/EFFICIENCY

We propose an activist architecture that addresses not only the physical but the social and economic well-being of slum dwellers. This requires an understanding of the economy of the favela, the community structure, and the existing skills of residents. The daily life of the favela lends itself to an interconnected web of activities: housing may exist alongside work, commerce, sport, and even farming; together these can create a dense, economically self-sustaining hub for a healthy community.

Urban agriculture—local, small-scale, and diverse—promotes healthy living and new economic opportunities. It can encourage pride of ownership, mitigate the pull of individualism through collective entrepreneurship, and mediate the effects of pollution, erosion, and runoff. Poor people in Caracas live mainly on carbohydrates and fat; urban agriculture provides inexpensive vegetables and fresh food. Indeed, Caracas, where the weather is mild, is becoming a leader in hydroponic food production; neighborhood microgardens feature tomatoes, salad greens, and spinach. Other profitable urban-agriculture projects that we are supporting through local NGOs include decorative crops like orchids. Some of these projects are group-owned or managed, but we remain convinced that the individual farmer is the most productive unit in the barrio. Dry toilets are useful in this context, as they produce cost-free fertilizer from human excrement.

We have conceived a kit of parts, whose assembly mimics the ad-hoc nature of slum construction and whose component materials are cheap, adaptable to a small footprint, and not easily removable. The last point is critical: slum construction is subject to intense salvaging, and a kit that can be disassembled and sold for scrap will meet a premature end. Components built in a factory measurably increase performance, enable future upgrading, and improve safety.

We offer the kit—and the concept of incremental, individual improvement within the existing fabric of the slum—as an alternative to the drastic and ultimately ineffective methods of the past. Clearing slum zones does not help the residents, who are merely displaced by new arrivals, and given the sheer numbers of units and the lack of political will to provide long-term solutions, clearance is nearly impossible to carry out. Therefore, at UTT we prefer to promote cultural and practical tools that enable and better define sustainable development. To this end the kit can either be a product in itself, like the emergency modular stairs, or a knowledge base, a set of skills and techniques that solves concrete problems in poverty-stricken areas. (For example, the dry toilet only works when the users know how to manage it correctly.) UTT's strategy is by nature based on upgrading; we preserve what is useful and animate self-help.

## BRINGING IT ALL TOGETHER: GROTÃO, A CASE STUDY IN COMMUNITY TOPOGRAPHY

In São Paulo, Brazil, we collaborated with the São Paulo Housing Agency (SEHAB), a city office, and the community to design a topographically driven building with a multiuse program in the hilly favela above the city. The site, Paraisópolis, is a large slum in the upscale Morumbi neighborhood. Home to some 70,000 residents, the slum extends over an undulating hillside that has protected it from development but now threatens the population with landslides and flooding. Homes are self-built and services are pirated, with residents plugging into power lines through illegal cable connections. A black-market economy thrives and drug lords self-police critical areas. Despite this, the community is home to a robust commercial and cultural street life; there are city schools and medical facilities and zones for sports and recreation. Isolated by extreme topography, the communities of Paraisópolis and Morumbi exemplify the world condition of extreme wealth existing alongside extreme poverty. The municipality, under leadership that privileges slum-upgrading programs, is undertaking a variety of works to mitigate the lack of services and to improve daily life in Paraisópolis. The Grotão neighborhood within the favela is in the zone of highest risk, both economic and geotechnical. Its residents are the poorest in the area and its steep physical access is the most precarious. In 2008 a mudslide destroyed more than 3 square miles (5,000 sq. m) of housing. The subsequent demolition of the remaining nearby units created an open space in the center of this dense favela that offered an opportunity to implement a new kind of development, intended to both discourage future occupation and provide new infrastructure and green space for the residents.

Our proposal is a multifunctional spatial hybrid that produces a thick, complex but organized section through the hillside of Paraisópolis. Construction must satisfy a multiplicity of demands brought on by the extreme nature of the site. The deteriorating landscape must be shored up, the frayed social fabric must be reinforced, and a sustainable set of technologies must sponsor renewed urbanism. These multivalent demands require a novel architecture that does not follow traditions and old habits.

If the scale and form of the project were determined by the landscape, the program was developed in concert with the community and geared toward education and the development of productive commerce. It will house the Grotão Music Factory and Educational Center, a community center for music-related activities and home to the Paraisópolis Youth Orchestra. The shaping of the steep slope into a series of flat, stepped surfaces will stabilize the ground and provide areas for urban farming and recreation, turning Grotão into a natural arena overlooking the urban landscape. This grand stair, well-furnished with

← / ↓ Grotão Project, Morumbi, São Paulo: Conceived to be implemented in two phases, the complex includes sports facilities topped by a multiuse pavilion and theater, a stairway, funicular, and bike path to provide easier transit into and through the neighborhood, terraced parkland (some of which may be dedicated to urban agriculture), and, at the top of the site, approximately twenty-five housing units.

→ A study for the housing units at the top of the Grotão site

↓ A rendering of social life at the complex

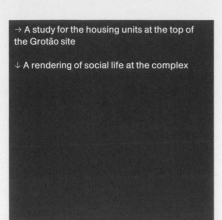

## typical aggregation
**multiple aggregation possibilities in order to respond to specific site conditions**

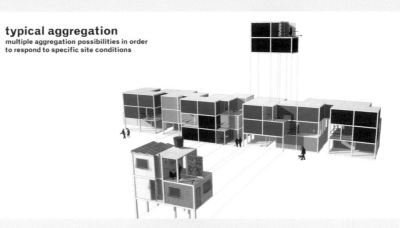

greenery and civic programs, connects the lower and upper parts of Paraisópolis and allows for further densification in the safer zones off the slope.

Water is the defining element of the project: since the favela as a whole lacks reliable, consistent sources of potable and gray water, the Grotão project must provide one and is designed to function off the city grid. We are creating a family of water-collection, purification, and delivery prototypes, including a combination of permanent and temporary rainwater collectors, cisterns, and pumps, to respond to changing environments and the social reconfiguration of the area.

Investment in infrastructure provides a perfect opportunity to add programs to buildings and services that are usually conceived of as having a single purpose. We plead for combined infrastructures: rain-harvesting roofs and solar panels to produce energy, stair systems that incorporate public communication lines, vertical sports facilities that incorporate needed social services. These ideas also allow temporary infrastructures to be deployed in emergencies, saving energy and reducing waste. This kind of thinking emphasizes the dematerialization of architecture, privileging instead buildings made of interchangeable parts—a flexible urban architecture that can function as a life-support system for developing city cultures.

The Grotão project exemplifies a new experimental and empirical approach to architecture, urban design, and development, one that uses retrofitting, stacking, bootstrapping, consolidating, and simple solutions that do not require engineering. It reflects our strong commitment to working with the local community and to using existing infrastructure, rather than an imposed plan, as the point of departure. Such designs are urban acupuncture—interventions based on contextual assessments.

The slums of Latin America, like the impoverished inner cities of North America and suburbs of European cities, cast doubt on the traditional notion of city growth as self-contained and rational, born from the logic of functional space. Architects must be advocates for slum residents and agents of change. But if change is to be viable and durable it must be accomplished thoughtfully, one step at a time. Our architecture manages pre-existing spaces—building over, under, around, and through—and creates new spheres that overcome segregation. It constructs bridges across a city's stratified sectors and eliminates contention at the crossroads by maximizing the potential of the borders. It is our hope and ambition that everyone in our cities will develop a consciousness of the culture of community that will endure for generations. This is the time to make a change for and with the people of São Paulo, Rio de Janeiro, Mexico City, and throughout the favelas of the world.

Notes

The quotation on p. 126 is from Michael Harrington, *The Other America: Poverty in the United States* (New York: Touchstone, 1962), 140.

1  Many urban renewal programs in the 1960s and 1970s built wide roads and intracity highways, which destroyed neighborhoods, increased dependence on automobiles, and weakened the public sector. New roads must be properly scaled and built in tandem with public transit.

2  Such basins are sometimes proposed for Latin American cities. A large area is simply allowed to flood; if it is placed and managed well (as part of an integrated ecological system), it can be an effective management technique, but governments are rarely willing to dedicate a large parcel of land to holding water.

"Global warming threatens to leave poorer nations even more vulnerable, and the already vulnerable poor more fragile."

# SUSTAINABLE COMMUNITIES: AVOIDING DISASTER IN THE INFORMAL CITY

ARLENE LUSTERIO
TAO-PILIPINAS, MANILA, PHILIPPINES

## THE PHILIPPINES

Located in Southeast Asia, the Philippines is the second largest archipelago in the world after Indonesia, with 7,107 islands and a total area of 115,831 square miles (300,000 sq. km) spread across three main island groups: Luzon, Visayas, and Mindanao. Sixty-five percent of the lands are mountainous, with a narrow strip of lowlands supporting 17,000 miles (27,000 km) of coastline. Unfortunately, this tropical expanse sits astride a typhoon belt, is highly vulnerable to earthquakes, and suffers drought, floods, and storm surges. There are twenty-six active volcanoes. In 2009 over 91 million people lived on these islands, where more than 11 million are residents in the National Capital Region of Luzon and Metro Manila, itself only 0.2 percent of the total geographical area. This means 4,748 persons settle every square mile of the greater capital. By 2015 experts expect that 68 percent of Filipinos will live in the cities, underscoring one of the most alarming rates of urbanization in Asia and the Pacific. At the same time nearly one-third of residents have no access to the formal water supply or public sanitation and live in informal settlements.

## THE SEARCH FOR RELEVANCE

In February 1986 the Marcos dictatorship was toppled and Filipinos carried out a peaceful revolution. For some of us the event kindled a renewed sense of responsibility and a desire to contribute to a country in dire need, especially in the urban centers. In August 2001 we founded TAO-Pilipinas, an organization dedicated to serving marginalized populations living in informal settlements. Today we are a multidisciplinary group—all women—of architects, engineers, planners, and geographers. We met initially under a mango tree on the grounds of the University of the Philippines in Manila; with the moon as our witness we promised to share our talents and training with the poorest members of our city. Our name, TAO, stands for Technical Assistance Organization, but also takes inspiration from the *tao,* the East Asian idea of *the way,* the right path. *Tao* also means "people" in Tagalog.

At the time poor communities living along the Pasig River in Manila were being resettled by the government, part of the Pasig River Rehabilitation Master Plan (started in 1994 under the Estrada administration) to clear 17 miles (27 km) of informal settlements. Families resisted and the process was disorderly; one member of a demolition team was killed in the chaos, which temporarily suspended work at the site. The Asian Development Bank, which had funded the master plan, took advantage of the slowdown to raise questions about the process and to insist that affected families participate in decision-making. We provided technical assistance.[1]

There is no question that people were living in unacceptable conditions. The Pasig is the longest river in Metro Manila; it links Laguna Lake to Manila Bay and passes through nine cities and municipalities. Nearly 150,000 people live along its banks. The settlers' lives are scarred by contrasting hues of poverty. There is no space, far too little light, too much noise, competing smells and odors, and a total absence of peace and quiet. We were shown hovels and multistory shanties and led along storage yards where 20-ton containers spin freely from cranes above people's homes. Narrow paths seamlessly turned into houses on stilts that bordered the riverbank. Drainage lines ran down the middle of walkways but led nowhere. Some paths had been paved; others were mud and puddles. There were sites so dense that two people could not find the space to meet. The basketball court doubled as a parking lot for tricycles, pedicabs, and jeeps.

3.3
SUSTAINABLE
COMMUNITIES

143

FIRM
TAO-PILIPINAS

PROJECT LOCALE
METRO MANILA, PHILIPPINES

## THE SAMAPI: ON-SITE REBLOCKING

Pineda is a *barangay,* a local precinct within Metro Manila, that lies along the Pasig River. A tract of the district is owned by the Philippine National Railway and a disused railway line follows the riverfront; the zone is some 10 to 50 yards (9.1 to 45.7 m) wide and more than a quarter-mile (0.4 km) long. The master plan required clearing a 10-yard (9.1-m) easement along the bank, which meant demolishing the houses there. The Council on Housing and Urban Development tried to ensure that the area would be transformed into a humane, decent, and affordable settlement. But the National Housing Authority proposed medium-rise housing units for the site and recommended clearing it for construction, with the promise that the residents would be allowed to return once the complex was complete. The amortized unit price, however, was prohibitive—three times what current residents could afford to pay. Residents of this strip of riverfront land were afraid that if they agreed to let their houses be demolished, they would never be allowed back. If they did come back, it would be to houses too expensive for them; as soon as they missed payments they would be thrown out. This process is common in slum clearance worldwide and often results in better housing and services, but the original residents are displaced and new residents move in. The evicted squatters do not return to the improved settlement but are shifted, ad hoc, to other informal dwelling zones. In the process communities with many social and mutual-aid systems are broken up.

The residents tried to negotiate to purchase the land and improve the site themselves through a *bayanihan* system of mutual self-help. They wanted to stay where they were, "as is, where is." They formed a coalition to deal with the government plan, the Samapi (the name is an acronym in Tagalog for Neighborhood Association of Manila Railroad, Pineda). For six years they argued with authorities. Then, in 2001, Gloria Arroyo

(previous spread) Houses along the old railway line in Pineda, Metro Manila

↑ The founders of TAO-Pilipinas at their first meeting, 2001 was elected president and her administration turned the site—still not cleared—over to the 400 families living there. At this point we were introduced to the community as architects who could advise them on developing an alternative plan that would be acceptable to the government and the Asian Development Bank. After our initial tour of the site we conducted meetings with residents and asked about boundaries, number of families, and how long they had lived there. These spontaneous conversations gave us insights into the social dynamics at work. We were filled in on the first settlers, who among the neighbors were considered trustworthy and who deemed corrupt, who agreed and disagreed with the process then under way. People told us about their struggle with the government, about being harassed and jailed, and about what had happened to the crew member who died:

At the time of demolition the husband was taking care of his wife, who was pregnant and had a sick child. It was raining. They asked to demolish their house by themselves when the rain stopped, but the demolition crew came with hammers and crowbars and started stripping their house. Some climbed onto the roof and started removing the [metal] sheets while others removed the walls. The pregnant wife was so traumatized and the husband so angry that he came out with a *bolo* knife and hacked a worker to death.

Community leaders were helpless; they were not on good terms with the local officials and for six years had lost one negotiation after another. To develop solutions *with* residents is at the heart of our mandate at TAO-Pilipinas. But we had to learn to communicate, to find the words and examples that would be meaningful to people. This was our first major project; we had to learn humility, to literally walk barefoot with the residents through the settlement, and imagine ourselves living their lives. We had to learn to listen. We call this *barefoot architecture* because it requires that we immerse ourselves in the community in order to create viable ways of bringing residents into the process so they can plan, design, and implement changes that improve their lives and—above all—that make sense to them.

We developed a base map from a seven-year-old government structures plan that gave us the data we needed to start. We measured houses, peering around every corner of the tiny homes, around dirty laundry, into garbage dumps and makeshift drainage lines, over collapsing walls and hanging ceiling boards, and into rotting gutters, smelly toilets, and dark alleys. We listened to arguments about who had been there first as we stood, crouched, knelt, and sweated. But as we became part of the household of Samapi, we were always fed.

Armed with basic data we started planning. In a process known as reblocking we traced roads across scattered houses to give some sense of order to the existing layout. River easements (the distance from the river that is considered unsafe for building) were established. Every house was located on the community plan. Owners affected by widening a road or realignment met to discuss their options. We earmarked open spaces to be given to families who would have to be relocated. Leaders were responsible for explaining the process, especially to families whose homes would have to be dismantled. We talked about planning standards, minimum lot area, and the need to increase the road right-of-way to allow small vehicles to pass in case of an emergency such as a fire. On the whole, residents agreed they could not stay where they are without some changes. "As is, where is," we all realized, is not an absolute. In this context people were more than willing to adopt a better settlement plan.

When the community presented their alternative scheme the National Housing Authority was the only dissenting voice.

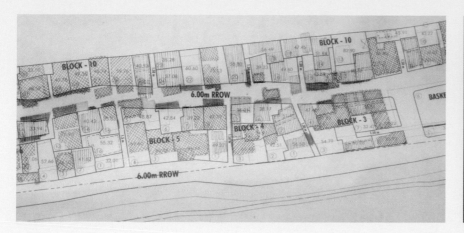

← Samapi People's Plan, 2001, detail

↓ Base map of the proposed Samapi People's Plan for new housing in Pineda, Pasig City, Manila, detail

LEGEND:

——— PROPERTY BOUNDARY

⊞⊞ EXISTING STRUCTURES

⊞⊞ PROPOSED LAYOUT

〰〰 RIVER

NORTH

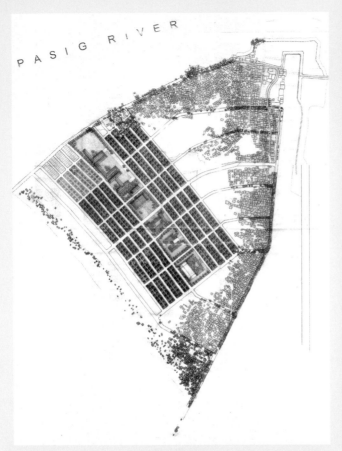

PASIG RIVER

↑ The winning scheme for the redevelopment of the Baseco squatter community includes centralized facilities and a combination of row-houses and duplex houses.

↗ A community living on the fishponds in Tanza Navotas, Manila

→ A volunteer community Solid Waste Management Team in Tanza Navotas collects segregated waste, sweeps litter, and reminds residents about the policies for solid-waste management in the area.

A special meeting was arranged with the mayor. We served as the technical consultant, supporting the viability of the community's proposal. The mayor approved the project with two provisions: increase the interior road and provide space for two basketball courts. After six years of struggle the people of the Samapi had convinced the government that their proposal was viable, legitimate, and possible. Redevelopment went forward without the displacement of the original residents.

## UNDERSTANDING THE ENVIRONMENT

Nine years later we continue to help informal communities strewn along mudflats and sandbars, and those situated near garbage dumps—the most critically vulnerable areas. We discuss how best to defend an area threatened by a master plan that will displace thousands of families. We work with the community to determine how it should be laid out, where facilities should be, what services are needed, and how to attach a value and a cost to their property commensurate with their means. We inform residents about minimum planning and design standards and requirements for compliance with laws. We move their proposals closer to reality and help develop conceptual plans and schemes that can be argued before local officials. For instance, we worked with the community at the Baseco Compound, the former Bataan Shipyard Engineering Company, now a shantytown housing thousands of families on Manila Bay. The winning scheme proposed rowhouse dwellings with centralized community facilities (daycare center, multipurpose hall, day market, health center, chapel, tricycle terminals at the entrance and in middle of the community, and fire station) that would displace few families.

Our aim at TAO-Pilipinas has been to help create sustainable settlements. Our master plans address housing as well as services. Metro Manila alone produces 6,000 tons of garbage a day. The Ecological Solid Waste Management Act was finally passed in 2002, two years after a mountain of garbage collapsed during heavy rains in Payatas, Quezon City, burying 150 individuals and displacing thousands of people who scavenged the trash for a living. The act mandates waste separation, recycling, and reuse, but this is not enough. The responsibility for solid-waste management cannot be left to the government; it belongs to everyone. But after years of doing this work we are convinced that people need to be actively taught how to manage trash and otherwise maintain their communities.

We launched our first solid-waste management program in 2005 with a community living in the middle of ponds used for fish farms. The community of Tanza Navotas, on Manila Bay in Metro Manila, is covered by 600 acres (242.8 ha) of fishponds and is prone to floods. Occupancy is very dense, so it is extremely important that everyone help manage solid waste. We trained fifteen members of the Federation of the United Urban Poor of Navotas to serve as leaders, demonstrating to the community how small, careless acts can have a massive negative impact on the environment. We then helped set up a local solid-waste management committee empowered to enact and enforce rules, restrictions, penalties, and guidelines about segregating garbage, and established a small fund to support a facility to collect and sell recyclables and reusable waste. Community training programs can make an enormous difference in the health of a settlement's immediate environment if the time is taken to raise awareness and help residents put a structure in place. Awareness leads to fewer health hazards, creates sustainable change, and provides opportunities for income to be generated from solid waste through work such as basket making, junk shops, and growing potted plants—all of which can substantially improve life in poor communities.

Typhoon Durian triggered a lava flow from Mayon Volcano that rolled boulders into this house, killing all its occupants.

# We now witness disasters throughout the country where before there were disaster-prone areas.

## THE INEVITABLE AND THE UNEXPECTED

Global warming threatens to leave poorer nations even more vulnerable, and the already vulnerable poor more fragile. The Philippines experiences an average of twenty typhoons a year, half of which are disastrous. In the last five years environmental hazards have become increasingly ferocious, though to be sure our risks are both natural and manmade: hurricanes, fires, trash slides, illegal logging that leads to mudslides and flooding, informal or unregulated construction along waterways, and the like. Many of these disasters can be avoided. But ignorance, lack of preparedness, and complacency lead all too often to catastrophe. We now witness disasters throughout the country where before there were disaster-prone areas. On November 30, 2004, a mudslide struck the three towns in Quezon Province—Infanta, Real, and Nakar. The slide was triggered by a typhoon, but it was massive logging in the Quezon mountains that made the storm so dangerous. A thousand people lost their lives. In 2006 Typhoon Durian battered the province of Albay in Bicol and triggered a lava flow from Mayon Volcano that swept molten ash and boulders into houses and over farmlands. Greedy developers who had reclaimed an ancient riverbed and sold it as a resettlement site to the poor were partly to blame.

Though disaster mitigation was not a part of our initial charter, we have been forced into relief and recovery work to better help our partner communities. At TAO we now have a dual strategy: to help identify viable sites for resettlement within the city and to mitigate conditions so people can stay where they are. To these ends we hold TAO-Pilipinas Young Professionals Workshops, which focus on disaster-risk management. In 2006, two years after the Quezon mudslide, thirty university students in architecture, engineering, and planning visited devastated neighborhoods in the region to survey the status of reconstruction and conduct education workshops for us. Some of the former residents were living in designated resettlement sites but others were still in highly vulnerable locations with no running water, no power, no drainage, no toilets, and only a mud road. We worked with community members on an action plan to mitigate future risk, though the absence of secure land tenure still threatens their future. Today, the resettled families are in safer locations but still lack basic services.

## REFLECTING ON OUR WORK

When Typhoon Ketsana hit Metro Manila in 2009, the water rose to 13 feet (4 m) along the inland waterways, covering the Pasig-Marikina River Basin and low-lying areas in the provinces of Rizal, Bulacan, and Laguna. But our assisted communities along the river, who are now trained in disaster preparedness, were spared calamity precisely because they have grown more resilient in the presence of water. People were not only prepared to pack their homes and evacuate safely; they were also capable of making damage assessments that reported what sort of help was needed. Other partners fared less well. In the Pasig-Marikina River Basin residents were under 6 feet (2 m) of flood water; a week after the typhoon they were still living in water waist-deep. Standing water promotes water-borne diseases—cholera, diarrhea, coughs and colds, and skin disease. There were several fatal cases of leptospirosis. Properties and appliances were destroyed. People had nowhere to go. The evacuation centers were packed and their conditions were scarcely better than in the flooded houses. The government ordered the sites cleared and the people removed. Demolitions are now scheduled, but not a single resettlement site has been prepared within the city. Some residents have been forced to move to Calauan, outside of the Metro area. At the moment, the people who stayed are still in a standoff with the government.

→ A man wades in waist-deep water a week after Typhoon Ketsana hit Metro Manila. Right after the storm, water had reached the top of the window opening (to man's left).

→→ Transport services are lacking in Tanza Navotas, so people make do.

↓ A week after Typhoon Ketsana struck Metro Manila, communities were in ruins.

At TAO our goal is for vulnerable communities to come to the table armed with viable alternatives—drawings, maps, schemes, plans—tools of negotiation. But the problem does not end with acquiring a site and receiving government approval of a plan. People disagree. The simple fact that people are poor does not necessarily lead to a shared vision of the future. What is achieved in negotiation can be quickly lost to factions and disagreements in the next stage. Community organizations must be strong and constant if they are to effectively challenge the government and then implement their projects when they win. This is very difficult. In one year, technical professionals—architects, engineers, planners, geographers—can develop an urban plan and building designs with community members who want to be involved. But to strengthen the social fabric and carry out these plans is a longer and more daunting process. Communities may need as much as five years to coordinate and professionalize their activism—to learn to act together, consistently, on their own behalf. Even then there are no guarantees.

Concrete, viable plans are a powerful means of persuasion, but they have limits. We need to vigorously promote understanding and awareness. Information must be up-to-date. Disaster response must now consider the impact of climate change. Rising water levels and the frequency of severe floods will dramatically affect the low-lying coastal areas and waterways of Manila, where most informal settlements are located.

Finally, residents and governments must consider viable ways to live with water in coastal settlements if people are to remain where they are. Since 2000 we have been working on this idea in a series of proposals for Navotas. We have presented concept houses to the mayor, raised on stilts for inner-city resettlement in flood-prone areas. Unfortunately, the land-use trend remains reclamation and control of such zones, rather than adaptable living. These policies can backfire and increase the likelihood of flooding. Landownership and the complexity of secure land tenure in urban areas also affects the possibility of building on water. No planning or design guidelines exist for land under water or development in or on water. Current laws and standards do not include water as buildable space. We need to advocate for fresh thinking and adequate regulations. And we need a staunch champion in government to support a pilot settlement on the water. We need a paradigm shift that accepts water as space for living; we need policies and laws that support new kinds of development, and eventually a new definition of urban life.

Note
1   For further reading see Solita C. Monsod and Toby C. Monsod, background paper for HDR 2003, *Philippines: Case Study on Human Development Progress Towards the MDG at the Sub-National Level,* United Nations Development Programme Human Development Report Office occasional paper, January 22, 2003; and Denis Murphy and Ted Añana, Pasig River Rehabilitation Program, 2004, published on the Habitat International Coalition website at www.hicnet.org/document.php?pid=2668, accessed August 21, 2009.

**0** miles
border: conflict between two border cities

"A 60-linear-mile cross-section, tangential to the border wall, between San Diego and Tijuana exposes the most dramatic issues challenging our normative notions of architecture and urbanism."

# CAMOUFLAGING DISASTER: 60 LINEAR MILES OF LOCAL TRANSBORDER URBAN CONFLICT

TEDDY CRUZ
ESTUDIO TEDDY CRUZ
SAN DIEGO, CALIFORNIA

"There is no such thing as a natural disaster," the landscape architect and theorist Anudartha Mathur has declared often, in the context of her work on the Mississippi River. Disasters, she implies, happen when the logic of natural systems is encroached on by stupid urban development. Every disaster yielding human loss, socioeconomic and environmental degradation, and political strife can be traced to a specific conflict between ecologies, natural and artificial. The many collisions in which top-down forces of urbanization and militarization clash with bottom-up natural and social networks are always the basis for territorial crises.

Much of my research on the transborder urbanisms that inform my practice began as a desire to critically observe and trace the specificity of such conflicts inscribed in the territory of the border between San Diego, in the United States, and Tijuana, Mexico, one of the most contested borders in the world. This observation has not only enabled a practice of research, a sort of projective forensics of the territory, but also has revealed the need to expand our narrow notions of architectural design.

The revelation was simple: without retroactively tracing and projectively altering the backward exclusionary policies that have been constructing the territory in the last years—the socio-political ground—our work as architects will continue to be a mere camouflaging (and decoration at best) of selfish, oil-hungry urbanization from China to Dubai to New York to San Diego. Conflict can be an operational device to transform architectural practice, while design can be expanded beyond building, engaging political processes and socioeconomic relations as well. Besides providing solutions that seemingly only seek to maintain the status quo and a certain lifestyle, or solve the problem in the short term, we need to understand the actual conditions that produced the crisis in the first place; we need to visualize the institutions, policies, and processes that got us here, because the very conditions that produced the conflict are material for design. For example, we must understand the mortgage crisis, the institutional lending and subsidy mechanisms that benefited big development while fooling small entrepreneurs with a third-rate notion of the American dream based on false ownership and ultimately leaving them without guarantees or protection. Unless we alter discriminatory zoning and lending, the official political and economic protocols that have enabled hyperprivatization and the spread of homogeneous housing pro-formas—that is, luxury condos—everywhere in the last few years, any efforts at providing emergency housing will remain short-term fixes rather than committed investment to build communities in the long term.

Moving from these broad conceptual meditations to the specificity of the San Diego–Tijuana border, one oscillates back and forth between two radically different ways of constructing a city. At no other international juncture in the world can one find some of the wealthiest real estate as on the edges of San Diego's sprawl barely twenty minutes from some of the poorest settlements, as manifested by the many slums that dot the new periphery of Tijuana. These two different types of suburbia are emblematic of the incremental division of the contemporary city into enclaves of megawealth surrounded by rings of poverty. I am interested in processes of mediation that can produce critical interfaces between and across these opposites, exposing conflict as an operational device to transform architectural practice. Critical observation of this border region transforms it into a laboratory in which to trace the current politics of migration and citizenship, labor and surveillance, the tensions between sprawl and density, formal and informal urbanisms, wealth and poverty. All these elements incrementally characterize the contemporary city everywhere. Border areas such as the Tijuana–San Diego region are the sites where the forces of division and control produced by these global zones of conflict are amplified and physically manifested in the territory, producing, in turn, local zones of conflict.

3.4
CAMOUFLAGING
DISASTER

FIRM
ESTUDIO TEDDY CRUZ

PROJECT LOCALE
SAN DIEGO, CALIFORNIA, USA,
AND TIJUANA, MEXICO

155

A 60-linear-mile cross-section, tangential to the border wall, between these two border cities exposes the most dramatic issues challenging our normative notions of architecture and urbanism. We can find along this section's trajectory a series of collisions, critical junctures, between natural and artificial ecologies, top-down forces of urban development and bottom-up organizational systems, all anticipatory of territorial disaster. These conflicts are made spatial as large freeway and military infrastructure collides with watershed systems, gated communities with marginal neighborhoods, formal urbanization with informal economies, dense slums with sprawling enclaves. This transborder cut begins 30 miles north of the border, on the periphery of San Diego, and ends 30 miles south of the border, at the point where the fence sinks into the Pacific Ocean.

## +30 MILES: SAN DIEGO

Top-down private development has been installing an oil-hungry sprawl of detached McMansions everywhere. The *conflict between master-planned gated communities and the natural topography* flattens the differential landscape of San Diego's edges and encroaches on the natural cycles of fire-prone areas.

## +28 MILES: SAN DIEGO

Large freeway and mall infrastructure runs the length of coastal San Diego, colliding with a natural network of canyons, rivers, and creeks that descend toward the Pacific Ocean. A necklace of territorial voids is produced out of the *conflict between large infrastructure and the watershed*. As the politics of water will define the future of this region, the recuperation of these truncated natural resources is essential to anticipate density.

**+15** miles

san diego:  conflict between the formal and informal

## +25 MILES: SAN DIEGO

Southern California's selfish urbanization generates an amorphous archipelago of private enclaves that amplifies the *conflict between privatization and everyday life*, exacerbating a land use of exclusion into a sort of apartheid of social life.

## +20 MILES: SAN DIEGO

The only interruptions along an otherwise continuous sprawl occur where the military bases that dot San Diego's suburbs overlap with environmentally protected lands. This produces a strange montage of housing subdivisions, natural ecology, and militarization. The *conflict between military bases and environmental zones* has been recently dramatized in mock Afghan villages, equipped with hologram technologies to project Afghan subjects, now being erected here as vernacular military-training sites.

## +15 MILES: SAN DIEGO

San Diego's downtown has reconfigured itself with exclusive tax-revenue redevelopment powers, becoming an island of wealth delimited by specific zoning and budgetary borders. Luxury condos and hotels, stadiums and convention centers, surrounded by generic commercial franchises compose this stew of privatization from New York to San Diego. The proximity of wealth and poverty found at the border checkpoint is reproduced here as powerful downtowns collide with the neighborhoods of marginalization that surround them. It is in these neighborhoods that cheap immigrant labor concentrates, conveniently becoming the service sector that supports downtown's massive project of gentrification.

The *conflict between the formal and the informal* emerges here as immigrants fill the first ring of suburbanization surrounding downtown, retrofitting an obsolete urbanism of older, postwar detached bungalows. Informal densities and economies produce a sort of three-dimensional land use that collides with the one-dimensional zoning that has characterized these older neighborhoods.

## 0 MILES: SAN DIEGO–TIJUANA

At the border itself the metal fence becomes emblematic of the *conflict between these two border cities*, reenacting the perennial alliance between militarization and urbanization. This territorial conflict is currently dramatized by the hardening, after the attack of September 11, 2001, of the border wall that divides this region, incrementally transforming San Diego into the world's largest gated community.

## -0.5 MILES: TIJUANA

As we cross the border into Mexico, we immediately see how the large infrastructure of the Tijuana River clashes with the border wall. This is the only place where an otherwise continuous metal fence is pierced and opened as the river enters San Diego. A faint yellow line is inscribed on the dry river's concrete channel to indicate the trajectory of the border. But as the channel moves beyond the fence and into San Diego's territory the concrete disappears, and the channel becomes the Tijuana River estuary, a US ecological reserve, which frames the natural ecology of the river as it flows freely to the Pacific Ocean. What dramatizes this *conflict between the river and the border fence* is the fact that the border checkpoint is at the exact intersection of both,

-30 miles tijuana: conflict between the natural and the political

-20 miles tijuana: conflict between density and sprawl

-15 miles tijuana: conflict between factories and er

punctuating the environmentally protected zone with a matrix of border-patrol vehicles, helicopters, and electrified fences.

## -10 MILES: TIJUANA

Adjacent to the checkpoint we can find many slums crashing against the border fence, which acts as a powerful dam, preventing the density of Tijuana from contaminating San Diego's picturesque sprawl. In many ways these shantytowns are built with the waste of San Diego, as the garage doors, bungalows, and rubber tires from older southern California Levittowns are recycled into Tijuana's periphery. These informal settlements are defined by the transplantation of urban debris from one city to another, as well as by the appropriation of high-risk, leftover zones untouched by urban development. The *conflict between the informal and natural ecologies* occurs here as people in search of emergency shelter invade steep canyons, seismic zones, and flood zones.

## -15 MILES: TIJUANA

These informal communities or slums dot the periphery of Tijuana and in turn are surrounded by enclaves of maquiladoras. The *conflict between factories and emergency housing* is

ousing

-10 miles
tijuana: conflict between the informal and natural ecologies

-0.5 miles
tijuana: conflict between river and border

0 miles
border: conflict between two border cities

produced here as these factories extract cheap labor from
nearby slums without contributing any infrastructural support.

## -20 MILES: TIJUANA

Many of the sites of conflict found in San Diego are reproduced
and amplified in Tijuana. As Tijuana grows eastward, for example,
it is seduced by the style and glamour of the master-planned,
gated communities of the US, and builds its own version—miniaturized
replicas of typical suburban southern California tract homes,
paradoxically imported into Tijuana to provide "social housing."
Thousands of tiny tract homes are now scattered around the

periphery of Tijuana, creating a vast landscape of homogeneity
and division that is at odds with this city's prevailing heteroge-
neous and organic metropolitan condition. These diminutive
250-square-foot (23-sq.-m) dwellings come equipped with all
the clichés and conventions: manicured landscaping, gate-
houses, model units, banners and flags, mini setbacks, front
and backyards.

The *conflict between density and sprawl* is reenacted here,
as these mini tract homes quickly submit to transformation
by occupants who are little hindered by Tijuana's permissive
zoning regulations. While the gated communities of southern
California remain closed systems due to stringent zoning
that prohibits any kind of formal alteration or programmatic

+15 miles
san diego: conflict between the formal and informal

+20 miles
san diego: conflict between military bases and environmental zones

+25 miles
san diego: conf

DANGER
OBJECTS
UNDER

PILEGRO
FIERROS

juxtaposition, residents in Tijuana fill in setbacks and occupy front and backyards and garages with more construction to support mixed use and provide more usable space.

## -30 MILES: TIJUANA

As we reach the sea on the Mexican side of the border territory, the metal border fence sinks into the Pacific Ocean. As the poles of this militarized artifact descend into the depths of the water, the site is simultaneously strangely poetic and hugely tragic, physically manifesting the contradictions that character-ize the border landscape and amplifying the most dramatic of all territorial collisions across this 60-mile section: the *conflict between the natural and the jurisdictional.*

This is where contemporary architectural practice needs to reposition itself: in the midst of these metropolitan and territo-rial sites of conflict. Each of these physical junctures needs to be unfolded to reveal hidden institutional histories, the missing information that can allow us to piece together our anticipatory research, enabling the reorganization o f the fragmented and discriminatory policies that have created this archipelago of division. In other words no meaningful intervention can occur in the contemporary city unless we first expose the conditions, the political and economic forces (of jurisdiction and owner-ship) that have produced these collisions in the first place.

gated communities and everyday life

+28 miles san diego: conflict between large infrastructure and the watershed

+30 miles san diego: conflict between top down development and the topography

## BEYOND THE IDEOLOGICAL DIVIDE: NEW COMMUNITIES OF PRACTICE

At this writing, politicians on the left and right in the US have collectively abandoned any attempt at national energy legislation to address climate change. The debate has been atrophied by special interests and the hijacking of the public by the politics of fear. In light of this stasis it is more pressing than ever that we come to see global warming as more than simply an environmental crisis: it is primarily a cultural crisis. This suggests the need to transform ways of thinking across institutions of urban development through a new kind of interface with the public, closing the gap between public policy and civic participation.

The conflicts found along those 60 transborder miles are local but are exacerbated by the general public's misunderstanding of them. For instance, the public does not notice that the recent strengthening of the infrastructure of surveillance along the US–Mexico border has an environmental impact. Currently, the US Department of Homeland Security is constructing a third border wall at San Diego–Tijuana, between the Los Laureles Canyon, a slum housing 85,000 people in Mexico, and the Tijuana River estuary on the US side. The destruction of canyons by Homeland Security systematically undermines the functionality of the existing transborder ecological systems of the Tijuana River watershed and specifically of the Tijuana River estuary, which has recently been designated by UNESCO as a vulnerable station in the migration of birds between Alaska and Chile. The destruction of the environmental stability of the border region by the new wall will in turn produce socioeconomic degradation, leading to future insecurity and risk. Here, the artifact of protection itself becomes the instrument that undermines security and the sustainability of cross-border communities. This exemplifies the need to rethink national security beyond the one-dimensional construction of physical borders. The need to reimagine the border through the logic of natural systems is the foremost task of this binational region. The absence of imagination is evidenced in the gap that exists in the public's perception of the problem and the backward institutional policies and strategies that attempt to solve it.

The revision of our own procedures as architects is essential today, as our institutions of architectural representation and display have lost their sociopolitical relevance and capacity to advocate. I am increasingly disappointed by the futility of design in the context of pressing sociopolitical realities worldwide. The conditions of conflict are redefining the territory of intervention, yet we are oblivious to them. It's been unsettling to witness some of the most "cutting-edge" architectural practices rush unconditionally to China and the United Arab Emirates to build dream castles, in the process reducing their innovations to mere caricatures of change, camouflaging gentrification with a massive dose of hyperaesthetic and formalist rhetoric. I hope that in the context of this euphoria for the Dubais of the world and the seemingly limitless horizon of design possibilities, we can also be inspired by a sense of dissatisfaction, a feeling of "pessimistic optimism" that can provoke us to address head-on the sites of conflict that define cities in the twenty-first century. So, as politics continue to be radically polarized between right and left, dividing institutions and publics, I would like to reflect on the pressing need to redefine three present, equally divided agendas in the architecture-urbanism spectrum that continue to perpetuate the division between social responsibility and artistic experimentation:

1. An apolitical formalist agenda, espousing hyperaesthetics for the sake of aesthetics, continues to press the notion of the avant-garde as an autonomous project, "needing" a critical distance from institutions to operate in the research of experimental form. Instead, we must cultivate new models of collaboration that depend on a project of radical proximity, engaging the social systems and the political and economic domains that have until now remained peripheral to it. Creative practices that infiltrate existing institutions in order to transform them from the inside out produce new aesthetic categories that problematize the status quo relationship between the social, the political, and the formal. As our recent unconditional love affair with a system of economic excess that legitimized architectural experimentation has come to a standstill, the new paradigms in architecture will emerge not from sites of abundance but from sites of scarcity, retaking the margins as the site for architectural experimentation.

2. The cheap politics of architectural identity continues to hijack the debate away from the true troubles of urbanization: the defunding of social and public infrastructure and the economic gap dividing enclaves of megawealth and the circles of poverty that surround them. This identity is packaged as a stylistic neoconservatism, serving an aspiring homogeneous middle class protected by picket fences and pseudo-Victorian porches—the *Truman Show*/Homeland Security of urbanism. Rather, social practices in architecture depend on a pluralistic democratization of the rights to the city across social and environmental networks. This suggests a future founded on an urban pedagogy that can produce new interfaces between cultural institutions and publics.

−10 miles

tijuana: conflict between the informal and natural ecologies

-30 miles
tijuana: conflict between the natural and the political

3. A project of social justice and activism in architecture usually translates into symbolic, problem-solving relief efforts that do nothing to interrupt the backward policies that produced the crisis in the first place. In this context, emergency-relief efforts are biased toward fixing short-term problems, not lifting communities in the long term. I believe that expanded models of practice depend on a reversal of thinking, embracing the idea that architects and artists, besides being designers of buildings and objects, can be designers of political processes, economic models, and collaborations across institutions and jurisdictions.

We must transcend the idea that building houses for the poor is the only way to solve the problem of poverty. If these relief architectures are not inserted into a meaningful socio-economic organizational system at the scale of communities, we will be perpetuating density as an abstract number of dwelling units per acre. Instead, practices of intervention into sites of crisis depend on the redefinition of density as a number of social exchanges per acre. At a time when the institutions of urban planning need to be redefined, that redefinition should recognize the value of social capital (people's participation) in urban development, enhancing the role of communities in producing housing.

It is here that a different notion of empowerment emerges, one that rejects the symbolic representation of people and architectural and artistic social practices that deploy only the symbolic image of the community and not its operative dimension. Empowerment here is not a one-directional effort. It signifies an act of translation and exchange of knowledge and political representation at the scale of neighborhoods. These communities' invisible urban praxis needs interpretation and representation, and this is the space of intervention that we are interested in occupying as architects. We must design the conditions that can mobilize this activism, applying them to new spatial and economic infrastructures that benefit communities in the long term, beyond the short-term problem-solving of private developers or the institutions of charity. Acting as facilitators of this bottom-up intelligence means translating the creative intelligence and ethical knowledge specific to a community into new communicational systems, radical urban pedagogy, and micropolitical and economic armatures.

Ultimately, it does not matter whether urban development is wrapped in the latest morphogenetic skin, neoclassical prop, or LEED-certified photovoltaic panels, if all approaches continue to camouflage the most pressing problems of urbanization. Without altering the exclusionary policies and economics that have produced the current crises, architecture will continue to be subordinated to the visionless environments defined by the bottom-line urbanism of the developer's spreadsheet and the neoconservative politics and economics of a hyperindividualistic ownership society. As architects we can be responsible for imagining counterspatial procedures, political and economic structures that can produce new forms of affordability, public culture, and activism.

# CULTURAL HERITAGE AND DISASTER MITIGATION: A NEW ALLIANCE

ROHIT JIGYASU
RESEARCH CENTER FOR DISASTER
MITIGATION OF URBAN CULTURAL
HERITAGE, RITSUMEIKAN UNIVERSITY,
KYOTO, JAPAN

Cultural heritage is constituted not just by monuments and objects but also historic cities, vernacular housing, and ecological systems, such as waterways and natural features. Traditional skills, practices, and languages are an important part of our cultural past as well, encompassing the skillful use of local resources and the living dimensions of heritage that come about, particularly in urban environments, as a result of the vibrant inter- action of people with each other and their surroundings. With half of the world's population now living in cities, urban centers are increasingly at risk. Natural hazards—drought, fires, land- slides, and floods—are becoming commonplace. Spectacular growth, chaotic development, and tourism are also adding to the pressures that irreversibly change the tangible and intangible value of cities.

Traditional urban systems are critical to successful disaster mitigation, and affording heritage a *proactive* role in preven- tion can lead to safer, more resilient cities. How do we as architects and planners intervene in complex urban environ- ments to make them more humane and livable, as they struggle to retain their social and architectural traditions while undergo- ing massive upheavals that lead to ever greater risk? Whereas experts tend to focus on megacities like Delhi, Tokyo, and London, the majority of people live in cities of 200,000 to half a million residents. These mid-size cities, which maintain strong ties with the rural hinterland, are the key to recasting the role of cultural heritage.

In Nepal over 11,000 people have lost their lives in major earthquakes in the last century; the seismic records for the region extend back to 1253. Over time, communities devel- oped structural features in their buildings that addressed the need for greater security, but these features never developed into a coherent system of disaster mitigation.

Today, many of these structures have been rebuilt over generations and the quality of workmanship has deteriorated significantly. Poor masonry and brittle, nailed joints have replaced the sophisticated wooden joints that once made build- ings flexible. Incompatible additions and alterations compromise a structure's performance. To reinvest these traditional building systems with new relevance, we cannot simply reintroduce certain artisanal practices. We need to draw upon past insights by reinterpreting and redesigning the once viable features as a dynamic, contemporary system of building techniques that is not only safer but also takes into consideration people's aspira- tions and ways of life.

The disaster-resilient structural features we find in small cities like Patan are not restricted to vernacular buildings; they extend to urban design and planning as well. Public, semi-public, and private open spaces serve a variety of roles at the city and neighborhood levels. These can be turned into places for staging secure relief operations and later used for disaster preparedness training. The public sheds that serve as rest stops and for small gatherings or playing music can be employed to store relief supplies and shelter the injured. The ancient water tanks and step wells located in public squares and at street junctions and village entrances are still used for bathing and religious ablutions. This system can double as an emergency water supply for extinguishing fires and washing. Unfortunately, in Patan and so many other small cities, these structures have diminished in number, and the ones that survive are nearly in ruins, the result of rising land values, haphazard, insensitive development, and limited resources.

We must bring the wealth of ingenuity, knowledge, and experience embedded in our historic cities back to life if cul- tural heritage is to be brought into the service of disaster prevention. This requires that architects and planners develop inspired, enterprising approaches and designs that cast the rich repository of the past in terms of a safer, vital future—for example, highly innovative retrofitting measures that would

strengthen an entire housing cluster, not just individual units. We should abandon our tendency, in contemporary disaster management practices, to artificially treat urban and rural landscapes as disconnected from each other. It is critical to keep sight of the fact that resilient urban systems rely on the interdependence of the city and the countryside, where livelihoods, land use, natural resources, and cultural and religious associations tie these evironments inextricably together. In addition, our disaster-mitigation tactics are misleading and failing enormous populations. We must apply the punctual solutions discovered by working in small cities to the risks citizens face in megacities as we move the practice of disaster mitigation forward.

↖ / ↖ The legendary city of Patan is located on a high plateau above the Bagmati River, just south of Katmandu. Local Newari culture, a mix of Hinduism and Buddhism, produced magnificent temples, monasteries, ornate shrines, and public rest houses, which dominate the landscape of the historic city.

← Wooden columns resting on stone bases split the brickwork into several masses, reducing its vulnerability during earthquakes.

Traditional Newari settlements were planned for resilience. ↑↑ Step well; ↑ interior courtyard; ↗ shrine; → public shed

# PART 4

# ENVIRONMENTAL RESILIENCE

"Everyone has the right to a standard of living adequate for the health and well-being of himself and his family, including food, clothing, housing and medical care and necessary social services, and the right to security in the event of unemployment, sickness, disability, widowhood, old age or other lack of livelihood in circumstances beyond his control."
—The Universal Declaration of Human Rights, Article 25

# GREEN
# RECOVERY

ANITA VAN BREDA AND
BRITTANY SMITH
WORLD WILDLIFE FUND,
WASHINGTON, DC

## ENVIRONMENTAL DEGRADATION AND (RE)CONSTRUCTION

We can now expect that in any given year 1 percent of the world's population is displaced. Of these, as many as 50 million people find themselves homeless in the aftermath of so-called natural disasters. Recovery and post-disaster reconstruction measures systematically fail to link disaster response with future environmental security. After Hurricane Katrina struck the coasts of the Gulf of Mexico in 2005, for example, it was clear that continuing to build residential neighborhoods on critical wetlands in Louisiana and Mississippi would again put people at risk. Wetlands are a natural protective barrier. But instead of addressing the problem of where to build, recovery strategies favored the right to build over risk aversion and long-term community safety, as if a future Gulf Coast were somehow hurricane-proof. Deforestation in Haiti, which has decimated 98 percent of the country's old-growth forests, caused hundreds of deaths during the 2004 floods; there was simply no topsoil left to absorb the rainfall. In some cases the subsequent environmental crisis does more damage than the initial disaster. After the Indian Ocean tsunami the World Conservation Union in Sri Lanka reported witnessing greater damage from reconstruction efforts than from the tsunami itself: mangroves were cleared haphazardly, trees decimated, sand dunes mined, and the debris that was dumped everywhere contaminated water supplies and blocked drainage canals.[1]

Such environmental degradation puts us at risk for generations. Conversely, environmentally sustainable reconstruction mitigates future risk and vulnerability. After a tornado destroyed most of Greensburg, Kansas, in May 2007, reconstruction proposals put homes above downtown shops, greenery along sidewalks and rooftops, and windmills on the prairie, and required all public projects to follow the US Green Building Council's Leadership in Energy and Environmental Design (LEED) Platinum standards. In line with the new city slogan, "Better, Stronger, Greener," an immediate plan to use eco-tourism to boost the town's economy complements a long-term focus on incorporating eco-technologies such as high-efficiency windows in all public buildings.

In principle sustainable reconstruction requires that each stage of development—technical, financial, social, and institutional—privilege sound ecological practices. The challenge is considerable. Buildings put an enormous strain on the environment and natural resources. Three billion tons of raw material are extracted annually from the earth for their creation. More than 3 billion cubic feet (85 million cu. m) of timber are harvested yearly.[2] Their water use amounts to 16 percent of the world's total water withdrawals. The energy buildings use accounts for 40 percent of the world's total consumption. Project managers must find ways to reduce the negative environmental impact of construction and build in ways that maintain long-term biological diversity and productivity. At the same time they must protect citizens at an affordable cost. The only way to bridge this gap is to make the environment a priority from the start.

## HOW TO MAINSTREAM THE ENVIRONMENT

**ASSESSMENTS:** After a disaster, and before reconstruction begins, strategic environmental-impact assessments should be integrated into the decision-making process. Assessments provide the baseline necessary to judge resource stability, determine natural-hazard risks, and predict the immediate and gradual consequences of proposed activities. At a minimum, rapid assessments can be applied. Although some agencies are standardizing the use of assessments, many more either do not use them at all or may manipulate the results to meet their

4.1
GREEN RECOVERY

ORGANIZATION
WORLD WILDLIFE FUND

PROJECT LOCALES
PAKISTAN AND SRI LANKA

175

needs.[3] In many cases intelligent use of assessments would have helped us avoid any number of the major shortcomings that resulted from recent global development schemes and disaster-recovery programs. For example, in 2000 floods killed 800 people in Mozambique and forced hundreds of thousands more from their homes. Much of the devastation can be attributed to poor initial development planning and lack of proper land use. Homes had been built in the floodplains and were rebuilt in the same location afterward; no assessments were carried out to call attention to this misstep. Assessments help identify potential problem areas and pinpoint nearby infrastructure and transportation systems that may affect or be affected by a proposed reconstruction project.

Subsequently, all solutions to foreseen problems should support actions that optimize eco-friendly placement of buildings, design techniques, materials, and construction-management practices. In addition to using assessments, policies that ensure that all reconstruction projects stay within their carrying capacity are extremely valuable.[4] Mandates can keep the scope of a project from straining existing local resources and infrastructure, for instance, preventing the overuse of aquifers. Exceeding carrying capacities may not cause problems immediately (but they will occur over time), so it is difficult to mandate preventive measures. In Kukes, Albania, during the Balkan wars of the 1990s, the concentration of Kosovo refugees in settlements surpassed local waste-handling capacity; as a result refuse dumps overflowed and raw sewage entered stream courses.

Keeping good records also assists future project proposals to incorporate successful techniques and avoid past mistakes. Standardizing ways to monitor and evaluate projects enhances the chance for fruitful consistency. The US World Wildlife Fund has created an Environmental Stewardship Report Card to assess the progress of approximately seventy-five projects in countries struck by the 2004 Indian Ocean tsunami.[5] The

(previous spread) Traditional brick factories consume enormous amounts of energy and pollute the air. Here, a factory in Gujarat, India

↑ Daniel Pittet, residence buildings at Kam For Sud children's home and organic farm, Katmandu Valley, Nepal

Human resettlement in conflict wih an elephant migratory route in Sri Lanka

data thus collected, which identify both a project's success and its shortcomings, highlight crucial information that may determine the potential of future projects in tropical areas affected by disaster.

SPATIAL PLANNING: When towns, villages, and settlements are reconstructed following a disaster, planners have an opportunity to ensure that their efforts have minimal negative environmental impact—and indeed to use techniques that positively serve and protect the environment. A spatial-planning assessment is a key tool in this. A spatial plan is a complete description of the physical configuration of the land to be developed and its resources. It can include drawings, geological surveys, written descriptions, and data sets. A good spatial plan will also consider features or conditions that may not be immediately evident, such as animal migratory routes or severe weather patterns. Communities and properties near the proposed development must be reviewed to determine what natural resources are being consumed and at what rate, how they are being managed, and how the proposed housing project might mitigate environmental strains or cultural tensions. Much of this assessment can be expressed in spatial terms: shelters and new homes should be kept at a distance from parks, wildlife preserves, and other ecologically sensitive areas, like proximate agricultural lands and aquifers, to discourage the possibility of residents extracting natural resources either deliberately or inadvertently. It is always best to avoid building in an area with a high water table, one that lacks sufficient potable water, land susceptible to flooding, and sites that show signs of heavy erosion. Planning should also address the local context, including weather conditions. For example, usage may adapt to seasonal changes, which in turn may dramatically influence the distribution of services.

When people are to be relocated, it is particularly telling to assess the past uses of a prospective site. If a site has not previously been cultivated for human activities, there may be a reason. Site preparation will likely require clearing vegetation and destroying habitats; the impact and viability of these processes should be measured. Clearance for construction, leveling the land, and adding infrastructure such as roads and wells often consumes excessive energy. In Sri Lanka after the tsunami communities were relocated away from the coast to what appeared to be underused scrubland. The site, however, was in the path of elephant migration; when cattle were grazed there, the route was disrupted, leading to dangerous encounters between wildlife and humans.

If a project proposal fails its spatial-planning assessment but relocating it is not an option, architectural solutions that address these obstacles become especially important. In 1975 major storms swept through refugee camps in Bangladesh, damaging many structures. Moving the communities elsewhere was not feasible. The nonprofit relief and reconstruction consultancy Intertect worked with university researchers from the United States to develop cyclone-resistant shelters out of locally available materials, mostly palm and bamboo. Each A-frame structure was cross-braced and performed well in strong-wind tests in the US. The floors were raised to prevent water intrusion. Use of bamboo and palm on a large scale to build shelters did not seriously affect the ecology of the area, as these plants are plentiful and can be replaced quickly.

Spatial planning should assess sources of construction materials. After the 2004 tsunami, an aim of many reconstruction efforts was to help people stay where they lived, rather than moving away from the coasts that provided their livelihood to inland sites whose environment could not support them. To do so, a more durable coastal-house model was needed. The Tsunami Design Initiative, made up of students from the Harvard Graduate School of Design, developed the Tsunami Safe(r) House, retaining the basic rectangular shape found in the region and using roughly the same amount of materials. The design restructures walls into a core-and-infill system, with four individual 10-by-4 ½-foot (3-by-1.4-m) blocks at each corner, rather than using four connecting exterior concrete walls, as had been typical before the storm. (Rigid, connected walls may pull each other down.) As a result the houses are five times stronger than the local structures, but still use materials that are familiar to local residents. After reviewing the plans, the Prajnopaya Foundation, an international NGO, adopted the project and, to date, has built 550 of the proposed 1,000 homes.[6]

In Pakistan the NGO Straw Bale and Appropriate Building, founded after the 2005 Kashmir earthquake, uses straw, a locally harvested, fast-growing crop, for home construction, leveraging its little-known capacity to resist earthquakes. The straw is compressed and tied into bales as building blocks. Straw-bale blocks are energy-efficient, nontoxic, and resist fire and pests.

The plan assessment should include a review of impact on the local ecosystem. After a disaster the urgent need for new homes leads to a huge demand for construction materials. The enormous pressure to act quickly discourages environmentally sustainable reconstruction practices and long-term thinking. In an emergency-shelter context, site planning is done by government authorities or humanitarian agencies that are doing the rebuilding. Good site planning will consider whether it is critical to revise material procurement if acquiring construction materials locally creates threatening conditions. For example, Indonesia suffers from massive deforestation. Sixty-five percent of forest on the mainland of Riau alone was lost to logging and clearing between 1982 and 2007. After the tsunami over 750,000 homes were damaged. Authorities anticipated accelerated deforestation from reconstruction projects. We at the World Wildlife Fund partnered with local, national, and international agencies to promote the Timber for Aceh campaign to use sustainable timber from outside Indonesia, sourced from supply chains that have been credibly certified as legal. We created public education activities and monitored illegal logging. A British Red Cross housing project also used only imported sources of wood. And the American Red Cross Rural Water Supply and Sanitation Project (with support from the Green Recovery Partnership) further enhanced the sustainability of these same homes by constructing individual treatment wetlands for wastewater disposal.[7]

In warm climates, planting to enhance the site's viability can help regulate indoor temperatures, increase personal comfort, and stabilize or renew the local ecosystem. The Swiss Red Cross, Swiss Solidarity, Swiss Resource Centre, and Development Alternatives together reconstructed tsunami-affected villages for 908 families in Karaikal, a village in Pondicherry, India, incorporating green spaces, kitchen gardens, and shade-tree planting. The houses used eco-friendly construction materials like fly-ash concrete blocks (using recycled residue from coal-fired power plants); storm-, gray-, and black-water management systems; placement of light sources along the solar path; roof water tanks and other rain- and groundwater harvesting systems. They established a nursery that would provide ten trees for each house built. Correct greening of a site should be part of every plan.

Not only the buildings but also the transportation infrastructure is part of a site-plan assessment. The need for roads and public facilities shapes the site plan; subsequent construction practices should plan for proper design and management of these to limit environmental impact. A lack of sufficient and adequate roadways limits livelihoods and encourages soil disruption and land clearing to accommodate new, impromptu passages; of course, it also hinders the construction process. In Dhamar Province, Yemen, in 1982 an earthquake destroyed some 25,000 homes and damaged an additional 18,000. The government announced

← ← A fishing net is used to reinforce this straw-bale wall in Pakistan for greater earthquake resistance.

← Workers from Straw Bale and Appropriate Building make building blocks from locally grown straw, an agricultural byproduct.

↑ A construction team has readied a straw-bale house for clay plaster.

↗ A finished straw-bale house in Hillkot, Pakistan

↗↗ Excessive clay mining in Indonesia is destroying the local resource.

→ / →→ Illegal logging and on-site milling in Indonesia

Our Green Recovery Partnership addresses major themes—livelihoods, construction, water and sanitation, and disaster management—in terms of environmental conservation.

that it was establishing a major rebuild-and-repair strategy to be completed in two years. Ten years later the project was still not finished. Only 10,300 houses had been built and 1,652 mended. The holdup was blamed on tribal conflict, but inadequate thoroughfares created the major obstacle. The area is so mountainous that only small four-wheel-drive vehicles could be used to transport materials. Several roads had to be specially built to reach the more isolated settlements. Road placement, design, and construction must, however, take into account the side effects of improved access in the long term. Will new roads encourage clearance of land and draw more new population to a district than it can support? Can the roads be constructed with minimum clearing of land and avoid invading fragile or protected territories such as wetlands, wildlife habitat, or forests? Do the roads benefit the people they most need to serve?

Water availability is critical to planning. The scope of a project influences the mode of water distribution. In addition to locating water sources, the site-plan assessment must ensure that withdrawals are easily replenished and water is kept sanitary, and where possible it must be saved, reused, or its use minimized even during the construction process. In Kenya flooding displaced hundreds of families from the Ifo refugee camp in 2007. The United Nations High Commission for Refugees erected 500 brick shelters and established methods for catching spilled water from tap stands to reduce water use in brick making. Rainwater collection is an underused and even more sustainable green practice. In 2008, when some 8,000 Rwandans were forced to leave Tanzania, a shelter project monitored by the Tanzanian Ministry of Infrastructure built 220 homes for them, each equipped with a rainwater catchment system that stores up to 317 US gallons (1.2 kl) of water. Project planners sited public boreholes (shafts to a water source) to improve access to drinkable water, expanding options for water distribution to include individual systems, communal watering points, and community systems, all of which may be viable if they are not depleted or contaminated over time. Proper assessment before siting boreholes is important, as unregulated or poorly sited boreholes can drain or contaminate a water table or aquifer.

Fuel availability is equally important. Fuels used for cooking and heating have an enormous impact on the environment. When planning a settlement it is important to determine if fuel can be collected and used sustainably. Moreover, if too much time and effort are invested in collecting fuel, there will be less time for recovery and the community's revival will suffer. Reconstruction plans that lessen fuel needs, using renewable energy systems or other fuel-efficient technologies, are highly advantageous. In the Rwandan project the Tanzanian Ministry of Infrastructure partnered with the Kigali Institute for Science and Technology to design and build a highly efficient wood stove for each house. It is difficult to convince people to stop cooking in their customary way, but the quantity of a resource can be reduced: an efficient wood stove uses much less fuel. Thus, the design limited the need for wood, protecting the community's natural resources from deforestation.

PARTNERSHIPS: Protecting the environment is integral to recovery, reconstruction, and development. After the 2008 Wenchaun earthquake in China an international workshop organized by the Ministry of Commerce and the United Nations found that environmental mainstreaming was successful when efforts were supported by policy statements, public awareness, technical capacity, good communications, and project monitoring. Partnerships also facilitate mainstreaming. They can reduce risk and vulnerability in construction, water and sanitation, disaster management, and restoration of livelihoods, because they permit groups (whether NGOs or government agencies)

# Earthquakes and tsunamis will always happen, but disaster is no longer inevitable.

to focus their expertise. The World Wildlife Fund and the American Red Cross created a five-year Green Recovery Partnership to integrate environmental management into the Red Cross's Tsunami Recovery Program in Indonesia, Thailand, Sri Lanka, and the Maldives. The partnership incorporates recovery practices that reduce risk and vulnerability in the region.

## DESIGNING A RISK STRATEGY

At present it is rare that a disaster-reconstruction program honors eco-friendly practices as the heart of its building mission. An exception is in Lagoswatte, Sri Lanka, where Sarvodaya, the largest NGO on the island, created an eco-village for the survivors of the 2004 tsunami. The project, known as Damniyangama, was inaugurated two years after the catastrophe. It includes fifty-five houses and a number of communal buildings. From preplanning to construction each step used environmentally sound building practices, incorporating community input into the design and bringing residents into the process of environmental management. The buildings are positioned to maximize use of sun, wind, and daylight. Drainage systems follow the natural slope of the land. New planted vegetation functions as a windbreak. Planners used local materials and labor, while avoiding toxins such as asbestos. The program relies on passive cooling measures, provides each house with solar panels, has rainwater-harvesting tanks and composting bins, is able to reuse gray water for plant irrigation, and recycles its waste. If struck by another hazard the community is equipped to rebound quickly, with little scarring.

Recovery must assume that disasters will recur and address their long-term effect on the environment. Nothing damages a local ecology more than building homes over and again due to poor hazard-preparedness. Prevention is the key to avoiding inadvertent unsustainable use: high-risk areas must be managed.

Combining local knowledge with environmental expertise generates good data that assist in preparedness. It is as important for communities and agencies to work together on the initial assessments as it is essential to partner with local governments and municipalities to ensure that disaster-mitigation procedures remain relevant over time. Disaster-risk mapping, resource mapping, and historical profiling help identify environmental concerns. Locations that are at low risk should be protected for the future. Planners should critique site selection and design, orient housing, and manage materials procurement. Designing with a built-in risk strategy reduces the long-term vulnerability of communities. Reconstruction programs must strive to ensure that if and when hazard strikes, people's lives are not severely disrupted. Earthquakes and tsunamis will always happen, but disaster is no longer inevitable.

Notes

1   See Karen Sudmeier-Rieux, Hillary Masundire, Ali Rizvi, and Simon Rietbergen, eds., *Ecosystems, Livelihoods and Disasters: An Integrated Approach to Disaster Risk Management*, Ecosystems Management Series 4 (Gland, Switzerland, and Cambridge, UK: World Conservation Union, 2006), 32.

2   See State of the World's Forests 2009 (Rome: Food and Agriculture Organization of the United Nations, 2009), ftp://ftp.fao.org/docrep/fao/011/i0350e/i0350e.pdf, accessed September 26, 2010.

3   See Eamonn Barrett, Sarah Murfitt, and Paul Venton, "Mainstreaming the Environment into Humanitarian Response: An Exploration of Opportunities and Issues," *Environmental Resources Management Final Report*, November 2007: 17–18, www.humanitarianreform.org/humanitarianreform/Portals/1/cluster%20approach%20page/clusters%20pages/Environment/ERM_%20Final%20Report_08%2011%2007.pdf, accessed August 12, 2010.

4   Carrying capacity, usually expressed as a ratio, describes the maximum number of individuals (humans or all species) that a given ecosystem or area of land can support without draining natural resources; it identifies the tolerance of a territory for sustainable development.

5   The Report Card reviews a completed project to determine whether it has achieved environmental sustainability objectives. It asks a series of questions in a simple Yes/No/Not Sure checklist format and asks for a description of any follow-up action that may be required. The checklist may be completed by the implementing agency, project coordinator, or World Wildlife Fund personnel. The assessment covers air and water quality, status of hazardous materials, impact on natural and cultural resources, and economic and social outcomes. Questions include: did the project result in the excessive emission of air pollutants (e.g., smoke, gases, dust particles)? Did the project result in the significant alteration of waterways (addition of spring catchments, drainage infrastructure, placement of rock along river bank)? Did the project result in pollution of rivers, streams, wetlands, or other waterways (e.g., addition of sediment, wastewater, hazardous materials, runoff from roads, soil movement, excavation)? Did the project restrict access to water sources or other public use areas or resources? Did the project result in the exposure of humans or the environment to toxic or hazardous materials at the project site? Did the project result in the disturbance of cultural, archaeological, prehistoric or historic resources at the site? Did the project result in an increase in local fees or taxes? Did the project result in the extraction of natural resources (e.g., fish, timber, water, sand, coral)? Did the project result in the disturbance of endangered species (e.g., sea turtles, orangutans) or their habitats?

6   For further detail on the Tsunami Safe(r) House project, see projects.gsd.harvard.edu/tsunami/proposal_TDI_Dec03.pdf and senseable.mit.edu/tsunami-prajnopaya, accessed September 26, 2010.

7   A constructed wetland system uses a natural process to filter wastewater.

"There was such disregard for housing culture in the way the new, post-disaster settlements were designed and built that serious physical and mental-health problems now trouble the fisher families of Tamil Nadu."

# THE HOME
# AS THE WORLD:
# TAMIL NADU

JENNIFER E. DUYNE BARENSTEIN
WORLD HABITAT RESEARCH CENTRE,
INSTITUTE FOR SUSTAINABILITY
APPLIED TO THE BUILT ENVIRONMENT,
UNIVERSITY OF APPLIED SCIENCES OF
SOUTHERN SWITZERLAND, LUGANO

The dwelling is the theater of our lives, where the major dramas of birth and death, of procreation and recreation, of labor and of being in labor play out. Yet in times of emergency, culture appears to be a luxury, beyond the means and priorities of response. Contrary to what was assumed by the scores of external agencies that came to the aid of Tamil Nadu, India, in 2005, following the Indian Ocean tsunami, the coastal communities had a strong housing culture. For families whose lives are based on fishing, housing extends well beyond the need for shelter.

Together with a group of graduate students from the Department of Social Anthropology at the University of Zurich I carried out post-disaster anthropological research in Tamil Nadu from 2005 to 2008. We visited twelve coastal villages, each with about 120 households, all Hindu and all from the fishing caste. We spoke with residents about how or if reconstruction practices had altered their culture. In these coastal communities men and women spend most of their productive and leisure time in the open—a lifestyle made possible by the warm climate and the thousands of mango, tamarind, nim, and coconut trees that offer shade and protection from it. In interviews and conversations, we discovered that the recovery process had moved forward with a complete lack of understanding of the communities' way of life on the part of external agencies. More importantly, there was such disregard for housing culture in the way the new, post-disaster settlements were designed and built that serious physical and mental-health problems now trouble the fisher families of Tamil Nadu.[1]

## HOUSING CULTURE AND WAYS OF LIFE

India's monumental architecture and housing culture are extensively described in the ancient doctrine of Vastu Shastra, a traditional Hindu system of astrological and mathematical calculations applied to construction design and aimed at enhancing the well-being of residents. The concepts behind house designs are the same as those for temples, reflecting the sacred and spiritual place a home occupies in people's lives. It is commonly assumed that only high-caste people apply Vastu Shastra principles to their houses. But in Tamil Nadu we found that the housing culture of even low-caste fishing communities is strongly influenced by the highly ritualized process.

Generally, a family begins the construction of a new house upon the marriage of a son. They first consult a *pandit* (priest, astrologer), who plays a key role in selecting the exact site and designing the house. The house must be symmetrical, with a central doorway and a well-made door. It must conform to specific measurements and proportions, which are defined on the basis of the horoscope of the oldest woman in the household. Further critical decisions are the orientation of the main entrance, the length of each wall, and the number of doors and windows. The pandit determines the most auspicious day and time to begin construction and participates in family prayers at the site, marks the positions of the corner poles, and breaks a number of coconuts in a ritual intended to ensure the safety of the building. All of this is important because even under normal conditions building a new house is a process that connects different but interdependent communities and whose value should not be underestimated in India's caste-divided society.

The fishing communities we analyzed are characterized by strictly defined gender roles. Women and men have different responsibilities and control different spaces. Men engage in marine fishery, while women traditionally market the catch and conduct most land-based activities. Accordingly, women also manage the process of building a new house. They mobilize masons or local small contractors, purchase construction materials, and supervise the work. Most of the work is done by specialized castes, but adult family members participate as

INSTITUTION
WORLD HABITAT RESEARCH CENTRE,
UNIVERSITY OF APPLIED SCIENCES
OF SOUTHERN SWITZERLAND, LUGANO

PROJECT LOCALE
TAMIL NADU, INDIA

unskilled laborers. The first house of a newly married couple is typically small, with a fully thatched roof and thatch (or sometimes brick) walls. Over time the family may build a new, larger or more solid house with brick walls and perhaps a roof made of artisanal or industrially produced tiles, occasionally using timber elements (though this is discouraged). Few families build the expensive, flat-roofed, precast-concrete houses found in other parts of India, as they are not well-suited to the local climate.

Doors, walls, and floors are generally decorated with bright colors and geometric patterns, flowers, or animals. Motifs are chosen by all family members in consultation with the artisans they employ for the task. Fishers spend significant amounts of money for decorations that give their house a unique character and identity.

Many fishers' houses consist of only two rooms: one inside, the other, a large semienclosed veranda, partly outside. The veranda, the intersection of private and public realms, leads from the front into the main room and is the most important space of the house. This well-ventilated area modulates the climate by allowing a cooling breeze to stream through small fretted windows or pierced openings in the walls. During the day, and in particular during the rainy season, people spend their leisure time and entertain guests here. At night the veranda is transformed into a sleeping area with straw mats rolled out on the floor. The inner room is primarily used as a secure storeroom and as a sleeping area for women during the monsoon season. Sometimes the house also includes a separate *puja,* or prayer room. The puja contains a small shrine but is also used for storage. The kitchen is a separate covered area, invariably located in the southeastern corner of the homestead plot. Most houses also have a small area for washing, screened by plants or fences.

Fishers spend most of their time outside, around their houses. The space around a house or a group of houses belonging to

(previous spread) Men tend their fishing nets outside a traditional house in Tamil Nadu.

↑ Painted decorations on a traditional Tamil Nadu house

kin-related families is often marked off by fences or trees and is used to keep goats and poultry, to dry fish, and to store nets or other utensils. This space is an essential element of home and vitally important to village livelihoods and well-being.

The settlements we studied are embedded in thick vegetation and trees. Trees provide valuable resources, such as tamarind juice, and cool shade in a region where daytime temperatures exceed 100°F (38°C) most of the year. These fisher communities associate trees with health, protection, beauty, and sacredness. The shaded areas under them constitute important private or communal spaces. Men mostly meet in the afternoons to mend their nets under the coconut trees near the beach, whereas women prefer to meet under the shade of tamarind trees, where their children climb and play in the strong branches.

## VERNACULAR HOUSING: POLICY, PERCEPTION, AND POST-TSUNAMI RECONSTRUCTION

The heterogeneity, functionality, and beauty of vernacular housing and traditional settlements quickly disappear behind official statistics, which list 87 percent of the houses in coastal Tamil Nadu as so-called kachcha dwellings. The Hindi word kachcha literally means "raw" and generally has a negative connotation. Its opposite, pucca, means "ripe" or "mature." Accordingly, kachcha is associated with poverty and backwardness and pucca with modernity. The words kachcha and pucca are officially used by the government of India to differentiate nonengineered vernacular houses built by local artisans with locally produced construction materials from engineered houses (houses built with industrially produced construction materials such as bricks, cement, and concrete). Roofing materials are of particular importance. Regardless of what materials are used to construct the walls, which in most cases in coastal Tamil Nadu are bricks

and mortar, all houses with thatched roofs are classified as kachcha. Homes with tiled roofs are semi-pucca, and only those with flat reinforced-cement roofs are considered pucca homes. A lack of appreciation for local housing culture has characterized India since its colonial period; present building codes, urban plans, and housing policies evolved not out of Indian culture and experience but as a result of western traditions. The imposition of western models becomes particularly evident today in India's social housing and post-disaster reconstruction programs.

On December 26, 2004, an earthquake measuring 9.2 Mw hit northern Sumatra, resulting in one of the most destructive tsunamis in recorded history. In India the tsunami killed nearly 16,000 people. A few weeks later the government of Tamil Nadu estimated that over 130,000 houses needed to be reconstructed and about 10,000 needed repair. These figures were not the result of an accurate damage assessment. Because the government intended to resettle all tsunami-affected communities at a safe distance from the coast, a detailed housing-damage assessment was not considered necessary. Stiff public resistance subsequently forced the government to relax its relocation policy. However, allowing communities to remain in their original villages did not compel the government to reconsider the number of new houses required. The unprecedented availability of humanitarian aid for reconstruction further complicated the process, as residents were encouraged to upgrade their kachcha houses even if they had not been damaged. The unexpected amount of aid encouraged the agencies' vested interest in building as many new houses as possible. This factor, along with the government's prejudice against vernacular housing and the vulnerability of fishing communities overwhelmed by new entitlements to free houses, kept the government to its original plan. The number of new houses was to be based on the number of families living in coastal villages affected by the tsunami, not on the actual number of houses lost.

←← This house, perfectly sound after the tsunami, was destroyed as part of the government's reconstruction program.

← A house on the Tamil Nadu coast destroyed in the tsunami

↓ A decorated house with a tile roof, which might have been considered semi-pucca by the government before the tsunami, but would have been designated kachcha after

State-built housing after the tsunami: an organic village structure was replaced by a strict grid of small cement houses with little air or light. There is no room for expansion, gardens, farm animals, or trees.

The most serious negative consequence of post-tsunami reconstruction in Tamil Nadu was the systematic demolition of undamaged vernacular homes and the felling of all the trees.

Housing reconstruction in Tamil Nadu was directed entirely by national and international NGOs, private corporations, and charity organizations. The government limited its role to defining the regulatory framework, coordination, monitoring, and quality control. Because the government strongly supported the people's right to a multiple-hazard-resistant house, it laid out detailed conditions with respect to minimum investments in housing, building technologies, and size of houses and homestead plots. According to official policy each family was entitled to a flat-roofed, reinforced-concrete house of 325 square feet (30 sq. m), a size that is barely sufficient to accommodate a nuclear family. The assumption that fishers live in independent nuclear families with a lifestyle similar to that of the urban middle class was also reflected in the design of the proposed houses, which in spite of their small size were typically divided into a dining room, two bedrooms, a kitchen, and an attached bathroom. None of the rooms was sufficiently large to allow an average family to stay together in one room. Because of this, the people we interviewed perceived their new houses as too small, even if the majority of the pre-tsunami houses were actually smaller. The veranda, the most important space in self-built houses, was generally omitted or so reduced that it was of no use. Government policy stipulated that plots were to be 646 square feet (60 sq. m) in urban areas and 1,300 square feet (120 sq. m) in rural areas. But land shortages forced families onto significantly smaller sites. Thus, even though the houses were conceived as extendable core units, there was no space to build extensions or plant trees.

None of the agencies involved in housing reconstruction in Tamil Nadu had worked with fishing communities before the tsunami. Many of those that built thousands of houses also had no previous construction experience, whether in post-disaster conditions or under normal circumstances. In spite of the government policy requesting private agencies to finalize house designs and settlement layouts in consultation with communities, in most cases the consultation took place on paper or exclusively involved the male village rulers.

The most serious negative consequence of post-tsunami reconstruction in Tamil Nadu, however, was the systematic demolition of undamaged vernacular homes and the felling of all the trees. There was a shortage of land and in many cases contractors refused to start building until the site was cleared completely. A cleared site was the prerequisite for rapidly and efficiently implementing a mass-housing approach to reconstruction. In one village 110 homes that had withstood the tsunami and had been repaired by an NGO were demolished to make room for the housing program of another NGO. As a result of these events most of the new coastal villages consist of endless rows of matchbox houses without a single tree.

## A LIFE WITH TREES

"Before, I could share my sorrows, now I cannot and it affects me mentally and physically; sometimes I cannot sleep and sometimes I cannot eat food, because I keep everything in my heart; sometimes I think about suicide and what is going to happen to my children."
—A young mother of three children

"The trees are missing. Now the friends are not sitting together and helping each other with the nets, and maybe this is why the people drink. The fact that there are not trees and that people are either inside the house or in the hot sun when they work on the nets leads to more tensions and this in turn leads to a higher consumption of alcohol."
—A middle-aged fisherman

Men and women used to congregate in separate groups under the trees surrounding traditional houses with steeply pitched thatched roofs and grillwork windows, but the government's program mandated the land be cleared so contractors could rebuild efficiently.

These two comments sadly summarize how the people we spoke to feel about living in their new homes.[2] Indeed, substituting concrete houses for vernacular houses and systematically destroying coastal habitats created dramatic consequences for the health of coastal communities. Besides the implications of demolishing vernacular houses, social conflicts over contractor-built houses, the nucleation of extended families, the marginalization of women in the house-construction process, and isolation of elderly people and widows from informal social-security systems, the consequences of cutting down the trees have been catastrophic.

Trees constituted an essential element of the natural habitat and notion of home in the coastal communities we studied. Thousands of trees are estimated to have been cut down to build the new houses—largely to clear land or burn as fuel, rather than for use in construction. The eradication of trees has dismantled livelihoods and social life, and has led to poor health. Many people believe that the absence of trees is responsible for increased rates of alcoholism, domestic violence, depression, and suicide in their communities. Because it is too hot in the sun, villagers no longer spend their leisure time together under the shade of trees, children no longer play outside, and men no longer mend their nets collectively outdoors. The lack of trees has created social isolation and solitude. Trees, moreover, were not only important for thermal comfort. Their vital products supplied communities with important livelihood resources such as fuel, fruits, vegetables, fodder, and plants used for medical purposes, and their presence was a prerequisite for keeping livestock. Before the tsunami most households owned a few goats. These produced milk and meat and could be sold in periods of crisis, to face an extraordinary expense, or to supplement a lean fishing season. Owning income-generating trees such as coconut palms and tamarinds was particularly important for elderly people who could no longer engage in marine fishery and related work. Social life and recreational activities for both men and women used to take place under the shade trees. During the tsunami trees even saved the lives of several people who managed to hold onto their trunks. Women we interviewed often referred to certain trees as their children. In addition, trees provide vital windbreaks to moderate storms.

Before the tsunami, the people we interviewed spent most of their time outside. They described their villages as "like a garden," with many different varieties of trees and flowers. Even though people could meet anywhere, certain trees or clusters of trees served as special meeting places where groups of men or women would regularly get together, particularly in the afternoons. They often took food with them and relaxed in the shade, ate together and sometimes slept under the trees through the night. Many people emphasized the importance of these communal places, telling us they actually rarely went home. People spoke about the times spent together under the trees as fun—time passed enjoying one another and joking around; though the communal space defined by the shade of trees was equally important for sharing sorrows and for mutual emotional support.

In the absence of shade trees people are forced to stay inside. They spend much less time together, as meeting friends is traditionally not associated with home visits, and their new houses are too small and not designed for entertaining. There is no veranda and none of the rooms is sufficiently large to accommodate guests. Men and women typically meet in different places, which restricts them from visiting each other in their respective homes. The absence of trees and open common space also limits the children's way of life. Without shade trees, children no longer play together outside. Parents fear that keeping their children inside is bad for their health and development and encourages them to do nothing but watch television and become lazy.

People have also noted a direct and measurable impact of loss of trees on their health. New diseases and the frequent occurrence of preexisting ones (fever, jaundice, and chicken pox) are ascribed to the lack of shade and fresh air. Even if ailments that people now associate with the absence of trees, such as headaches or chest and abdominal pain, are psychosomatic, they hint at the likelihood that many people are suffering from depression.

Eliminating the trees of Tamil Nadu's coastline cannot entirely be countered by replanting; it will take ten to thirty years before any newly planted trees reach a pre-tsunami size. But it is not simply a question of time. The homestead plots in the newly constructed grid-patterned housing colonies are too small to support either large numbers of trees or a few large trees, which need space to spread and grow. So public lands along the water have been replanted with kajurinas, a fast-growing needle tree that provides a windbreak and roots well in sand but offers little shade, produces no marketable products, and renders the soil too acidic for anything else to grow.

## FROM RECOVERY TO WELL-BEING

Helping communities restore their livelihoods after disasters is a complex task, not fully resolved simply by building hazard-resistant houses. The case of Tamil Nadu shows that people have the capacity to build environmentally sustainable, culturally expressive houses that meet their practical needs. A respectful and dignified approach to reconstruction would entail giving financial and material support to people rendered homeless by the tsunami, allowing them to rebuild their houses according to their needs and preferences, and encouraging communities to ask for the sort of help they need.[3]

Unfortunately, the consequences of ignoring people's housing culture and livelihoods within the framework of post-disaster reconstruction are coming to light in failed projects all over the world—in abandoned villages, ecological damage, new health problems, and dangerous buildings. Many agencies involved in housing reconstruction—in spite of their discourses of empowerment, participation, and sustainable and equitable development—remain, in practice, notoriously oblivious to these issues. Long-term safety and security begin with understanding housing as a living system, an expression of a way of life. To think otherwise is to repeat the sad and irreversible fate of the coastal villages of Tamil Nadu.

Notes

1  See Jennifer Duyne Barenstein, "Earthquake-Safe: Lessons to Be Learned from Traditional Construction," International Conference on the Seismic Performance of Traditional Buildings, Istanbul, Turkey November 16–18, 2000, posted at www.icomos.org/iiwc/seismic/Jigyasu.pdf, accessed July 10, 2010; Paul Oliver, ed., *Encyclopaedia of Vernacular Architecture of the World* (Cambridge, UK: Cambridge University Press, 1997), 15; Jennifer Duyne Barenstein and Sushma Iyengar, "India: From a Culture of Housing to a Philosophy of Reconstruction," in M. Lyons and T. Schilderman, eds., *Building Back Better: Delivering People-Centred Reconstruction to Scale* (Rugby, UK: Practical Action Publishing,  2010), 163–88; Jennifer Duyne Barenstein, "Post-Disaster Housing Reconstruction: Approaches, Challenges and Risks," keynote paper presented at the Regional Conference on Owner-Driven Reconstruction, cofunded by the Swiss Agency for Development and Cooperation, Bhuj, Gujarat, India, July 16–18,.2008; and Jennifer Duyne Barenstein, "Owner-Driven and Agency-Driven Post-Disaster Housing Reconstruction: Issues and Experiences from Gujarat and Tamil Nadu," in C. M. Madduma Bandara et al., eds., *Traversing No Man's Land* (Colombo, Sri Lanka: Vijitha Yapa Books, forthcoming).

2  The interviews were carried out by Jasmin Naimi-Gasser during fieldwork in a reconstructed village in coastal Tamil Nadu in 2008. See Jasmin Naimi-Gasser, "The Socio-Cultural Impact of Post-Tsunami Housing Reconstruction Programs on Fishing Communities in Tamil Nadu: An Ethnographic Case Study" (thesis, University of Zurich, 2009).

3  The World Bank is now promoting the idea of owner-driven reconstruction (within a series of standards) as the most viable option for governments to support, rather than large public reconstruction programs. See Jennifer Duyne Barenstein, Abhas Jha, Priscilla Phelps, Daniel Pittet, and Stephen Sena, *Safer Homes, Stronger Communities: A Handbook for Reconstruction after Natural Disasters* (Washington, DC: World Bank, 2010), and online at www.housingreconstruction.com.

The heterogeneity, functionality, and beauty of vernacular housing quickly disappear behind official statistics, which list 87 percent of the houses in coastal Tamil Nadu as kachcha dwellings.

"Our priorities tie in with the educational
mission of the school: students and
the community can see how traditional
architecture and craftsmanship can be
kept alive when adapted to sustainable
and appropriate design."

# DESIGN AS MITIGATION IN THE HIMALAYAS

FRANCESCA GALEAZZI
ARUP ASSOCIATES, LONDON

There are rare opportunities in the career of a designer to do something truly special, to create unique designs that help to sustain entire communities, while offering them protection against the impact of external elements. This impact is not only material change due to natural disaster, war, or drought, but also societal change such as cultural impoverishment and globalization, which may, over time, lead to a profound sense of loss—loss of identity and sense of community.

The Ladakh school project has given us at Arup and Arup Associates a chance to develop a site that is inherently resilient in the face of these complex external forces.[1] This extraordinary project is, as well, an opportunity to propose a model—appropriately modern and sustainable—for other communities and cultures in the world under pressure to change.

## LADAKH, A REMOTE COMMUNITY

Sometimes known as Little Tibet, Ladakh is an ancient kingdom located high in the Indian Himalayas, close to Tibet's western border. In a remote high-altitude desert that lies some 11,500 feet (3,500 m) above sea level, Ladakh is an environment of extremes surrounded by the splendid mountain ranges of the Karakoram to the north and the Great Himalayas to the south. For nearly six months of the year the valley is cut off by prolonged snowfall, with winter temperatures dropping as low as −22°F (−30°C). In the summer the intense solar radiation at this altitude forces temperatures up to above 100°F (38°C), and the snow-melt brings the rich fertile valleys alive. The rainshield formed by the Himalayas prevents the Indian monsoon from reaching this region, resulting in minimal year-round precipitation. The little water available for use comes from winter snowfall, which melts in the spring and flows down the valleys toward the Indus River. The retreat of Himalayan glaciers and abnormal climatic patterns, both attributed to global warming, increasingly threaten the availability of this precious resource.

Ladakh is one of the few remaining mountain societies where a traditional Tibetan Buddhist way of life is practiced. Despite being remote, isolated during the winter by the closing of the only road that connects it with the other Indian states to the south, it is a place of strategic importance, located in the contested Kashmir region between Tibet (whose border with China is disputed) and Pakistan. For the past sixty years it has been the scene of regular fighting between India and Pakistan, both of which claim Kashmir. Since 1974 Ladakh has been open to tourism and the small military airport has grown to operate daily summer flights to Delhi, bringing a growing number of tourists. Today, this fragile community is under immense social pressure, principally due to the rapid changes that are shaping a modernizing India, but also due to the impact of western lifestyles (real and perceived) on younger generations through tourism, technology, and mass communications.

This, in brief, is the complex environmental, cultural, and social context in which the idea was conceived to create a model school for best educational practices and sustainable development.

## THE IDEA OF THE DRUK WHITE LOTUS SCHOOL

Local communities that wanted their children educated in their own language and culture requested help from their spiritual leader, His Holiness the twelfth Gyalwang Drukpa. Under the patronage of His Holiness the fourteenth Dalai Lama, the Drukpa Trust was formed in the UK in 1992 to raise funds to design and build a new school. A site in the Leh district was chosen.[2] Arup and Arup Associates were responsible for the master plan, concept design, and detailed design for the entire school

4.3
DESIGN AS
MITIGATION IN
THE HIMALAYAS

199

FIRM
ARUP ASSOCIATES

PROJECT LOCALE
SHEY, LADAKH, INDIA

project; since 1995 our teams of architects and engineers
have worked on the project primarily as volunteers. The school
complex is located in the village of Shey, thirty minutes' drive
from the capital, Leh, on a gently south-sloping desert site surrounded by two important monasteries and close to the Indus
River and its adjacent irrigated crop fields.

Designed to provide education from preschool and kindergarten through secondary education and vocational training,
the school includes a phased building program for 750 students
and has become the new heart of the community. It also provides facilities for some 200 residential students from remote
areas who would not otherwise have access to education.

The mission of the school is to give students the confidence
and skills required to succeed in a changing world, together with
a sound foundation in the Ladakhi language, culture, and traditions. The concept of a child-centered education is at the heart
of the curriculum. The preschool is based on the Montessori
system, which recognizes that children develop in different ways
and have different learning needs. The primary and secondary
school has a more structured curriculum; students have access
to teaching laboratories for physics, chemistry, biology, and
computing and a large library.

In 2001 the first preschool and daycare block was completed, followed by the Junior School for primary students in
2006. Currently the construction of more school buildings and
residences is under way, with a target to complete the whole
complex by 2013. Phased construction permits adaptation to
the difficulties of building in an extreme environment and
allows the school to grow organically, with the student population year by year.

(previous spread) The Druk White Lotus
School offers a sustainable model for other
communities and cultures that are under
pressure to change.

↑ The canteen at the school

↑↑ The school's opening ceremony

↑ The school courtyard

→ Master plan

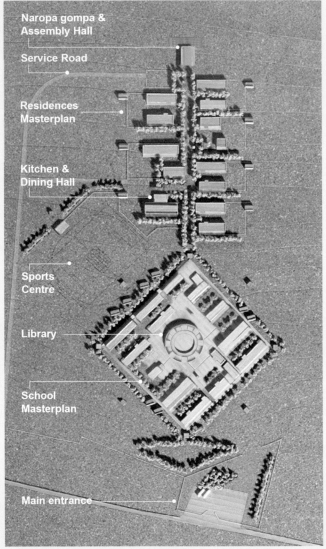

Naropa gompa &
Assembly Hall

Service Road

Residences
Masterplan

Kitchen &
Dining Hall

Sports
Centre

Library

School
Masterplan

Main entrance

## DESIGNING FOR LADAKH

The Druk White Lotus School is designed to be sustainable at every level. This includes architectural and engineering design, construction, operations, and the educational mission of the school—which together aspire to a progressive educational model in harmony with local traditions. The ecological context is extremely fragile, so site strategies were planned to achieve a nearly zero-impact system for water, energy, and waste management

Our design approach may be summarized as innovative, clever low-tech. Engineers and architects have worked together closely from the outset; we believe that this integration is necessary for success. The extraordinary environment of Ladakh has required great sensitivity to site. The buildings and site must respond to the evident signs of climate change in the region, especially drought, retreating glaciers, and less predictable weather patterns.[3] We had to minimize the use of resources and make as little impact as possible on the environment in both construction and operations. The location is in a highly seismic area, vulnerable to powerful earthquakes, so earthquake resilience using simple construction techniques was a fundamental goal. The buildings are designed to be easy to operate and maintain, while its spaces are simple, flexible, and comfortable, celebrating local culture and the unique heritage of Ladakh and fostering learning. These principles are in clear contrast to the high-tech approach adopted in the area in recent years, especially by foreign firms, which have produced buildings that are difficult to use and expensive to maintain, requiring abundant skills. As a result many of those new buildings have decayed rapidly or stopped functioning properly.[4]

Innovation does not consist in loading a building with technology and complicated systems but in developing simple, passive, yet sophisticated means that can be easily communicated to the people who use it and are intuitively operated. In the strategies we adopted simplicity, robustness, adaptability, and appropriateness were prioritized over pure aesthetics or style.

To make the construction techniques and passive systems as efficient as possible, the engineers used the latest analysis software to develop earthquake-resistant construction, passive solar-energy systems, and the optimum use of natural ventilation, natural daylight, and double glazing. The real challenge for the design team arose each time the analysis results had to be translated into construction techniques. Designing for Ladakh, with its unreliable power supplies and consequent limitations on the use of machinery, meant that materials had to be simple to procure and buildings simple to build and run.

## A RESILIENT MASTER PLAN AND BUILDING DESIGN

The master plan is divided into four main areas by function: the first—the site entrance, caretaker's house, visitors' center, and bus drop-off from the road to the south—gives pedestrian access to the second, the daytime teaching area, and the third, the residential buildings. The fourth area, comprising the water and energy infrastructure and the sports facilities, is located separately alongside a service track to the west.

Learning from the arrangement of daytime spaces in local monasteries and houses, we designed the school with passive solar heat systems. The master plan places the buildings along two key orientations. Those in the teaching area are oriented 30° toward the southeast so that they get morning sun, which at this altitude is abundant even in winter. The residences are oriented along a north–south axis, with all buildings facing due south to receive sun throughout the day.

Large glazed facades to the southeast act as solar-caption elements, while heavy masonry walls with high thermal inertia store the heat gained throughout the day. This removes the need for other heating methods during the majority of the winter and eliminates dependence on external fuel sources.

The schoolrooms are primarily one story high, separated to avoid overshadowing, and grouped in two parallel buildings around an open courtyard, which provides play areas and additional secure outdoor teaching spaces. Each classroom has a quiet warm corner with a small stove on a concrete floor that is available as a supplementary heat source, only needed on extremely cold days. In summer windows and roof lights allow cross-ventilation for cooling and fresh air.[5]

The residential blocks are also arranged around a landscaped courtyard with play areas and planned vegetable gardens to introduce variety to the students' diet while they learn agricultural skills. Because the residential buildings are predominantly used at night, they can use a Trombe wall, an enhanced version of a simple passive solar wall that stores solar energy collected during the day and releases it in the form of heat during the evening, when the dormitories are in use. The Trombe system has thick walls coated externally with dark, heat-absorbing paint and faced with two layers of glass, separated by a small gap to create an air pocket. Heat from sunlight passing through the glass is absorbed by the dark surface, stored in the wall, and conducted slowly inward through the masonry. Adjustable openings on the top and bottom of the wall transfer heat from the air cavity to the room inside. This increases the efficiency of the system and ensures that the rooms are constantly kept comfortable. There is no need for the wood- and dung-burning stoves or gas heaters commonly used in Ladakh households. Thick stone walls on the three sides of the block that do not face south act as thermal storage and keep the internal conditions almost stable, even when outdoor temperatures drop well below zero. In summer the Trombe walls are shaded on the outside with planters of

flowers and the external glazing units can be opened to allow built-up heat to escape the air cavity to prevent overheating. One central window provides daylight, cross-ventilation, cooling, and fresh air.

## USING LOCAL MATERIALS AND RESOURCES

An initial challenge for the design team was the lack of resources and materials near the site. Each imported building element makes its way into Ladakh on polluting diesel trucks across the unspoiled passes of the Himalayas. So the first step was to study the traditional local architecture to understand what available materials could be used in a contemporary way, while avoiding the imitation vernacular pastiche that is widespread in Ladakh.

We were particularly inspired by the superbly rendered mud-brick and stone construction of the ancient monasteries. The materials—stone, mud mortar, mud bricks, timber, and grass—are mostly indigenous to Ladakh. Using these allowed us to radically minimize the use of imported products. The stone for the walls is found close to the site and the mud for mortar, bricks, and roofing is excavated nearby. Timber is grown locally: poplar and willow from nearby monastery plantations and local producers. Glass, structural timber, cement, and steel must be bought and delivered from other parts of Kashmir or India. All buildings have cavity walls on three sides: granite blocks set in mud mortar are used for the outer leaf, while traditional mud-brick masonry is used for the inner leaf. This increases thermal performance and durability in comparison to the locally rendered mud-brick walls.

The project includes, and indeed celebrates, local expert craftsmanship, traditional construction skills, and the symbolic aspects of architecture. We interpreted traditional techniques

← View of dormitory room, with vents in Trombe wall

↙ Manual construction methods are efficient at a site where electricity to run power tools and machinery is scarce.

↓ Trombe wall construction

↓↓ The living room of a residence, with large windows for ventilation in the summer

in a contemporary pioneering spirit, in contrast to the trend among local architects and engineers to design new buildings in steel and concrete, inappropriate to the topography and climate, but wrongly perceived as better because identified with western modernity. Such buildings too often are poorly constructed and deteriorate rapidly. Our priorities tie in with the educational mission of the school: students and the community can see how traditional architecture and craftsmanship can be kept alive when adapted to sustainable and appropriate design.

## EARTHQUAKE-RESISTANT CONSTRUCTION

Durability, flexibility, and earthquake resistance must govern structural design, since Ladakh is classified as seismic Zone 4, the second-highest category of seismicity in the Indian Building Code. Although there have been no recent major earthquakes the region has frequent tremors. The disasters caused by earthquakes in Gujarat (2001) and Pakistan (2005) show all too well the devastation that results from lack of well-engineered, earthquake-resistant buildings. Thus, a strong seismic strategy was developed for the school.

Traditional Ladakhi buildings are not engineered for seismic design but with the application of some simple structural principles and details we have been able to improve earthquake safety greatly. The project aims to act as an educational tool—we want to demonstrate that seismic design can be applied appropriately to traditional construction techniques.[6] To this end all structural solutions, such as steel plates for the beam-column connection and cross-bracing cables, are exposed. The buildings have timber frames that absorb seismic loads. The Ladakhi-style heavy mud-and-straw roof is used, but is supported by a timber structure that is independent of the walls. Steel connections and cross-bracing provide earthquake stability.[7]

Despite the complexity of the structural analysis, the design uses simple solutions that are easily understood and replicable by local craftspeople and constructed within the constraints of local materials and techniques. (Steel plates, rods, and bolts are readily available in Ladakh.) Once the school is fully built, vocational courses, including carpentry and construction training, will be offered to the older children and adults in the community. A team at the Trust is currently planning that program.

## WATER AND SANITATION

Water is a scarce resource in Ladakh. Water for irrigation comes from the snowmelt in a complex network of shared open channels in the intensely cultivated fields along the Indus River. A new hydroelectric-energy plant is under construction on the Indus; to preserve the fragile balance of water use the government may impose a ban on drawing water from the river, which will force more households to rely on groundwater abstraction. Unfortunately, over time this will reduce the capacity of the aquifer and directly affect the groundwater supply at the school.

In this complex scenario, in a location that would otherwise be desert, the water cycle of the site relies on a solar-powered pump that delivers potable groundwater by gravity feed. When the pump is not in operation the solar panels charge batteries. The electricity generated can be used as a small power supply for lighting and other purposes. The anticipated water demand of about 16 US gallons (60 l) per day per resident and 2 US gallons (8 l) per day per student is high by local standards, but is seen as a key aspect of promoting hygiene and an important part of the children's education.

Key to the public-health strategy for the school, traditional dry latrines have been adapted and enhanced to Ventilated

A freshwater fountain in the school courtyard

Improved Pit (VIP) latrines, which require virtually no maintenance. They eliminate flies and odors and do not require water. The innovative design again exploits the strong sun at this altitude. A double-chamber system with an integrated solar-driven flue allows them to function as composting toilets that produce humus for fertilizer. The solar flue is constructed as a chimney with a large south-facing metal sheet painted in a dark color. The intense sunshine causes the air in the cavity behind the metal sheet to warm and rise. This induces a continuous air flow from the toilet into the pit and through the solar flue, which keeps the toilet well-ventilated and healthier.

Wastewater from domestic uses is infiltrated via underground slotted pipes (which pass wastewater directly to trees planted nearby) and a traditional open-channel system along lines of planted trees that provide shade and green in the otherwise bleak high desert. A second solar-powered pump feeds a tank that then provides additional irrigation water by gravity feed to the site's gardens.

## WASTE STRATEGY IN HARMONY WITH NATURE

In Ladakh everything is typically reused. The population has survived for centuries by using natural resources carefully, without abusing them. For example, despite the long, frosty winters the scarce trees—apricot, willow, and po plar—are not used for fuel. Rather, wood is used only for construction or for tools. Dried animal dung provides fuel and human waste is used as fertilizer; traditionally, every house has a composting toilet and all waste is recycled.

However, in recent years Ladakh has started importing packaged goods from India, including plastic bottles and food wrapping. This has generated an escalating problem of inorganic waste disposal in a region with no recycling facilities. Most plastic is currently buried or burned, giving rise to pollution—a new phenomenon for the Ladakhis. A ban on plastic bags exists but does not suffice to alleviate the worsening situation. In this context the school is designed to reduce waste production: all waste streams are separated; waste materials are reused where possible and only the residue is sent to a local landfill. Plastic is buried in a nearby location that can be excavated in the future, when a recycling facility is available. All paper and organic waste is composted and glass is reused. Wastewater from cooking feeds a reed-bed system, which breaks down some organic waste before irrigation in order to prevent pollution. The reeds absorb and filter the water, which is then infiltrated in the ground.

## OVERCOMING THE ELECTRICITY SHORTAGE

Electricity in Ladakh is scarce and extremely unreliable. In the capital, Leh, a large diesel generator provides homes with electricity at night, when the national grid becomes unavailable, but in villages power may be lacking for weeks. Construction of the large hydroelectric plant on the Indus has advanced slowly and it is uncertain when the project will be completed. This fact led our team to come up with an alternative: a phased photovoltaic (solar) installation that, when complete, will create a stand-alone local electricity grid to provide the electrical load for the whole site. The system is green and modular: photovoltaic cells and inverter systems are being installed in each building and connected to the site's electrical supply to provide daytime power generated from sunlight. A modular battery system will provide power in the hours of darkness. The full scheme will include 270 solar panels and an expanded battery system. Future buildings will be similarly outfitted and integrated into the grid as the school grows and funds become available.

The first stage of installation took place in summer 2008 and included 54 monocrystalline solar panels, each rated at 170W peak power. These have been installed across the south-facing roofs of three buildings, each with its own local inverter. This phase was donated by Arup Associates as a way to directly offset the carbon emissions generated by the business operation of the firm at its home offices. At Arup Associates we avoid using third party offsets because many carbon-credit projects lack proper controls and transparency. With a direct offset such as this one, we can ourselves monitor the actual carbon reduction achieved on-site. This way we can confidently become carbon neutral as we link our practice ever more closely with green projects in the local Ladakhi community, raising awareness and providing exemplars of good environmental design over the long term.[8]

## CONCLUSIONS AND REFLECTIONS

The Druk White Lotus School clearly demonstrates the value of progressive and sustained international collaboration. Such a project can support local cultural traditions, both symbolically and materially, by way of an approach to design and resources that is both contemporary and sensitive to traditions. We have deliberately avoided both the widespread internationalism of architecture and the practice of mimicking local vernacular styles.

We learned that it is fundamental to be aware of the varying expectations of all parties involved, which, in a cultural context so different from our own, can create unexpected complexities during the design and construction phases and when a building is in use. This process of assimilation and adjustment is not always simple. For the Druk White Lotus School we needed continually to simplify construction details and operational elements,

↑↑ A Ventilated Improved Pit dry latrine with dark painted metal solar flue

↑ Photovoltaic panels power the pump that delivers potable groundwater.

preparing clear manuals and, most important, working closely with local teams. It was also crucial to properly train teachers and students in the correct operation of the buildings and facilities.

The Arup design team is engaged in a long-term journey of dynamic partnership and exchange with the local community. It has been critical for us to be open to learning from local experienced and skilled craftspeople—a posture that lifts the aspirations and expertise of both teams. The imposition of western designs and technological solutions on developing countries, especially in isolated communities, has proven ineffective and even harmful. Instead, the Druk White Lotus School demonstrates that intelligent and durable buildings are those that draw upon the skills and knowledge developed over centuries in a community. Resilient buildings should arise from local culture, climate, and resources. Interpreting these conditions in a responsive and appropriate way and bringing innovation and improvement forward without depriving the design of its indigenous roots are the principles of an extraordinary partnership.

Notes

1   Arup is a global firm of designers, planners, engineers, consultants, and technical specialists offering a broad range of professional services, with more than 10,000 people in 38 offices globally. Within Arup, Arup Associates is the design studio of integrated architecture and engineering, with 150 staff in London, China, and the Middle East. Further information on Arup Associates can be found at www. arupaassociates.com and www.dwls.org.

2   The literacy rate in the Leh district of Ladakh is relatively high at 62 percent (72 percent for males and 50 percent for females, according to the 2001 Indian census) and schools are well distributed throughout the region, but the majority of them provide only primary education. Until a few years ago students were taught in Urdu until they were fourteen, then shifting to English. Lack of instruction in Ladakhi broke their bonds with their own cultural heritage, while poor English skills reduced their chances of admission to higher educational institutions in India to almost nil. Thus it was important at the proposed new school to start education in English at age five.

3   Flood risk was considered, too. However, the massive floods that occurred in the regions around the Indus River in August 2010 were unprecedented in scale and caused an entirely anomalous mudslide at the school. Five feet (1.5 m) of mud poured over the site; despite this the school held up well, with no major structural damage and no loss of life. The event was shocking because Ladakh is a desert; it never rains there. We need to assess whether this is a new risk related to climate change and unpredictable weather patterns or if it was a singularity, unlikely to recur.

4   For example, at a school not far from ours a European firm subsidized a huge installation of solar heaters. The buildings are of normal concrete construction and rely heavily on this system to provide heating in the winter. When the management contract with the firm was terminated due to tensions with the school administration, there was nobody on-site able to repair and maintain such sophisticated machinery. Poorly constructed concrete buildings may be found throughout Ladakh. Because of the extreme climate, concrete decays quickly, curing too fast in summer or too slowly in winter. Further, it is often poured by hand, so that air pockets form in the structure. By contrast, local techniques have proven for centuries to be the most appropriate to the environment; we should learn from them.

5   The glazed facades do not generate excessive summer heat because they are slightly recessed and the high-angle sun is mostly occulted during the hottest part of the year. Timber beams that protrude over the glazed elevation were originally intended to support an external shading system of woven willow, but this has never been required because the buildings remain quite fresh. The heavy thermal mass of the masonry also acts as a heat buffer, helping to maintain a pleasant internal temperature.

6   Some elements of the school, such as the ventilated toilets, have already been replicated in new local government buildings.

7   A key principle of earthquake resistance is that the roof should not be supported entirely by the walls and that the points of connection between roof and support should have strength and also some give or flex. See Andrew Charleson, *Seismic Design for Architecture* (Oxford, UK: Architectural Press, Elsevier, 2008).

8   The solar-power scheme was independently audited and approved by TICOS, the Travel Industry Carbon Offset Service. Travelers around the world can purchase Carbon Offset credits to compensate for the carbon emissions their journeys generate, thereby funding the purchase of further photovoltaic panels for the school. See www.ticos.co.uk/projects/project_id/tp049.htm and the school website, www. dwls.org/carbon-offset.html, accessed September 27, 2010.

A kindergarten classroom has a butterfly roof, which provides ample natural daylight and captures rainfall.

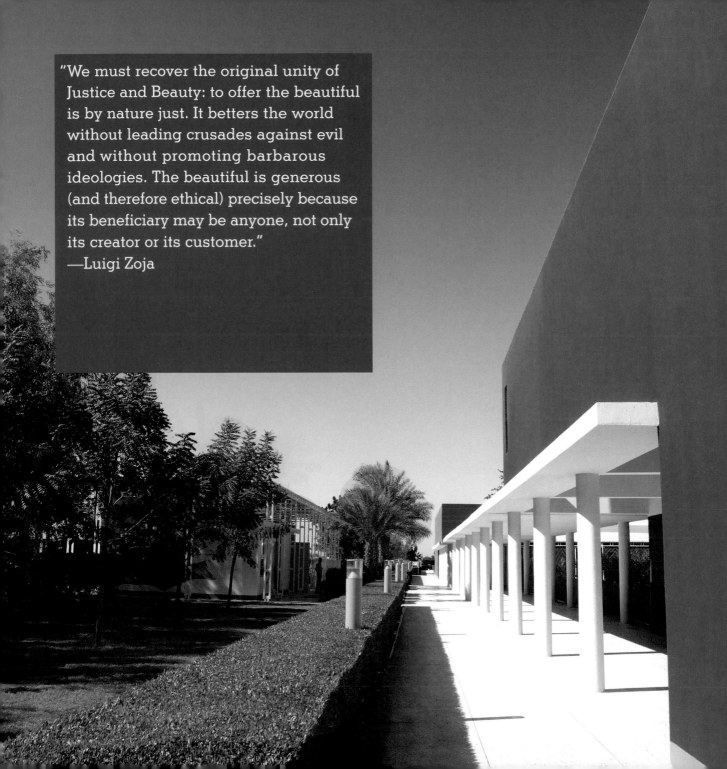

"We must recover the original unity of Justice and Beauty: to offer the beautiful is by nature just. It betters the world without leading crusades against evil and without promoting barbarous ideologies. The beautiful is generous (and therefore ethical) precisely because its beneficiary may be anyone, not only its creator or its customer."
—Luigi Zoja

# ON BEAUTY, ARCHITECTURE, AND CRISIS: THE SALAM CENTRE FOR CARDIAC SURGERY IN SUDAN

RAUL PANTALEO
STUDIO TAM ASSOCIATI, MILAN

To share with the countries of the world's southern hemisphere a part of the wealth that has been taken (and continues to be taken) from them is not really a *humanitarian* gesture; it is, simply, an act of justice.

To build an outstanding hospital in the heart of North Africa has meaning. For us at Tam Associati it was an extraordinary opportunity to reflect on the meaning of the word *right*, starting with the *right to health*, as a point from which to construct a culture of equality and justice. But we should also reflect on the more ample front of *rights*, particularly the *right to the environment, to what is beautiful,* and *to memory* as the necessary premises for a sustainable and pacific coexistence at local and global scales.

The cardiac-care center, named Salam (peace in Arabic), is the only African hospital of heart surgery that guarantees free-of-charge assistance and highly specialized care to patients with both congenital and acquired heart diseases. Amid war and a growing humanitarian crisis in Sudan, an Italian aid organization, Emergency, launched a regional Africa program in Sudan and its nine neighboring countries, where 300 million people are spread across 3.8 million square miles (10 million sq. km)—an area equal to that of western Europe. Cardiac pathologies are the second leading cause of death in children in Africa.[1]

Since opening in 2007 the Salam Centre has become a concrete example of what cooperation, inspired by a commitment to excellence, can achieve, no matter how difficult the context. It has become a regional catalyst for other new resources and processes aimed at responsible forms of social transformation. Tam Associati started working with Emergency in 2003 as site technicians. That affiliation has consolidated into a permanent collaboration. Over the past seven years we have been the architects responsible for all of Emergency's new projects in Africa: Sudan, the Central African Republic, and recently Sierra Leone. As architects we want to uphold the principles of ethical and responsible project planning and prove that design

professionals can serve and foster civil rights and sustainable development—even during crises and in the most difficult conditions of displacement and armed conflict.

## GUIDING PRINCIPLES

With these principles in mind, we imagined the Salam Centre as a place that is *hospitable, domestic,* and *beautiful,* where the surgical and convalescent patient, almost always a victim of poverty and war, can feel what it's like to receive treatment as a true subject of care, entitled to the fundamental rights that are too often denied on this continent. The main hospital building is noninvasive, silent, and friendly. It comprises a single ground floor in a U-shape that embraces a large open space with two enormous mango trees and is situated at the center of a larger hospital complex. The trees were thus a generating premise of the architecture and plants soon became a literal, integral part of the building's thermal apparatus: large tree-filled areas and planted lines of shrubbery provide screening and reduce heat.

The center, which trains local medical staff as well as treating patients, is in the village of Soba, about 12 miles (20 km) south of Khartoum, the capital of Sudan. The site has 130,000 square feet (12,000 sq. m) of indoor space on 430,000 square feet (40,000 sq. m) of land along the banks of the Blue Nile. The structure is a system of buildings and related open spaces: hospital blocks (operating theaters, wards, offices, pharmacy, clinics, labs) are connected by airy, external shaded passages and set around a large courtyard, together with an admissions area, a guest house for relatives of patients coming from outside of Khartoum, a meditation pavilion for people of all creeds, a residential compound for staff, and facilities and maintenance buildings, including a solar generator. The design mitigates the feeling of being lost and away from home that is typical of hospital environments. Its philosophy is to create a place of work and healing, a cozy space where patients are respected, are not isolated, and are cared for as individuals rather than treated as objects. The project, especially in its details, highlights the idea that preserving life requires not only expertise and technology but also decency, humanity, and beauty.

In light of these concerns, we followed three principles: to create a hollow, open space at the center of a network of freestanding buildings; to work with the best technology available, given the context; and to develop an architectural language imbued with an ethics as well as an aesthetics. The hospital unfolds around the empty courtyard occupied by the two mango trees. This open, green area is the central physical and symbolic space from which all the trajectories of the complex begin. As in many traditional North African houses, the configuration creates angles, perspectives, and sensations that are varied and changing and, we hope, less monotonous than the utilitarian cubes that define traditional hospitals. The hospital's courtyard is a world of its own, an ideal internal microcosm—bound by the buildings, protected and protective, dominated by the symbolic

4.4
ON BEAUTY,
ARCHITECTURE,
AND CRISIS

FIRM
STUDIO TAM ASSOCIATI

PROJECT LOCALE
SOBA, SUDAN

213

(previous spread) The Salam Centre patio with cafeteria at right

↑ A corridor in the Surgery Centre, painted in cool hues and naturally lit

← The cafeteria is made from seven large recycled shipping containers with an attached terrace shaded by bamboo roof screens.

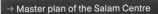

→ Master plan of the Salam Centre

↘ Residences for medical staff, each with a terrace giving onto a shared courtyard

↓ Corrugated-metal shipping containers in their raw state

↓↓ The components of a container residence

| | |
|---|---|
| 1 | SURGERY CENTRE |
| 2 | MAIN ENTRANCE |
| 3 | TECHNICAL BUILDING |
| 4 | RELATIVES HOUSE |
| 5 | SERVICE BUILDING |
| 6 | FACILITIES BUILDING |
| 7 | SOLAR PANELS |
| 8 | PRAYER AND MEDITATION PAVILION |
| 9 | MEDICAL COMPOUND |
| 10 | CAFETERIA |

sheltering figure of the trees. It is separated from the external macrocosm, hostile and scorched, of Soba, Khartoum, and impoverished, war-weary Sudan. We kept the height of the buildings low to inspire a sense of homeyness, which we then translated into many of the building's details.

Nonlocal and visiting medical staff are hosted in a compound next to the hospital, consisting of ninety individual lodgings and a cafeteria. These buildings are all made from recycled and refurbished metal shipping containers. Each lodging is some 215 square feet (20 sq. m), configured from one-and-a-half containers, and has a bedroom, bathroom, and a small veranda giving onto the courtyard. Six containers were converted into services units and eight larger containers comprise the cafeteria, which also has an open-air dining terrace.

Temperatures exceed 100°F (38°C) for long periods in Sudan and can reach above 120°F (50°C). The extreme climate, together with the presence of a fine dust generated by the strong desert winds, required that we adopt the right type of insulation, cooling, and filtering technologies. These technologies allowed us to reduce the energy consumption of the hospital while at the same time guaranteeing maximum levels of comfort.

For example, the containers used for the staff dwellings are insulated with a layer system: 2-inch- (5-cm-) thick interior insulating panels and an outer skin of metal panels. The roof also has two metal layers, with a bamboo brise-soleil panel system over all. As a result the sun's rays never strike the containers, keeping the interiors cool despite their metal construction and saving an enormous amount of energy.

The hospital itself must be kept cool and its needs are substantial: it uses nearly 1 million cubic feet (28,000 cu. m) of air per day. A traditional cooling system would have used a great deal of electricity, powered by fossil fuel. Instead, a number of passive-mitigation measures were taken during construction: the walls are 23 inches (58 cm) thick, made of two layers of

bricks separated by an insulating air cavity, with small windows to prevent the building from heating up. These windows are closed by double glass panels; the external pane is reflective. In a country rich in both oil resources and sunlight, Emergency chose to use the sun as the cleaner source of energy. Solar panels were imported from Italy, bringing an almost unknown technology to the country—one that indeed is very seldom used in Europe. Today, the hospital has its own generating facility with 288 solar panels, producing 3,600 kilowatt hours—enough to cool and light much of the complex and run its machinery—without producing one gram of carbon dioxide.

Solar power doesn't just produce electricity. Solar collectors also cool water that is then used to lower the temperature in the rooms that need to be chilled for medical or other purposes (for example, to maintain sensitive equipment). The water is heated by the sun in copper-and-glass insulated tubes and then transferred to a large insulated tank that keeps it at about 185°F (85°C). The water is then cooled down to 46°F (7°C) in two solar-powered chilling machines. (Two regular boilers have also been installed as backups, in case solar power is not sufficient to run the two chilling machines.) The cool water then cools air in a heat exchanger and a second system of tubes transports the cool air to various hospital rooms according to need. Electric power is used only to run the water-circulation pumps. Solar power thus runs the primary cooling system without discharging any particulates into the atmosphere. (Standard electric air conditioners have also been installed.)

Shrubs and trees protect the buildings from the heat and mitigate the effects of the harsh climate. For practical as much as aesthetic reasons we placed traditionally crafted thatched roofs over paths and rest areas to provide additional shade. We derived the technique from traditional woven beds. In all, we greatly reduced reliance on energy-consuming cooling technologies. This has meant a greater and more efficient use of locally available resources such as Nile water and solar power. The latter is largely able to cool the air of the entire hospital.

The next important task was to understand how to best filter out large quantities of dust and sand from the air without having to rely on costly and complicated filtering devices. Khartoum is the dustiest city in Africa, and a particularly unfriendly environment for performing surgery. We found a simple mechanical solution: air is pumped through a series of labyrinthine brick tunnels before reaching the air conditioners. As it flows against the tunnel walls the impact shakes the sand and dust out; at the same time, the air grows cooler as friction with the walls reduces its speed. A fine spray of water at the end of the tunnels eliminates the finer dust from the air and cools it down further. The system needs very little maintenance (cleaning the tunnel network is sufficient) and the air reaches the conditioners well filtered and 48°F (9°C) cooler than when it entered.

These technological solutions are context-specific. In a country with very low levels of technology and with particularly harsh conditions, the key features of the work are simplicity and innovation. Rejecting the practice of providing "third world" structures for "third world" countries, we proved that with creativity and low-cost technology the same standards of health care can be guaranteed as in any western health-care center.

## AN ETHICAL ARCHITECTURAL LANGUAGE

The Republic of the Sudan has been troubled for more than twenty years by interethnic and interreligious violence. Patients and their families are under great stress. We wanted to accommodate prayer, as is customary in hospitals, and at the same time welcome the spiritual complexity of the country. Our choice was not to privilege any specific religious practice or group, but rather to create a space that would invite the prayers and meditations of

peoples of all faiths. We had to consider, of course, the fact that the Muslim faith is practiced by the majority of Sudanese and calls for the separation of men and women, as well as ablutions. Still, we tried to limit the impact of difference by concealing the symbols specific to any one religious practice.

In addition to the sense of inclusion, in designing a hospital it was important for us to imagine a face that would best represent the underlying philosophy of the project—to care for and preserve life. Every detail of the building—the colors, nature of the light, and small accents such as the placement of the windows—is aimed at helping make patients and staff feel safe and at home. We wanted patients, doctors, and family members to feel that here, no matter their sex, race, color, or beliefs, they come together under the common roof of hospitality. Since the facility is still quite new, it is difficult at this stage to gauge its social and cultural impact on local health care; Emergency developed the project as a pilot, which would not only respond to the urgent health-care needs of the country, but—above all—set a precedent for free health care as a fundamental and universal right. The special care given to the details of the project is our architectural response to this intention.

## THE ETHICS OF BEAUTY

The relationship of values to design, to beauty, is not tangential but essential. Yet since the word *beauty* evokes the ethereal distance of pure aesthetics, to discuss the elegance of the Salam Centre's design, its appealing light and air and colors and the underlying ethics of these elements, I have coined the word *beautiness:* an imperfect word that includes in its meaning the aspirations, longings, and desires of life. Beautiness is the ethical sense inherent in the beautiful. To choose three colors that go well together, that have a sort of grace, does not cost any

← The hand-woven screens are installed around the periphery of the central courtyard, helping cool the patio.

↓ A weaver making screens for the courtyard

↓↓ Traditional woven bed

more than leaving the choice to chance or accident. It does not take any more energy to place openings rhythmically against the facade than to design a wall with holes in it. It is simply a question of culture and attention. As designers of hospitals we do not speak often enough about beauty: yet what else is a hospital in a war zone if not beautiful? By its nature it defies its context and injects positive human and ethical values into a negative environment. To do so has no rational motive, no practical justification; we may make hospitals in desperate environments because they are needed, but we make them beautiful because we can. Our hospitals are beautiful because they are based on the principle of equity. Beautiness is a moment of truce and must be made accessible to those for whom each day is a battle. *Poverty, despair, abandonment* are labels that westerners have fixed to Africans. Yet these words do not in any way represent the life of the people on this vast continent. It is a matter of urgency as well as an act of justice for us to free our imagination from the reductive tropes that limit it when we speak of Africa.[2] Africa needs something else from the west: simple respect.

The Salam Centre is now staffed by more than 300 people, most of whom are local and trained on site. The goal is to perform 1,500 annual cardiac surgeries in Soba and treat more than 234,000 children from the nine countries in Emergency's regional network of pediatric clinics.[3] Ultimately, the high-tech hospital, with its network of high-quality pediatric and cardiac screening clinics, will be handed over to the local authorities and integrated into the national health-care systems of each country. Transferring the facilities to local administration is an absolute necessity for the long-term sustainability of the project.

In fifteen short years Emergency has treated more than 3 million people, free of charge, in some of the most volatile regions in the world. As Dr. Gino Strada, the organization's founder, insists, "If you see in the bed next to yours the man that you were shooting at the day before, you start thinking that what you were doing made no sense. You rediscover the common denominator, that of being human."[4] Architecture in Africa, as in Europe, must speak the language of a new modernity, a modernity without arrogance that respects a changing world in this moment, in all its variety. The social and environmental impact of this project is embodied in its architecture, which articulates a vision of the future in which rights take root as a shared legacy of humanity, perhaps leading to new forms of globalization.

Notes

The quotation on p. 210 is from Luigi Zoja, *Giustizia e Belleza* (Turin: Incipit, 2007).

1   Emergency is an independent and neutral NGO that provides free, high quality medical and surgical treatment to the civilian victims of war, landmines, and poverty while promoting a culture of solidarity, peace, and respect for human rights.

2   Here, too, beauty plays a role. The medical ethicist Daryl Pullman argues that since people in pain suffer also in the loss of their human dignity, the alleviation of suffering, which is an ethical act, also has an aesthetic dimension: "History, culture, tradition and experience combine to inform particular perspectives on what constitutes dignified lives and actions. In this respect, personal dignity informs a model of ethical action that is analogous to aesthetic experience. . . . the idea of personal dignity is in many respects akin to an aesthetic notion. To have a sense of personal dignity is to live a harmonious life. At the social, affective level our sense of personal dignity is contingent upon how nearly our lives comport with various social and cultural expectations of how we should live. At a deeper psychological level it is contingent upon how nearly our moral activities comport with our own expectations of what morality demands of us. Personal dignity and personal integrity merge at this point in what might be described as the ethically beautiful life; a life in which reason, emotion and will converge." Daryl Pullman, "Universalism, Particularism and the Ethics of Dignity," *Christian Bioethics* 7, no. 3 (August 9, 2010): 333–58, DOI: 10.1076/chbi.7.3.333.6876.

3   The hospital has already had a significant impact: between April 2007 and June 2010 24,228 patients were triaged, 15,913 cardiological examinations were carried out, 3,067 patients were admitted, and 2,351 surgeries and 818 catheterization procedures were performed. Patients were from all over Sudan as well as Eritrea, the Central African Republic, Congo, Rwanda, Tanzania, and Somalia.

4   Quoted in the Emergency USA blog, entry for July 25, 2007, at http://blogs.myspace.com/emergencyusa, accessed August 31, 2010.

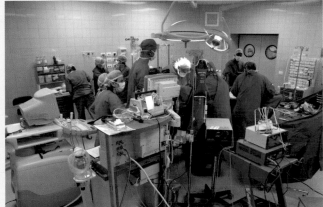

← / ↑↑ Interior and exterior of prayer and meditation pavilion

↑ Operating theater at the Salam Centre

# PART 5

# TEACHING AS STRATEGIC ACTION

"For many decades, architectural educators and practitioners have observed with increasing alarm the decline in significance of architectural work. Especially acute is the diminishment of architecture's power for social and cultural transformation. . . . Our profession, verging on irrelevance, has reached a critical juncture. Architecture schools must move quickly to respond seriously to the complexity of divergent and varied social demands."
—Frances Bronet

# CULTIVATING RESILIENCE: THE BaSiC INITIATIVE

SERGIO PALLERONI
INSTITUTE FOR SUSTAINABLE SOLUTIONS,
PORTLAND STATE UNIVERSITY, OREGON

There is a human crisis in the world that despite its urgency and the vast scale of its impact rarely reaches the headlines. Though taking a back seat to the attention and investment that natural disasters garner, poverty is a growing condition for populations worldwide. Interestingly, it may also be the most important reason for the staggering numbers of victims that natural disasters claim. Poverty is on the rise even in the supposedly booming countries of Asia. The United Nations estimates that the lives and futures of two out every five citizens will be defined by poverty by 2025. Despite the urgent need for immediate solutions in moments of crisis, we would be more successful if we approached disaster relief by ameliorating *anthropic* risk, the day-to-day condition of the poor. For it is their condition that condemns the poor to second-class status; it is their pervasive vulnerability that turns the poorest peoples into the overwhelming majority of the victims of natural hazards.

Take Haiti as a case in point. In January 2010 a 7.0 Mw earthquake flattened much of the island's built fabric and killed 225,000 people immediately (and more in the aftermath). The horrifying loss of human lives and the damage to physical infrastructure could have been avoided. A nearly contemporary 8.8 Mw earthquake in Chile was a hundred times stronger but claimed 507 victims, 0.2 percent of the loss Haiti suffered.[1] Why? Because Chile has invested in its building industry. Education and technology have met the challenges of living in an earthquake zone. But this kind of education—or, more fundamentally, the economic and social resources that build expertise and secure homes and communities—is something most Haitians have not enjoyed in generations. As in much of the developing world, the vast majority of construction in Haiti is done piecemeal by the poor, as they marshal their tiny resources over time. It is only in tragedies of sufficient scale (those brought to our attention by the media's inclination to exploit horror) that we become aware of the poor. In this

moment we do not recognize them for their economic or political condition but as victims, fellow humans afflicted with the thing we fear for ourselves: vulnerability. And this brings out a sudden, if fleeting, compassion for people we would otherwise rather ignore.

Today, few experts doubt that education and investment in improving the condition of those most likely to be affected by natural disasters are the most cost-effective long-term strategy to limit risk and foster greater capacity to recover. Indeed, this view is at the heart of a movement of nonprofits and NGOs to increase the assets and social capital of marginal communities while bolstering their ability to improve their own condition and resilience. The latter is an interesting concept, one that has gained a growing following both in the environmental movement and in the world of development work. It focuses on identifying and strategically building upon a community's physical, human, and social resources. A development approach that focuses on the condition of human beings rather than grasping at numbers—numbers of homes, numbers of roads, numbers of latrines—which are still the traditional metrics of development aid, can save and better lives.

But educating communities in need can be a minefield, particularly when it involves clients and professionals from different economic, educational, cultural, and national backgrounds. As Paulo Freire reminded us in *Pedagogy of the Oppressed*, educating the poor can propagate dependency and the very power relationships that have historically defined the relationship between the developing and industrialized countries. These hierarchies are often at the root of the poverty of the very people we are trying to serve. Freire advises us to redefine the traditional power relationships of development work in ways that promote equality and reflection for both parties.[2]

In architecture the idea of educating professionals to address the needs of a broader, more diverse audience is gaining

5.1
CULTIVATING
RESILIENCE

ORGANIZATION
BaSiC INITIATIVE

PROJECT LOCALE
MEXICO

225

ground. But in practice only a small percentage of the academy properly addresses the needs of the poor and vulnerable. Unfortunately, many architecture programs continue to teach creative expression disconnected from pressing realities and to envision the successful architect as an independent practitioner working on individual great buildings, rather than emphasizing collaboration—especially with communities and professionals outside of the sphere of architecture and engineering. In 1996 the Carnegie Foundation published a major critical study of architectural education with recommendations and goals for reform.[3] To succeed in an environment in which clients are not only wealthy individuals and corporations, architects, the foundation recognized, need to be more connected to real-life issues and better collaborators and communicators; in school they must develop a philosophy of caring for and service to the community. Architecture schools have been slow to adopt the measures recommended more than a dozen years ago. Yet a strong trend in architectural education is beginning to emerge.

## BaSiC INITIATIVE: BUILDING TO LEARN, LEARNING TO BUILD

The BaSiC (Building Sustainable Communities) Initiative is an international academic service-learning program that each year challenges students in the design fields to help solve the problems faced by communities in need. Evolving from a University of Texas foreign-study program in Mexico that began in 1988, BaSiC Initiative programs have become increasingly multidisciplinary in response to the challenges faced by our client communities. The extraordinary collaboration with other disciplines (such as health, finance, environmental conservation) has introduced our students to new forms of knowledge, new methods of inquiry, and alternative pedagogical approaches that

(previous spread) Visitors center, Ladakh, India, 2010

↑ Haiti after the earthquake, 2010

← Visitors Center, Tamil Nadu, India, 2002

↓ Peace Pavilion made from military parachutes, Ladakh, India, 2010

Katrina Furniture Project, New Orleans, Louisiana, 2006. → A wrecked house is stripped and →→ the salvaged lumber is made into furniture.

continue to change the nature of the BaSiC Initiative design studios. Based broadly on theories of Thomas Dutton and Paolo Freire, the studio has taken as its challenge the sustainable development, survival, and betterment of marginal communities worldwide. We are now working in India, Taiwan, Mexico, New Orleans, Chile, Colombia, and Haiti, and have completed nearly 100 built projects—libraries, community centers, schools, homes, pavilions, a solar bakery, and the like. At the end of a residency in the community, students have helped create and build a clinic, hospital, school, home, or other facility that serves and belongs to the community. Along the way they discover the potential of collective knowledge and dynamic exchange and become citizens of the world.

The program integrates intellectual exploration and firsthand experience, giving it a richness and realism not often found in the traditional academic design studio. The schedule is demanding. A community submits a proposal for a new building; projects are selected on the basis of need, viability, partnerships, and community commitment. Students spend the first year at their home institution, investigating the physical and cultural characteristics of the client community, documenting the site and programmatic requirements, and engaging in group design charrettes. The students then create schematic design and construction plans for the community to review. During the residency period, which varies from project to project but can last several months, each student makes a commitment to spend six days a week

# In the Design/Build Mexico program students experience architecture as a cultural activity.

working on-site. Days off are staggered so that we are always present whenever community members have time to participate. Seminars, design, and research fill at least five out of seven evenings. Typically, there are about thirty students on-site for each project.

The class is divided into small groups, each one taking responsibility for the completion of an aspect of the project. Teams convene every morning to discuss their progress and to ask for help from faculty when they need it. The process of consensus-building in the initial design charrette provides students with a common basis from which to discuss and develop ideas. The community is both our client and collaborator. This insures that the project addresses both immediate and long-term needs. In our first program, Design/Build Mexico, this was our seminal insight as we struggled to negotiate the sometimes conflicting demands of academic education and social action in a fast-growing squatter community. That experience has become the foundation for all seven of the BaSiC Initiative's ongoing major programs.[4]

## SQUATTER COMMUNITIES

Squatter communities have significantly transformed the urban landscape of Mexico since the 1960s. They remain a very present reminder of the effects of globalization on this rapidly modernizing country. Some cities have been so consumed by these settlements that their edges are no longer distinguishable. Jiutepec-Tejalpa is a squatter community that stretches along the edge of CIVAC, a tax-free industrial zone for international companies southeast of Cuernavaca in central Mexico. There are now more than a million people living here. The city continues to grow at one of the fastest rates of any major urban area in North America, as farmers no longer able to compete in a global economy are drawn away from agriculture by the promise of a living wage and education for their children. But the problems of communities like Jiutepec are grave. The lack of basic physical infrastructure creates areas with little clean water and few paved roads, poor sewage systems, and no local schools or government systems.

Along with the physical transformations that follow from extreme need come massive shifts in the social fabric. For every two male migrant workers in the US, one woman is left behind in Mexico with the family's children, as well as with those too poor, sick, or old to make the journey. The tremendous strain on daily life calls into question whether such communities are physically and culturally sustainable. However, despite the cultural fragmentation and pressure resulting from their current circumstances, a longstanding community tradition of building remains the backbone of these informal settlements. This building tradition, along with an eagerness for community empowerment, is an indispensable resource for positive development.

For more than twenty years we have been collaborating with women's groups in Jiutepec-Tejalpa who are intent on improving the health and education of their children. We started in 1989 by building schools and then clinics and children's libraries, the first in informal settlements in Mexico. In Cuernavaca's squatter communities 300,000 to 400,000 people are without easy access to books. In the Juana de Asbaje y Ramirez Library, the south side of the 2,000-square-foot (186-sq.-m) building is punched to create a loggia along the access road. The curving roof rises toward the north to bring maximum natural daylight into the building (at this latitude northern light produces little heat.) It dips to the south to provide shade on the hot side of the building. The roof also captures rainwater and distributes it to channels in each of the four thick walls, where it is carried into a reflecting pool that lies above a cistern. The pool reflects light (but not heat) to the underside of the library roof, balancing the northern light for reading.

## SOLAR KITCHEN INITIATIVE, 2002–5

We returned to Jiutepec-Tejalpa in 2003 to address the issue of nutrition for children at school. Comunidad AC, a local non-profit organization that had formed out of our collective efforts to build the first schools, was again our client. Our eighteenth project for this community consisted of retrofitting the José Maria Morelos School with a solar kitchen.

Cooking school meals is one way that mothers can supplement their children's diets and reduce costs. Before the solar kitchen was built they prepared lunches for their kids on the street near the school. In 2002 we had experimented with a design for a solar condenser stove and oven for the kitchen of an elementary school about a half mile (1 km) away. The design, built from bicycle parts and small vanity mirrors, uses a counterweight, much like a grandfather clock, to track the sun. The solar parabolic mirror concentrates the energy of the sun on a pot or stove in the kitchen. The device is a simple and inexpensive way to harness the free energy of the sun (plentiful in this climate) to reduce the cost of cooking meals for children in very poor communities.

Our task was to reinvent the kitchen as an ecological response to the broader needs and conditions of the squatter community. Our students took on the challenge as a means to rethink the energy requirements of a traditional kitchen (water use, fuel, lighting, sanitation, cost and impact of manufacturing appliances), as well as an opportunity to improve nutrition and homebuilding in the community. In other words they posed the problem of the school's kitchen as a question of how best to effect change in the homes of the parents. Thus, the initial project to build a little kitchen was expanded to become a pilot project that would show off alternative means of energy, water treatment, and sanitation that could then be developed in homes.

As the students discovered, home kitchens use most of the fossil fuel and are often the source of a great deal of the ecological waste (wastewater, used cooking oil, organic and inorganic solid waste) in a rapidly growing informal settlement with little infrastructure. The design of our kitchen responded to these concerns by incorporating alternative, nonpolluting (and economical) technologies such as solar cooking, solar hot-water heating, gray-water filters to treat dishwater, and natural light as the main source of lighting. The addition of an open-air dining pavilion allowed the incorporation of a rainwater catchment and eventually photovoltaic solar panels for electricity generation, which essentially takes the kitchen off the grid. The outdoor pavilion uses local materials (bricks, stone, cement, and recycled glazed pottery and tiles) to create healthy responses to the environment: cross-ventilation, the use of solar power, and water recycling. A hand-washing fountain at child height stands at the entrance. It uses rainwater collected in a catchment and held in a cistern below the floor of the dining room, so that water is available even during the annual dry period.

We had the project designed within ten days of arriving on-site. The students submitted construction documents for a building permit, which was expedited to allow as much time for construction as possible. The design phase of all BaSiC Initiative programs is intentionally short; this allows us to focus on the site and the construction phase, where many of the details are better resolved. This is when the community really starts to take an interest, and time must be allowed for discussion and revisions. As the students become familiar with local building technologies and resources, they are better able to finalize the details in ways that are pertinent and resonate with local culture.

For example, extensive green walls fed by gray water provided necessary shade from the western sun on the building's

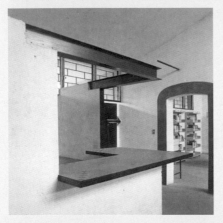

↑↑ / ↑ Juana de Asbaje y Ramirez Library, Colonia Joya de Aqua, Jiutepec-Tejalpa, Cuernavaca, Mexico, 2001

↗↗ Before they had a solar kitchen mothers prepared lunches on the street, using propane gas or wood as fuel.

↗ / ↗↗ / → Solar kitchen, José Maria Morelos School, Jiutepec-Tejalpa, Mexico, 2003–5. The solar condenser swivels to follow the sun and captures and directs its heat to an oven and stove in the kitchen. The kitchen is lit by skylights and windows. The outdoor dining area can handle 150 children eating at a time, but the kitchen can accommodate food preparation for the entire school population of 360.

long facade. The trellises themselves are made of angled sections of salvaged steel, a material readily available in Mexico that can be easily adapted for reuse. Found and salvaged materials such as the leftover tiles and broken dishes used in the countertops help the project become part of the local fabric in the eyes of the families.

The solar parabolic array turned out to be a greater challenge to design, build, and install than originally anticipated, which kept the students on-site longer and gave them more time to resolve other design questions and initiate a series of weekend workshops. They conducted seminars with the community on the value and use of the new technologies. We also offered classes on nutrition, health, solar energy, water use, and food contamination. These were very popular, especially the ones related to cooking, nutrition, and health. At the end of the courses Comunidad AC and the Ministry of Education of the State of Morelos awarded certificates to those who had attended.

Our prototype solar kitchen is now the basis for a regional program funded by the government of Morelos with federal assistance. The project represents one of our most successful integrations of cultural, economic, and environmental concerns. In its broad adoption throughout the region, it is an example of how architecture students can collaborate to help reinforce community resilience and health.

## ARCHITECTURE AND CULTURE

No single act can capture the complex, dynamic relationship between architecture and culture. To live and work in a community grounded in a tradition of building, to be conscious of culture and its relationship to the physical environment, to design cooperatively with fellow architects, and to use one's own hands to bring a design to completion are all acts that reveal architecture's inseparable connection to culture and environment.

In the Design/Build Mexico program we have applied these principles to encourage students to experience architecture as a cultural activity. They learn that sociocultural conditions and ecological considerations are as important as technology, history, and formal composition. The social process of building community is a common heritage among Mesoamericans, whose historic capacity to deal with scarcity and lack has helped them to survive. For the squatters, being part of this process creates social capital. In turn, understanding the social protocols behind local building practice allows students to engage in an exchange of mutual respect, learning, and responsibility.[5]

Confronted by globalization, urban poverty, cultural hegemony (and resistance to it), and the realities of budget, time, client relationships, and group design dynamics, students quickly come to grips with the community's concerns and needs. This requires listening, finding the questions that open the conversation, giving residents the time to articulate their needs and priorities, more listening, and reaching consensus.

The buildings we leave behind must contribute to the livability of the community and function as an agent for change. But the value they accrue is not simply in the fact that they help alleviate urban problems. Each project reaffirms architecture's role as a cultural product that facilitates dynamic exchange, while acting as a constant reminder of the power of communities to provide for themselves. For a project to be successful our work together must produce a serviceable building *and* an artifact of collaboration that itself becomes a member of the community.

# BUILDING TOWARD RELEVANCE

The informal sector accounts for more than 90 percent of construction in many Latin American countries, including Mexico—a reality on which a significant educational experience can be founded. To recognize and legitimize the informal sector is in itself a fundamental critique of the current state of high architecture and its emphasis in the design studio. The choice to situate one of our major programs in a Mexican squatter settlement is a response to the rarefied way in which architecture is taught, practiced, and understood in the developed world.

Squatter settlements, it could be argued, have a healthier connection to building than does most of the industrialized world, where economic prosperity seems to have divorced architecture from the basic issues of civic life. In a squatter community architecture is neither isolated nor autonomous—it is a direct response to the realities affecting much of the world's population. Our approach reestablishes relevance in architectural education; it fosters building as well as social skills such as communication and compassion. These experiences equip students for a valuable professional practice that connects them to the 2 billion people living in poverty around the world, including those at home.

We ourselves must continue to adapt. More than twenty years after we founded Design/Build Mexico, the forces of globalization, frequent and severe natural hazards, and climate change challenge our notions of architecture, our commitments to sustainable, resilient growth, and the very pedagogy that drives the program toward ethical action and change.

Notes

The quotation on p. 222 is from Frances Bronet, review of Thomas A. Dutton, *Voices in Architectural Education: Cultural Politics and Pedagogy,* in *Journal of Architectural Education* 49, no. 1 (Sept. 1995), 50.

1 Data provided by the US Geological Survey (USGS) Earthquake Hazards Program, online at http://earthquake.usgs.gov/earthquakes, accessed August 12, 2010.

2 See Paulo Freire, *Pedagogy of the Oppressed,* trans. Myra Bergman Ramos (New York: Continuum, 1970, 2006).

3 Ernest L. Boyer and Lee D. Mitgang, *Building Community: A New Future for Architecture Education and Practice* (Princeton, NJ: The Carnegie Foundation for the Advancement of Teaching, 1996).

4 The program areas today are Design/Build Mexico; Global Studio (building infrastructure based on microcredit lending strategies, such as Yaqui housing programs); Build a Village/Save a Life (village-building programs for homeless coffee-picking communities in Central America and native communities in Tunisia and South America); the American Indian Housing Initiative; Urban Communities Studios (such as Sustainable Taiwan, programs focused on sustainability and economic strategies that improve the living conditions of the poor, elderly, and children in cities); Design/Build India Programs (focused on cultural preservation and sustainability); and Disaster Relief Programs (in Nicaragua, Haiti, Mexico City, New Orleans, and the US Gulf Coast). I direct the programs at Portland State University, except for the American Indian Housing Initiative, which is directed by Penn State University, a founding BaSiC Initiative member school.

5 Recently, in Mexico the term "squatter settlement" has been replaced by "informal settlement" to reduce the stigma imposed on these communities. Squatter settlement is used here because it aptly reflects the traditional land politics continually enacted in Mexico, where squatters occupy land with the hope of eventual ownership, as promised by Article 27 of Mexico's 1910 Constitution.

"As a studio we had never before confronted a situation like that in Greensburg. The decimated town was still being assisted by the Red Cross when we arrived. The site itself was devastated, but at the same time it was central, located right downtown, and had enormous potential to rally the community."

# STUDIO 804 IN GREENSBURG, KANSAS

DAN ROCKHILL
ROCKHILL AND ASSOCIATES,
LECOMPTON, KANSAS

JENNY KIVETT
UNIVERSITY OF KANSAS, LAWRENCE

Studio 804 is a nonprofit corporation dedicated to producing high-quality, sustainable modern architecture in marginalized neighborhoods throughout Kansas. At the same time, we offer a comprehensive educational experience to graduate students entering their final semester of the master's program at the University of Kansas School of Architecture and Urban Planning in Lawrence. While the studio is affiliated with the university, our nonprofit status allows us to run projects independently, without university funding. This, it turns out, is a blessing. We have the freedom to pursue interesting opportunities and run our operations on schedule, as well as the legal status to receive the donations, grants, and loans that fund each endeavor.

Every year a new group of graduate students produces a fully realized residence or public structure that grapples with the challenges of bringing quality design to affordable housing in an urban-renewal context. Accessibility, modular prefabrication, and sustainability are among the requirements. The entire process is compressed into a single semester: fund-raising, site acquisition, drafting of design and construction documents, permits, client meetings, hands-on construction (done entirely by the students), and the eventual sale of the building all happen in five short months. The semester is unlike any other in their academic career. It's my job to engage students; to give them the sense of urgency that comes from critical, direct experience; to help them prepare for a future in a rapidly changing, difficult profession; and to supervise each project to ensure that it is executed well.

## ON THE ROAD TO GREENSBURG, KANSAS

After twelve years of slowly and steadily building Studio 804, in 2008 we had a successful curriculum, international recognition, nine completed housing projects, and students clamoring to participate. While we didn't have enough money to develop our own projects, this had never been a primary aim. We had a local sponsor, industry contacts, material suppliers, and consistent donors. Everything, it seemed, had fallen into place.

Then we put all of our accrued credit on the line to aid a small farming town in south-central Kansas. On May 4, 2007, one of the largest tornados in recorded history had destroyed over 90 percent of Greensburg, Kansas (population 1,574), and killed twelve people. The devastation was massive: no public buildings or services remained; schools, churches, markets, government buildings, cultural centers, and meeting halls were wiped out. Even the trees were gone. The disaster caught the attention of communities across the state and they responded with an outpouring of support.

We knew that Studio 804 had the potential to make a contribution to the reconstruction effort. But to do so we would have to forfeit much of what the program had gained in experience and practice. We had to cut our ties with our usual sponsor and local material donors in order to work in the new location; the students had to relocate from Kansas City to a rural disaster site with few comforts; and we expected to build a public building rather than a private house. We also had to agree that for this project we would abandon our design and social agendas, which aim to strengthen Kansas City's urban core.

Our original idea was to erect one new building, as we had done in other years. Before preparing a proposal for the Greensburg city council, twenty-two graduate students made a series of visits to the town, nearly 350 miles (563 km) away. Studio 804 hoped, optimistically, to partner with the township, but in the immediate wake of the disaster the city was neither prepared for this sort of assistance nor anxious to fund a new building. At the same time, it was under considerable pressure from the governor of Kansas to rebuild in an environmentally sound and responsible way: she had made a commitment to

5.2
STUDIO 804 IN
GREENSBURG, KANSAS

ORGANIZATION
STUDIO 804

PROJECT LOCALE
GREENSBURG, KANSAS, USA

237

turn post-disaster reconstruction into an opportunity to rebuild the entire city according to the principals of green design. The city council ultimately mandated that all publicly funded buildings over 5,000 square feet (465 sq. m) be LEED Platinum certified, the highest measurable level of sustainable construction. No precedent existed anywhere in the state for this standard. The Leadership in Energy and Environmental Design (LEED) Green Building Rating System, developed by the US Green Building Council, "encourages and accelerates global adoption of sustainable green building and development practices" by creating and implementing universally understood and accepted tools and performance criteria.[1] Focused on the choice of materials, natural resources, and energy, the reconstruction of Greensburg would thus show off the potential of sustainable practices.

Unfortunately, nothing can be done architecturally to circumvent the dangers of a tornado. Short of moving to another state, there are no architectural or engineering safeguards and no standards that prevent or mitigate a punishing tornado. The winds of an EF5 tornado are unbiased in their destruction, pulling up trees and bringing down stone structures. Although precautions such as tornado shelters or a full basement save lives, the residents of Greensburg have learned to live with a certain precariousness. So they focused the rebuilding process on factors within their control, such as developing an environmentally sustainable civic plan and conserving energy.

Initially, the city managers didn't quite know how to respond to our offer to build them a building, and were especially leery of our unusual designs. Looking at samples of our past work, most members had a hard time imagining such nontraditional architecture as part of their new town. Our buildings look modern—that is, different from what most people have come to expect from builders in Kansas. This look is generated out of our desire to design buildings that reflect their materials and

(previous spread) The Arts Center modules in place on the site. The street grid was all that remained in much of Greensburg after the storm.

↑ Convoy: the components en route to the building site

function in creative ways, which sets us apart from most local architects, who tend to mimic past styles. We reason that architects reflect culture—and architecture, like all of the design arts, moves forward with a certain edge, analyzing and interpreting the latest trends and tendencies for their relevance and staying power. As a studio we prefer to situate ourselves along that edge. For us architecture is not unlike the clothes we wear, the newspapers we read, or the cars we drive: its design is vulnerable to changes in taste, fashion, and perspective over time. Beyond our dedication to supplying good structures to communities that need them, the studio's mission, whether in the context of urban renewal or post-disaster reconstruction, is to contribute critically to the conversation about innovative, relevant design. The city was unwilling to accept too foreign or artistic a design for a principal government building, but welcomed the idea of an art center. And so, despite the fact that the town had been obliterated and there was great need for other facilities, the council enthusiastically embraced the plan to build one, though they did not agree to provide the funding. We therefore continued to search for a client and sponsor.

The 5.4.7 Arts Center, a fledgling group interested in the arts and named for the date of the tornado, emerged as eager supporters in the early rebuilding effort. They were willing to accept the building in principle, but as a nonprofit corporation they didn't have the money to back the project. So in the beginning there was not even the promise of funding. What's more, the students strongly supported the governor's mandate to use the LEED Platinum standard as a means of insuring future environmental sustainability. Studio 804 would have to do massive fund-raising on its own. Somewhat miraculously, we secured enough seed money from multiple sources to start working.

Before we could begin developing the design, we needed to purchase an appropriate site for the building. The students knew that a sustainable building would need to rely heavily on passive solar technology for day lighting and energy absorption. This requires a broad southern exposure. Due to the layout of the city, we had to acquire four contiguous lots. The site for the Arts Center is conveniently located adjacent to the new town center, making it a tourist destination as well as the local community center.

The timeline is consistent for all our projects. Students give up their winter break so that we can begin a two-week design charrette in early January. Each student develops and presents a three-dimensional model of the proposed building. Within a few days, designs with similar characteristics are clustered and each group of students works to refine the ideas that are ultimately combined into a single scheme. I refer to this as a shell game intended to maintain a high level of interest without compromising the fledgling designers' self-esteem. No single individual takes responsibility or credit for the design; instead, the design emerges from the group. Construction documents are completed next and, typically, a building permit is acquired by the end of the month. That leaves students two months to physically construct the building and six weeks to finish, once the prefabricated modules have been brought to the site and assembled.

## THE BENEFITS OF PREFABRICATION

On the whole the design process for Greensburg was no different from that of our previous housing projects. The initial construction was prefabricated in our warehouse. To work as efficiently as possible and complete the building on time, we then all moved to rural Greensburg for two months. By the time we got to central Kansas we had been refining our process of prefabricated construction for nearly four years. Because of the distance from the university and the students' living arrangements, we built the whole building inside our warehouse in

←← 5.4.7 Arts Center, detail with exposed wood salvaged from a disused ammunition plant

← Opening day of the Arts Center attracted townspeople, tourists, and officials from several counties interested in the application of sustainable technologies in the region.

↓ Greensburg after the tornado of May 4, 2007

Lawrence. We then broke it into modules for shipping. The unit breaks coincide roughly with the major room divisions, and each component needs structural support, which must be part of the design. Once the modules are separated, students move them out individually and prep each one with supplies and materials before wrapping it for transport.

We had learned how to do this in 2004 when we moved a three-bedroom, two-bathroom house from Lawrence to Kansas City. The city was not far enough away to warrant resettling the studio there, but it was just far enough to put a strain on our efficiency, patience, and interest. We wanted to avoid adding a midnight drive to the late hours of student life and minimize delays due to the uncertainties of winter weather, so we found a warehouse in Lawrence that could be leased cheaply. This meant that the students had to figure out how to construct the building at a distance and then dismantle and ship it. Together we created our own system of prefabrication based, in all honesty, on the creativity and lack of inhibition that only naivete can supply. The building was finished inside and out—floors, drywall, and siding—broken into sections, and loaded by crane onto trucks. It is crucial to have each unit prepared before the crane arrives to avoid expensive delays. We try to run the operation like an efficient business and time is a major consideration. This is especially true for the few pieces of rental equipment that are used on contract, such as a 70-ton crane. Given the way we work, prefabrication imposes discipline on both the design and construction processes.

Nonetheless, prefabrication has a bad reputation, especially in disaster relief, where prefabricated buildings are siteless, provisional structures made with cheap materials and hastily put together. What we do is different. Our buildings are not meant to be temporary, and our use of materials is never intended to leave the impression of an unfinished, makeshift solution. Our process relies on a profound sensitivity to the location. The goal is to show off the function of the building and the beauty of materials in the landscape while providing clients with a building they appreciate. We prefabricate our buildings because we can produce them during inclement weather in a convenient location and then set them in place more expediently than if we were to build directly on-site. Immutable restrictions, such as the size of our warehouse door, bridge heights along the transport route, the length and width of the flatbed truck used for shipping, and the dimensions of the lot, constrain the design. This has the benefit of leaving less room for argument and keeping the design simple. It is within this simplicity that the students discover the project's beauty. Moreover, we have found that this process creates a physically stronger building, often more durable than those built on-site. We have to take so many precautions to safely transport each piece of the structure that our buildings tend to be a little more robust and easily exceed minimum standards. Once finished and detailed on-site, the building is permanent, bearing no resemblance to either a temporary structure or to more typical prefabricated construction.

## A SUSTAINABLE PROTOTYPE

The 5.4.7 Arts Center is also designed as a prototype, an example of sustainable features that can easily be included in any building of this size, including houses. We implemented passive and active techniques to reduce the overall heating and cooling load on the building. We incorporated sustainable materials as often as possible, including salvaged wood. An important source was the Sunflower Army Ammunition Plant, located between Lawrence and Kansas City. Established in 1941, it was one of the world's largest powder and propellant plants and is now an excess federal property. Sunflower Redevelopment, a private firm, is cleaning its tainted brownfields and converting the site for public and private development. It took months of discussions, agreements, compromises, and bureaucratic entanglements for the students to make their way through the complexities of securing the right to harvest structurally sound lumber from the property. It took only four days to dismantle one of the 1,000 derelict ammunition buildings. The exposed wood on the outside of the Arts Center is a product of that effort.

Cross-ventilation keeps the building from overheating In summer, while the concrete floor absorbs heat from the sun in winter, helping to warm the space in the evening. On the south side there is space for trees to be planted to add shade. Although passive attributes provide for the majority of thermal comfort within the building, we also installed a forced-air heating and cooling system. A geothermal heat pump was used instead of a conventional electrical pump; in conjunction with active systems these technologies offset energy use from the grid. The latter include three horizontal-wind-axis turbines that generate half the necessary power for a typical small commercial building. The Greensburg area is ideal for wind turbines: prevailing southerly winds reach an annual average speed of 10 to 12 miles (16 to 19 km) per hour. A photovoltaic array, mounted on the roof and angled to provide maximum output, provides a second active system.

Our projects employ green procedures at all levels. The materials used to construct the building as well as on-site construction waste were recycled as far as possible. The interiors use water-saving low-flow faucets and low-level volatile organic compound (VOC) adhesives and paints. A water-reclamation system was installed for use in watering the lawn of native buffalo grass, and concrete with a high fly-ash content (recycled industrial residue) was used for the plinth and sidewalks.

The building is elevated on a plinth so as to overtly engage the public. This is particularly important since the 5.4.7 Arts Center has had to serve many functions. The gallery acts as a

↑↑ The Arts Center gallery, set on a plinth, serves many purposes in the community.

↑ The south facade is faced with Hydroswing glass hangar-style doors, which are energy-efficient and have a great capacity to withstand high winds. In front of it stand six solar-powered lights; behind the building the tops of the three wind turbines are visible.

↑ Older housing stock in Kansas City

↗ 216 Alabama Street, Lawrence, Kansas, 2000, was the first house built by Studio 804 for the nonprofit organization Tenants to Homeowners. It uses recycled and innovative materials, including tires for the bathroom floor and okume (a plywood from an African hardwood used in boat building) for the siding.

→ 1603 Random Road, Lawrence, Kansas, 2001, is clad in maintenance-free Corten steel; a cooling tower was recycled to create the exterior screen on the two long facades. The interior includes gymnasium flooring salvaged from a demolition site in Kansas City.

↓ Mod 2, Kansas City, Kansas, 2005, tested the viability of prefabrication in all aspects of production—siting, material, accessibility, transport, coordination. Its success has led us to use prefab elements regularly in our designs.

↘ Mod 3, Strawberry Hill, Kansas City, Kansas, 2006, is clad in Douglas fir and corrugated aluminum.

space for meetings, art classes, lectures, and other public events; in the hope of eventually attracting tourists to the downtown district, it becomes the town theater on weekends, when movies are shown on the lawn.

It was important that the many communities within driving distance be able to use the building not only as the local arts center but also as a resource and a firsthand demonstration of the advantages of sustainable design. Ours was the first permanent building completed in town, so we hoped residents and members of local government would take our work as an example of what they could achieve. In fact we were so overwhelmed by visitors that we had to turn away all guests during the construction period in order to finish the project on time. Even before we left, the building had become a destination for intrigued Kansans from surrounding counties. While we have no way of documenting exactly how many people have taken inspiration from the building in their own reconstruction efforts, we are constantly reminded by the Arts Center board of directors of the building's popularity. Since its completion three other buildings have been certified LEED Platinum, and almost every other new project in town uses sustainable features to some degree.

As a studio we had never before confronted a situation like that in Greensburg. The decimated town was still being assisted by the Red Cross when we arrived. The site itself was devastated, but at the same time it was central, located right downtown, and had enormous potential to rally the community. We were distinctly different from the other groups working on the ground: we were the only workers there from the beginning to the end of the project who were not residents of Greensburg. As the project progressed we realized that our presence in the middle of town was a powerful visual statement. Our lights came on at 6:30 in the morning and stayed on until well after midnight. Our commitment and sense of urgency reinforced the community's own resolve to rebuild. This sense of partnership was particularly rewarding for the students. They saw that we were providing a service that would have lasting benefits for the town. As for Studio 804, our partnership with the 5.4.7 Arts Center allowed us to construct our first public building, the first LEED Platinum building in Kansas, and, indeed, the first LEED Platinum building designed and built by students.

## STUDIO 804 TODAY: MITIGATING URBAN FLIGHT

In 1995 "Studio 804" was the name of the final design studio for students completing a master's degree in architecture at the University of Kansas. In the following fifteen years approximately 200 students have contributed to the program as it moved from small-scale design/build projects to more challenging, low- to moderate-income single-family homes. We try to create a friendly, competitive spirit in the program that encourages students each year to live up to the success of their predecessors. It is immensely gratifying for students to see their designs built as a capstone to their education. To date we have completed five single-family homes in Lawrence, Kansas, all dedicated to sustainable, affordable housing. Our reputation for using reclaimed materials is secure. In 2004 we moved the project to Kansas City, Kansas, ready to tackle the problems of urban sprawl, abandoned properties, and neglected neighborhoods. As in other desolate urban landscapes of the Midwest, the entire core of Kansas City had been vacated in favor of suburbia. Many areas have not seen new construction in more than thirty years. Houses sit abandoned and boarded up until they become a danger to the neighborhood. Yet the city has great potential for its residents.

Over the years local community-development corporations that had initially been either indifferent or outright hostile to our

3716 Springfield was the first LEED house in Kansas City.

work, and uncomfortable with its modern look, have been forced to acknowledge that we serve a vibrant interest in urban living that they had overlooked. Young hipsters want to move back into the city but find few options that suit their tastes. This group is willing to put aside the usual measures of real-estate value, such as curb appeal and capacity for quick resale, in favor of something more interesting and modern. We have found that young professionals looking for the amenities of urban life—entertainment, dining, art, social opportunities, and public transportation—are drawn to marginal neighborhoods in transition, where land is less expensive and lifestyle choices more exciting. Additionally, they don't have the skills, time, or inclination to buy a fixer-upper; they want something new and in good condition. They are willing and able to spearhead neighborhood revival.

In response we have developed a strong market base and now have a waiting list for our next student-designed house. The Mod 2 house (named for the modular nature of its constituent units) sold before the students could get it out of the warehouse. For Mod 3 we partnered with El Centro, a Kansas City community development group with which we continue to work. Today, we are running smoothly; class size is increasing and with it the

manpower for more advanced design and research projects. We have industry contacts and financial support. All of the homes we build comply with accessibility guidelines for disabled and elderly residents. Mod 3 and Mod 4 nearly doubled not only their own market value but also that of housing in their respective neighborhoods—places where houses have typically sat unsold for over a year. This newfound interest in forming vital urban communities surprised even the residents.

We hope eventually to fund our own projects. Each year we show a small profit and use that to underwrite our capacity to take on complex urban problems. We sell our projects for market value without compromising our commitment to sustainable building practices. After fifteen years we may still be struggling to step out on our own, but after Greensburg we have now built the first LEED Platinum residence in the Kansas City metropolitan area.

Note
1  US Green Building Council website at www.usgbc.org/DisplayPage. aspx?CMSPageID=222, accessed July 10, 2010.

# SUSTAINABLE KNOWLEDGE AND INTERNET TECHNOLOGY

MEHRAN GHARAATI, ARCHITECT, MONTREAL

KIMON ONUMA, ONUMA, INC., PASADENA, CALIFORNIA

GUY FIMMERS, BaSiC INITIATIVE, TORONTO

The post-disaster context—especially in developing countries—is often in conflict with the conditions that are required for sharing technical knowledge. The environment is too chaotic and imperfect to cultivate understanding that ensures good practices are sustainable. In fact, structural systems fail most often for lack of know-how. This is as true for vernacular building methods as it is for modern construction. And yet as soon as the training programs and payments have stopped and the inspectors are gone, the construction industry will often quickly mix and match safe building practices with old habits. As a result, in many cases around the world the new post-reconstruction buildings become dangerous hybrids. Bam, Iran, is a case in point.

On December 26, 2003, a 6.7 Mw earthquake struck the city of Bam, killing more than 26,000 of its 120,000 residents. The town, famous for glorious earthen architecture that dates back some 2,000 years, was completely destroyed. The disaster revealed that builders and masons, especially those using materials new to the region, did not know how to build to basic safety standards. Essential junctions between structural elements failed. Heavy secondary elements flattened first stories. Reinforcement was inadequate or virtually nonexistent, and the bonding elements that would join different materials together were either used improperly or left out completely. Even after the earthquake, in the midst of a massive effort on the part of the government to ensure future safety, it was common practice to oversize structural elements and overdesign reinforcements, especially in the housing sector. Typically, homes were over-built under the misconception that the bigger the structural elements, the stronger the building, but this only makes them brittle or too rigid. Moreover, the majority of households planned to extend their homes in the near future, though there was nothing in place to ensure proper practice once external constraints and pressures had been removed.

How knowledge is shared and exchanged among professionals should not be misconstrued as a simple choice of techniques or materials. Indeed, how we share our expertise with one another is the basis of sustainable safe building practice. Knowing *what* to do or *how* to do something may get the job done. Yet to guarantee that resistant building practices are applied with aptitude and conviction over the long run, builders need to know why what they are learning is critical to future safety. This requires *tacit* knowledge. Whereas explicit knowledge refers to knowledge that can be expressed in the form of hard data—words, numbers, drawings, and so on—tacit knowledge is a deeper level of understanding that involves intangible factors, such as personal experience, belief systems, and intuition. Acquiring tacit knowledge is also time-consuming, based on patience and long-term commitment, and requires different sorts of conversations. *Sustainable knowledge,* knowledge that can be adapted and interpreted without losing track of the essential priorities that ensure safety over time, implies tacit understanding.

As professionals reflect on what we can do better, we need to commit to long-term, knowledge-based processes that redress what it means to know how to build in a range of materials, processes that promote communities of practice within the building trades. One way to do this is through the Internet. When Haiti was struck by an earthquake on January 12, 2010, Internet technologies were galvanized into action. Social networking sites, blogs, and forums sprang up, creating hubs of information and resources. These technologies are proving to be effective tools for humanitarian development.

Haiti Rewired, a social network created by the daily technology news website Wired.com, rethinks the way aid and development have traditionally been delivered. Evan Hansen at Haiti Rewired observed how a few frenzied months of media exposure and an onslaught of money and resources following the Indian Ocean

↑ Bam, Iran, after the 2003 earthquake: a collapsed two-story building

↗ Home owners in Bam prepared for additional construction by extending columns above the roofline, so that another floor could be added once the family had saved enough money for it.

↗↗ Improper reinforcement in a structure in Bam

→ / ↓ / ↘ Using web tools BIMStorm helps professionals find solutions to complex problems in a shared environment that is immediate and responsive, helping predict the viability of building design and energy distribution. The system encourages participatory knowledge and creative input, changing how we as an industry respond to post-disaster reconstruction.

tsunami and Hurricane Katrina did not achieve sustainable results. Haiti Rewired's mission statement lists five simple principles that can change the way experts and stakeholders approach Haiti and respond to crisis in general: collaboration, transparency, innovation, design, and DIY (do it yourself).

Approximately 1,600 members active in twenty-two groups ranging from architecture, information technology, and economics to education and healthcare make up the Haiti Rewired community. Information and expertise are freely shared and exchanged as people with knowledge and experience weigh in on questions that address everything from the problems of land tenure and debris removal to housing materials and community resources. One can share and compare experience via the blog, pose questions, raise issues in the forum, and post updates from the field.

The excitement of participants in an environment where geographic distance is no longer an obstacle is palpable. Communication takes place in a way that has the potential to promote transparency, encourage debate and reflection, as well as allow us to double-check assumptions, correct misunderstandings, and ensure that the best ideas go forward. This is a basis by which sound, sustainable knowledge can be passed on to those who need it.

Building information modeling (BIM) takes online collaboration up another level. Not only is it an online tool; it is real-time collaborative planning and design networking technology. BIMStorm founder Kimon Onuma believes that the network's Plan Haiti has revolutionized real-time BIM collaboration by mobilizing thousands of people around the globe. Emergency responders, architects, planners, government agencies, and citizens alike are able to view the current state of projects and participate in the rebuilding and recovery efforts in real time.

The real-time aspect of BIMStorm technology allows experts to verify, through on-the-spot brainstorming, whether designs are efficient, have structural merit, and are cost effective and deliverable. Not unlike Haiti Rewired, resources related to the Haiti efforts are linked and include articles and manuals on post-disaster reconstruction. Maps and reports from NGOs on the ground are also compiled. Excel grids, buildSMART, GIS data, Google Maps, and Picasa photo albums help mobilize the platform.

The browser-based network invites experts from a range of disciplines to consider the outcomes and implications of their proposals in the immediate present and over time—five, even ten years from now. Site data, image databases, forums, and calendar functions interact on the fly. Users can edit, revise, and populate site plans and floor plans, test for thermal efficiency, and predict energy performance through the life cycle of the project. BIMStorms open up serious opportunities for exploring and implementing sustainable, appropriate practices as the reconstruction process in Haiti unfolds. It is a remarkable tool that has the capacity to test and challenge the intelligence and integrity of future programs, *before* the money is spent.

Internet technologies have become an effective filter to test the interrelations of communication systems and analyze the potential application of innovative materials at all scales—home, community, citywide. These networks are an integral link to understanding the impact of decision makers on the culture and the people in need. Out of these conversations communities of practice are forming among professionals that hold the promise of sustainable knowledge.

But technologies on their own do not provide the answer; it is how they are used as tools to critique, analyze, and enable us to achieve sustainable solutions that will endure. Empowering Haitians is an integral part of the discussions occurring on the Haiti Rewired and Plan Haiti networks. The challenge will be to maintain momentum in a time when media attention is short and efforts to keep interest and funding from waning are difficult.

# PART 6

# IS PREVENTION POSSIBLE?

"One of the shared lessons from our experience in Vietnam and Myanmar is that principles of safe, storm-resistant construction can be quickly and easily transferred to new communities precisely because they can be adapted to any local construction technique."

# MORE TO LOSE: THE PARADOX OF VULNERABILITY

JOHN NORTON AND GUILLAUME CHANTRY
DEVELOPMENT WORKSHOP FRANCE,
LAUZERTE, FRANCE

The cruel paradox of vulnerability among the poor is that as one invests more scarce resources in one's home the cost of recovery from damage caused by natural hazards also increases—there is more to lose and repairs cost more as well. This increasing vulnerability can be reduced if families and builders integrate a few key principles of hazard-resistant construction when they build. Poor communities worldwide face risk bluntly, exposed to repeated cycles of loss and recovery. They build on fragile, compromised sites along fault lines and slopes and in the paths of hurricanes and typhoons. Recovery from the effects of extreme weather and climate is getting more and more expensive and the need to recover more frequent. For many families this means backsliding further into poverty.

This situation overwhelmingly characterizes conditions in Thua Thien Hué province, central Vietnam, where Development Workshop France (DWF) has worked for more than twenty years to help prevent typhoon and flood damage to people's homes and public buildings.[1] Our long-term, intimate involvement with some of the poorest communities on the planet has been rewarding insofar as we have been making headway in addressing this innate paradox. But extreme climatic events (storms, wind, floods, droughts) are now occurring with a frequency and force that make it impossible to predict whether our current approach will be relevant for more than a generation. We therefore place great emphasis on constant reassessment, adjustment, and review of our methods.

In rural central Vietnam poor families have virtually stopped building their houses out of locally gathered materials—bamboo, rice thatch, timber for poles. Today, they use rigid-walled structures of cast cement brick. They make their own wall blocks and roof tiles on-site, using cement and sand purchased from small local suppliers, or buy processed building materials at local markets. The shift to new materials and techniques is almost universal, as poor communities come to associate new building practices with a better lifestyle. But this change in habit has never translated—in either material or economic terms—into safer homes or more stable futures. Buildings made in the modern mode do not withstand punishing winds and water well, and the cost of recovery when a home is damaged has gone from almost nothing to several hundred dollars for the average family. At the same time our experience demonstrates that risk can be avoided, especially in zones under constant threat—the hotspots for which we lack good practice.

Twenty-five years ago most poor rural families in central Vietnam lived in thatched pole-frame houses, which were easily destroyed by storms but quickly rebuilt with help from neighbors and family. In the mid-1980s a new economic policy in Vietnam changed this. Families, though still poor, began to have a little more disposable income, so they improved their homes, making them better and stronger—or so they thought. Nearly 100 percent of the rural housing stock in the region has been replaced in the past twenty years. Some 70 percent of these houses will be either heavily damaged or destroyed by the next major storm, and such storms now come every year.

Most Vietnamese houses are built a little at a time and are the result of years of savings, borrowing, and the owners' own labor. The cost of building an average 375-square-foot (35-sq.-m) house, if it were done at once (or what it would cost a family to replace a destroyed home), is about 25 percent of a family's extremely modest income.[2] A damaged home is therefore a considerable setback and can trigger a downward financial spiral. Families risk their health, their ability to send children to school, and even their capacity to earn a living in order to rebuild. Some families have rebuilt their homes four or five times in a decade—a terrible effort and strain. Many families never fully recover, but instead live at greater risk in homes that have been poorly repaired.

6.1
MORE TO LOSE

ORGANIZATION
DEVELOPMENT WORKSHOP FRANCE

PROJECT LOCALE
THUA THIEN HUÉ, VIETNAM

255

Development Workshop works closely on disaster-risk reduction with communities in Vietnam. Since 2000 we have aggressively promoted prevention—strengthening houses and public buildings so that they resist the impact of recurrent floods, typhoons, and whirlwinds. Reducing the risk of damage means that families can channel their scarce resources to more productive uses instead of diverting them to repairs over and again. It can be difficult to convince people with little means that they should spend more on a safer future. Sadly, the ultimate argument is made when a devastating cyclone passes and only the strengthened houses are left standing—a lesson lost neither on the local people nor the authorities.

At the same time, while donor and development institutions eagerly embrace disaster prevention, risk reduction, and mitigation and debate best methods, it is difficult to measure the impact and value of prevention. How does one quantify the value of preventing death and destruction? What priority should be allocated to prevention? It is easier to obtain funds to rebuild one house after a disaster than to strengthen many beforehand at the same cost.

This does not mean that reconstruction guarantees safer building—far from it. When tremendous resources are mobilized fast, quality control and best practices may be lacking and there is a terrible risk of rebuilding vulnerability. Yet it is during the recovery period that disaster-risk reduction practices should be integrated—at a time when people understand the necessity and the work can be done at low cost. It is far more costly to go back later to replace badly built "temporary" buildings (which typically remain in place for a long time) with better ones that do not repeat past hazardous building practices. That is not the best way to help communities build safely.

Our approach is pragmatic and specific: we deliberately promote generic principles of risk-resistant safe construction that are suited to the context of a region or individual building

(previous spread) In Vietnam, the house of Nha Tam Vuong dai Phu Da before it was reinforced

↑ The house of Nha Gia Co Tho, after it was reinforced using DWF guidelines and raised above flood level

and can be adapted to each family's needs. No two houses or public buildings have the same weaknesses, so applying principles rather than a specific technology is key. Moreover, generic principles can be applied to both existing and new structures. This is not to say that Vietnamese building regulations play no part, but rather that in the predominantly semiformal construction sector legislation is not the best route to reach the poor and help them make their homes safer.

Our program in central Vietnam promotes Ten Key Points of typhoon-resistant construction. These principles highlight specific technical safety measures: diagonal bracing, good connections among all components of a building, the best shape and angle of pitch for the roof, separation of high-risk veranda roofs from the main roof, and firm anchoring of the roof covering (such as tiles or corrugated-metal roofing sheets). In addition, they point to basic rules of safe location, good building shape, the value of doors and windows that close securely, the importance of placing matched openings (doors and windows) in opposing external walls so that wind can blow through the building and not build up internal pressure, and the benefits of planting trees as windbreaks.[3]

These simple concepts can be interpreted or adapted according to the nature of a building and its construction materials. For example, a roof made of corrugated-iron sheeting can be held down with supplementary metal retaining strips that run along the length of the roof, and in the case of tiled roofs, these should be anchored with thin vertical reinforced-concrete ribs. Ironically, these ribs were a traditional Vietnamese technique that has long been abandoned. We have helped families strengthen more than 2,000 houses in central Vietnam; the average cost of preventive strengthening is 15 to 30 percent of the building's reconstruction cost.

While preventive strengthening of homes in high-risk areas may seem an obvious good idea, the concept was not embraced immediately. In 1998 our proposal to reinforce homes of the poor in Thua Thien Hué was greeted with derision by provincial authorities. Fortunately, we had already demonstrated the advantages of safe construction techniques in a small pilot program in the province and had long-term partners there.[4] Our long-term relationship with local partners, including people in the provincial and communal local authority structure, proved to be a major strength. In some cases individuals who had worked with DWF in 1989–90 had risen through the ranks of local government and the official Communist Party system and were able to provide staunch support for our work.

In addition we work with an almost exclusively Vietnamese team and have very little staff turnover. Indeed, many of our key staff in Vietnam have worked on DWF projects for more than ten years. This longevity affords us collective institutional memory and a depth of local knowledge that is precious and relatively unusual among foreign NGOs. Ten years after our initial proposal we now have wide provincial backing. Families and authorities have seen for themselves that using our Ten Key Points is an efficient and cost-effective means to resist the impact of typhoons and floods. Seeing is believing.

## DEVELOPING A CULTURE AND PRACTICE OF PREVENTION

The process of preventive safety practiced at DWF is broadly based and involves many different local actors and actions. At its heart is a straightforward message: Prevent Storm Damage. We form partnerships with local governments and the families whose houses will be improved. To start with, we train advisors from area villages, or communes, to draw up a list of the work that needs to be done for each house. Then we tell the family how much it is going to cost. The family decides whether it can

1. Make use of the site to reduce the impact of wind and flood

2. Keep building shape simple as this reduces wind pressure

3. Build the roof at an angle of 30° - 45° to prevent covering being lifted off by wind suction

10. Plant trees and bushes as wind breaks and to reduce water flow

### PREVENT CYCLONE DAMAGE

### Ten key points of cyclone resistant construction

4. Avoid wide roof overhang; separate lean-to roof from main roof

9. Put in window & door leaves that can shut properly

5. Make secure joints between foundations, posts, bracing, trusses, rafters, purlins & battons

8. If there are no window leaves, make sure there are openings on both sides of rooms

7. Fix the roof covering down with bars over the roof covering, to stop sheets lifting

6. Use diagonal bracing in the roof & walls to stop the structure losing shape & breaking

**DW Development Workshop**

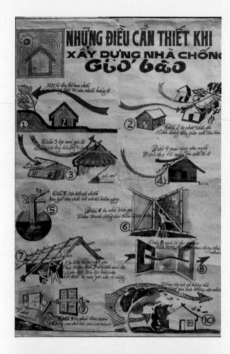

← Ten Key Points of Cyclone Resistant Construction: this poster, in Vietnamese, Thai, Myanma Bhasa (Burmese), English, and other languages, represents DWF's core principles of good construction. It is a simple, inexpensive tool, easily distributed.

↑ The original poster was drawn by a local artist in 1989. The ten points were not only displayed but sung.

We offer training sessions in which nearly all the builders in a commune learn about safer construction alongside community leaders. This is the first formal training many builders have had.

afford the work and whether to go ahead. In the first years of the program we provided a subsidy to cover some of the costs, but families have always contributed cash and labor. The average cost of strengthening a rural home is roughly $250. If a family cannot undertake the work itself, the project will ask the People's Committee, officials of the provincial government, to help by assisting in organizing and supervising the work. However, most families do the work themselves. More than 30 percent of the households we have assisted are headed by widows and economic widows who have lost a husband either to the sea or to a city in search of work.

We later discovered a drawback in our process. Follow-up interviews revealed that families were placing so much value on strengthening their homes that they were willing to borrow money from moneylenders and relatives at ridiculously high rates of interest. This sort of borrowing causes problems down the road. So we started a pilot program with our partner communes in 2002, using project funds (and later grants) to provide low-interest loans for house strengthening; it ran for two years. We wanted to demonstrate that people were willing

to borrow for a purpose that would not generate income, such as prevention, precisely because it would save them money later on. We also wanted to prove that very poor clients would and could pay back their loans. In 2008 we negotiated with the Vietnam Bank for Social Policy to launch a new, low-interest, no-collateral credit product that specifically targets house strengthening with repayment over five years. Because of its success the DWF subsidy has largely been superseded. The loan program, which relies on existing lending records and borrower repayment capacity assessments and works with each commune's People's Committee and the Farmers' and Women's Unions, is critical to making preventive strengthening sustainable and replicable.

The People's Committee is the local authority in each commune and an important partner. With it we develop a damage-prevention committee in each district, charged with coordinating our efforts. This is where we address the idea of prevention for the first time in a village or town. While preparedness has long been a Vietnamese strength, the prevention of damage at the local level has not. The communes each prepare

←← A DWF staffer trains builders.

← Bamboo huts are erected on school grounds to demonstrate that safe building techniques can be applied at home as well. Here, an example in Myanmar

→ A full-size mock-up of a strengthened roof is transported throughout neighboring communes to show safe construction techniques.

→→ Opening ceremony for a new strengthened kindergarten facility in Myanmar a five-year damage-prevention action plan that covers a wide range of kinds of work needed. DWF provides support at this stage by helping the communes identify priorities. For example, we build bridges, construct safe harbors for families living on boats, and ensure safe access and escape routes. The committee also identifies the neediest families. Families are selected democratically, by a vote organized at the hamlet level.

These activities are directed and guided by some twenty local DWF staff based in Hué city, divided roughly into one team tasked to raise awareness and one with technical skills. We have put wireless radio communication systems in place and integrated storm-resistant construction techniques into the government-sponsored temporary house-replacement program.

Building on this experience, DWF has encouraged the communes' disaster-prevention committees to work as a network, sharing their knowledge, successes, and failures with communes in neighboring provinces that would like to join our program. During a typical 15-month program we work closely with some 12 communes, selecting approximately 550 families (or 2,750 people) to receive direct help and training; 250 builders and village cadres (commune and hamlet leaders) participate, as well as eighty primary-school teachers, who in turn reach 1,200 children. At the district level we train eighty construction technicians. Overall, 100,000 people are exposed through vigorous public-information campaigns to our Prevent Storm Damage message.

This wall-to-wall approach is the key to generating a common understanding of prevention among local builders and hamlet leaders. We offer one-and-a half-day training sessions in which nearly all the builders in a commune learn about safer construction alongside community leaders. This is the first formal training many builders have had. They learn why storms damage buildings and how to build for the future.

In order to emphasize the long-term value and savings of preventive strengthening, DWF members actively participate in the process, ensuring quality control. Where possible we work on buildings that will be seen and used by many, in order to further our educational mission. We have reinforced schools, cultural centers, markets, and other public facilities. We have also built kindergartens because they are similar in size to

→ Child's painting of a house blowing away during a storm

→→ *The Mountain King against the Storm Genie*, a folktale reenacted by schoolchildren

↓ Boat races are part of raising awareness

↓↓ A Cham and Man spectacle adapted to promote typhoon-disaster prevention

↘ A risk-reduction slogan on a chin strap

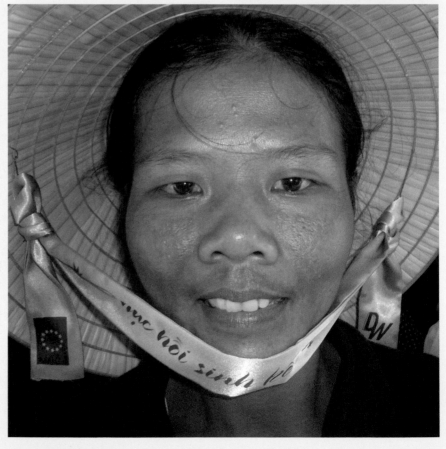

Vietnam typically suffers some six typhoons a year, but in 2009 there were ten before the season was over.

261

homes and thus offer a good way to expose parents to safe construction techniques. These new, safe public buildings can also serve as a refuge in times of disaster.

Our work in schools goes beyond making buildings safer. DWF works with teachers and children to integrate the issues of prevention into school curricula and involve children in risk reduction. School activities include drawing and poetry competitions on the theme of storm-resistant building. Children are a big help because they share these ideas with their parents—and of course, they are the house-builders and home owners of the future. Every year primary-school children perform in a play about the need to take action. The plays are videotaped so that we can reach a larger audience. One is *The Lazy Builder,* about a husband who is more interested in drink than safety, despite the exhortations of his wife and daughter, and whose home is destroyed by a typhoon. And in the traditional tale *The Mountain King against the Storm Genie,* the mountain king triumphs over the threat of typhoons.

The important role of children in communicating our message is part of the bigger, sustained Prevent Storm Damage campaign, which aims to inform and motivate the public. Repeated and regular participatory activities, designed to raise awareness, take our prevention message directly to the community. Here we use any and all opportunites to attract attention and gather a crowd—from loudspeakers to wireless FM transmission. We make audiotapes about prevention. We use television, posters, the press, and cartoon strips. We even organize activities that bring the communes together: boat races, soccer matches, rock concerts, and puppet shows all get the message across. Puppets shows in particular have great appeal, as traditional puppetry in Vietnam has always been used to convey social messages.

Vietnam typically suffers some six typhoons a year, but in 2009 there were ten before the season was over. Ketsana, on September 26, destroyed 17,000 houses and 772 square miles (2,000 sq. km) of cropland across ten provinces. Warmer oceans have made storms more fierce worldwide. As the typhoons become more frequent and ferocious, the country is at increasing risk from rising sea levels, which threaten 40 percent of its land mass. As concern increases about the known and unknown impact of climate change on coastal Vietnam, a growing public is ready to listen to messages that help them address the risks of adverse weather.

The Development Workshop project is above all community-based. Its success is predicated on enabling communities at the local level to take measures to reduce their own vulnerability. In 2006, when houses and public buildings strengthened by our methods performed extremely well during the deadly Typhoon Xangsane, families were inspired to copy and apply the Ten Key Points of safe building practice. Thua Thien Hué province then issued an edict exhorting local authorities, provincial services, and the general population to adopt our principles. The government built demonstration houses in three different geographical contexts and produced its own handbook. Support at the provincial level has made it possible for us to train local architects and engineers. Our strategy is intended to complement Vietnam's very good, longstanding, broad national approach to controlling floods by building dikes. Thus, we also collaborate with the Provincial Committee for Flood and Storm Control. An important result of this collaboration has been the first interactive disaster website in Vietnam.[5] Information is posted in real time: communes have access to official data on storms and disasters as they happen and can contribute local information as well. Where the local authorities are supportive and are working with the population to reduce vulnerability on several local fronts, communication campaigns are raising awareness, while financial and administrative structures back the process.

## EXPORTING THE TEN KEY POINTS

In Vietnam the work we have done to prevent and limit destruction has stood up well. In nearby Quang Nam province during Typhoon Ketsana the buildings strengthened using our system served as refuges for the most fragile communities. Recent typhoons are the best test. After one such storm two similar buildings stood side by side: one, with its distinctive DWF bars on the roof, tying down the covering, remained intact; the other was a roofless shell, virtually blown away. People have taken notice. Now, after more than two decades of incremental work, careful coordination with the existing political structure, and development of a reputation for probity, our program is expanding into new provinces. Make no mistake: this is in large part because the concept is simple and easy to export.

In spite of our successes our work in Thua Thien Hué province is not enough, on its own, to redress the degree of vulnerability people face in central Vietnam. We are a good model of what can be achieved, and we have managed to influence decision makers; we have even been recognized internationally.[6] But so much more has to be done. Exporting safe principles (and the myriad ways to reinforce them) to other provinces and regions is critical if we are to have an impact in Southeast Asia, where the cycle of weather-related destruction is accelerating.

In May 2008 Cyclone Nargis hit the delta region of southern Myanmar; 800,000 houses were destroyed, along with 4,000 schools and public buildings. The NGO Save the Children, well-established there since 1995, was familiar with our work in Vietnam and invited a team, including Vietnamese staff, to come and see how we might adapt our process to local conditions. Together we developed the Safer School program, based on our Ten Key Points, and produced a version of the posters in Myanma Bhasa, the official and primary language of Myanmar. Some details were revised—for example, to address local pole-and-bamboo construction techniques. In the ensuing project several hundred schools, as well as early child-development centers and new homes, were strengthened to resist the impact of storms and cyclones.

The program was systematic: first, engineers from Myanmar trained in our office in Thua Thien Hué; they then identified target villages, assessed buildings, ordered materials, and trained local builders and residents. As in Vietnam, the first task was to retrofit the most fragile buildings—in this case schools. To date, work has been carried out entirely in schools hurriedly rebuilt after Nargis, not one of which included a single feature that would resist a future cyclone. In addition we built a small bamboo-frame house, about 10 by 10 feet (3 by 3 m), on a school playground to make it clear to parents that the Ten Key Points can be applied to any rural home. Some of our schools have already stood up to fierce whirlwinds, convincing residents that, indeed, they are safer. Families also unanimously consider our model of a reinforced-bamboo house an extremely good example of how to make their own homes storm-resistant. People have quickly grasped the principles of safe construction. We held dozens of one-day workshops in the villages, and although some people said they had already known something about safe building practices, this was the first time that they received information in a systematic manner. Many beneficiaries learned the key points by heart.

One of the shared lessons from our experience in Vietnam and Myanmar is that principles of safe, storm-resistant construction can be quickly and easily transferred to new communities precisely because they can be adapted to any local construction technique. To our way of thinking it is critical to work with a relevant set of principles that are easy to assimilate, adaptable to any local context, and effective. Preventive strengthening is not free, and families are put off by this, but prevention is much cheaper than repeatedly rebuilding one's damaged or destroyed house, and much safer than risking one's life.

Today, in the wake of an exceptionally lethal earthquake in Haiti, the UN is calling for long-term measures to rebuild the island more safely. "Hopefully," declared an official, "no new hospital, school, or public structure will be built without integrating disaster risk reduction principles into its design and construction. Disaster-risk reduction is the best investment that nations and communities can make to reduce future disaster impacts and protect their people and assets."[7] Only time will tell whether her hope will be realized. Extreme poverty still limits the opportunity for poor families to make their homes safer or, indeed, their lives better. In the meantime Development Workshop will continue to demonstrate through practical action that the very poor can and, with minimal help, *will* step forward to protect themselves.

Notes

1  Development Workshop France is a French nonprofit organization, one of a group of NGOs originally founded as Development Workshop (DW) in London, UK, in 1973. Our first projects in Vietnam began in 1989; the current program promoting disaster-resistant construction methods began at the end of 1999 and continues today.

2  Costs are difficult to quantify in western terms, but a typical Vietnamese family might earn $50 a month (a single individual $12), and the cost of a new house might be in the range of $2,000—an astronomical sum.

3  These points were developed and tested by DWF in 1989–91 in consortium with the Groupe d'Echange et de Recherche Technologiques (GRET) of the United Nations Development Programme/United Nations Centre for Human Settlements (UN-Habitat), program VIE/85/019, "Demonstration of Typhoon Resistant Building Techniques." DWF's current program is supported by the European Commission on Humanitarian Aid, the Canadian International Development Agency (CIDA), the Ford Foundation, and local contributions.

4  In projects in 1989–92 DW had incorporated typhoon-resistant construction details in public buildings in what later became Thua Thien Hué province and in other provinces farther north (Quang Binh, Quang Tri, and Thanh Hoa).

5  http://www.ccfsc.gov.vn/KW367A21/Home-page.aspx.

6  DWF received the World Habitat Award in 2008 and the Sasakawa Award Certificate of Distinction from the United Nations International Strategy for Disaster Reduction organization (UNISDR) in 2009.

7  Margareta Wahlström, Special Representative of the UN Secretary General for Disaster Risk Reduction, quoted in a press release, United Nations International Strategy for Disaster Reduction Secretariat (UNISDR), January 22, 2010, posted at www.unisdr.org/news/v.php?id=12398, accessed August 18, 2010.

"The original vision for the Gola Forest Programme highlighted the importance of preserving the integrity of the forest. Yet it is only by respecting the integrity of its residents that the forest can be preserved."

# BUILDING PEACE ACROSS AFRICAN FRONTIERS

ROBIN CROSS AND
NAOMI HANDA WILLIAMS
ARTICLE 25, LONDON

"We know how to organize warfare, but do we know how to act when confronted with peace?"

This question, posed by the oceanographer Jacques-Yves Cousteau, lies at the heart of the contemporary debates swirling around post-conflict reconstruction and development. If the goal of building a true peace is to attain stability that permits growth, health, and progress, what steps after the formal peace is announced will ensure that this accord becomes a way of life?

Today, the global spotlight is focused as never before on strategies to reduce the risk of disaster in developing countries. In their most obvious form such strategies lead to technical guidelines for earthquake- and hurricane-resistant buildings that will help protect people against another Hurricane Katrina or Haitian earthquake, of which, unfortunately, there will be many. Natural disasters worldwide are increasing in number and severity. Natural disasters generate a dramatic public response. The robust and immediate nature of the event instantly whips up global interest, stimulates intense media coverage, creates a broad and diverse platform for debate, and leverages financial and policy support. Even if all this interest is often short-lived, it is still very valuable.

There is no such momentum behind the response to areas emerging from armed conflict. The event that sets off a conflict may attract attention, but our interest and our humanitarian support for the civilians caught up in the fray soon die off, until a ceasefire presents another brief media opportunity. As a result the very important and ongoing domestic and global implications raised by the extreme vulnerability of a post-conflict state are often ignored by the international community. As wars wear on we simply lose track; and no one seems interested in peace, once it is declared.

To be sure, there are no quick fixes for states after the conflict has quieted down. Longevity and sustainability of rebuilt institutions and infrastructure are the keys. This is why disaster-risk reduction during the rebuilding process—and in this case the disaster would be another conflict—must be a component of the decisions made when a nation or war zone is physically reconstructed, and these decisions must take the form of a *process* of peace building. At every stage of this process—from decisions on land use and planning to architectural design and construction—the priority must be to build a secure and lasting peace, brick by local brick. Research tells us that 40 percent of post-conflict states invite war within a decade. This staggering figure suggests the urgent need for a debate on the advantages of peace building as opposed to conflict prevention. International aid agreements are complex and often fail to reach those at the bottom. For a fragile country that finds itself left to its own resources, it is a struggle to navigate these complexities, which can fast become an intractable problem.

Article 25 of the Universal Declaration of Human Rights, from which our office takes its name, asserts that adequate shelter and housing are a fundamental human right. Our team of architects and engineers provides construction solutions to some of the world's most vulnerable people in ways that put the development process firmly in the hands of the local community. It was in the context of these challenges that our practice, Article 25, a United Kingdom charity operating as a construction-design consultancy service to NGOs, first became involved with the Gola Forest Programme in eastern Sierra Leone. Sierra Leone has suffered terribly from a recurrent pattern of civil war, violent changes in government, the missteps of foreign intervention, and, ultimately, the world's indifference. We in the west hear little about what is going on there now.

The Gola Forest Programme is a collaborative initiative that unites the government of Sierra Leone, the Conservation Society of Sierra Leone, and the UK's Royal Society for the Protection of Birds for the productive preservation of an

6.2
BUILDING PEACE
ACROSS AFRICAN
FRONTIERS

ORGANIZATION
ARTICLE 25

PROJECT LOCALE
GOLA FOREST, SIERRA LEONE

267

expansive rain forest that covers 290 square miles (750 sq. km)—the largest and most diverse remaining forest in the country. The land runs in a long tract along the Liberian border and comprises parts of seven chiefdoms. This is the same stretch of prime West African rain forest that (with the neighboring Lofa and Foya National Forest of Liberia) was used as a corridor by rebel soldiers and for the export of blood diamonds during eleven years of civil war.[1] Now the rebels have departed and the forest is at peace. Yet beneath the lush tranquility a grave danger lies waiting.

## SURVIVING THE PEACE IN THE GOLA FOREST

Threats to the forest ecology in Sierra Leone include a rise in demand for timber, which will most likely escalate the current deforestation rate of 2 percent per annum and devastate the remaining fourteen threatened bird species currently known to inhabit the rain forest. Endangered birds such as the Picathartes and rare species such as the forest elephant and giant mollusks (which look like they should be deep in the ocean but instead crawl the forest floor) are among the threatened fauna. The so-called natural-resource curse, the phenomenon by which nations rich in natural resources tend to have poor economic development, has ample opportunity to take hold here, in a fragile post-conflict society. Mining companies and timber merchants eye the forest jealously for the goods it may yield. High profits tempt the urban elite. And the prospect of exhaustion of resources, should these resources be exploited, threatens rural communities. Indeed, resource inequality was one of the causes of the long civil war. Years of conflict have stripped civil society bare. National unemployment in 2006 was at 57 percent; it is probably much higher in rural areas.

(previous spread) The future construction site for the Peace Park headquarters, with a backdrop of dense rain forest

↑ Participants in a community workshop in Lalehun discuss needs for resources and infrastructure.

The seven Gola chiefdoms that make up the region are extremely vulnerable—heavily plundered and severely depleted. Three hundred and fourteen people live here, but the population along the wider forest edge is thought to comprise more than 130,000 residents. There is no potable water supply and there are no health-care facilities. A generation of uneducated youth, accustomed to nothing but violence and warfare, has come to adulthood bereft of skills and purpose with which to forge a livelihood; even those with skills find few employment opportunities. This "youth bulge" represents one of the most critical symptoms of a postwar state, one that time and again has led countries back into chaos.

In a promising step toward a more lasting peace, in 2009 the presidents of Sierra Leone and Liberia met at Lalehun, a settlement in the Gola Forest, to shake hands over a new Management Plan that codified the Gola Forest Programme and established its stewardship of the transboundary Gola Forest Protected Area, which brings together the Gola Forest in Sierra Leone and the Gola National Forest in Liberia into a single protected district; together, the two zones form an expanse of 770 square miles (2,000 sq. km). The idea of such a partnership had been in the making for some twenty years, despite the frequent disruptions of war and political crisis. The goal is "to conserve the integrity of the Gola Forest in perpetuity, ensuring that local people living around the Gola Forest will have enhanced livelihoods as a result of income generating schemes which remove the need for the unsustainable use of the Gola Forest resources."[2] In a decisive move away from years of civil unrest, the two presidents pledged at their historic meeting to work together for peace. The day demonstrated their commitment to protecting a transboundary area for ecologically and socially sustainable settlements that will provide secure environments from which livelihoods can be generated. Current and new residents will build their futures here. This endorsement by two heads of state was momentous.

Article 25 began to work in Gola in 2009. Our role was to provide the master planning and construction design for new conservation facilities and sustainable settlements within the protected zone, dubbed the Peace Park by locals.[3] The crucial question we faced was how to build in a way that would reconcile the interests of national government and regional powers and the competing demands of human development and environmental conservation. How can a small team of architects and engineers make a difference on both the international and human scales in the face of such formidable challenges?

Our principle was simple. Rather than build from the defensive posture of fear, we would build *for* peace. Our design steered clear of impenetrable concrete blocks in which residents might barricade themselves, fearing that conflict might return. Rather, we wanted to create something transparent and positive, a building strategy that celebrates peace and capitalizes on the rich diversity of the local environment—something the local community would actively want to take hold of and protect as its own during the peace-building process.

The general idea was to incorporate transparency and community accessibility into the design of the buildings themselves. This had been the approach taken in Belfast, Northern Ireland, where a city traumatized by armed conflict was transformed from a streetscape of blast-proof concrete buildings into a city of glass—a symbol of a healthy, peaceful society that intends to stay that way. Similarly, the transparency and accountability symbolized by the glass dome of the rebuilt Reichstag (1999) in Berlin has undoubtedly had immeasurable impact on the city's transformation from the front line of international confrontation to the cosmopolitan hub of a prosperous democracy.

To reconcile the conflicting interests and needs of all the stakeholders, our Article 25 team had to engage the different parties in a process of negotiation. This took the form of workshops, as opposed to information sessions. This is a key

🡔🡔 The communities living at the edge of the Gola Forest are some of the poorest people in one of the world's poorest countries. Here, a house in Old Lalehun

🡔 Former commercial buildings were adopted by new residents of the area who had been displaced during the ten-year civil war. This house in New Lalehun probably originally housed workers from the logging industry.

← Men and women often have very different perceptions of their surroundings. Men mapped their community in geographic terms while women mapped the environment according to its constituent elements.

↑ For construction projects to successfully contribute to the peace-building effort, the capacity on the ground must be understood and developed. At Gola the local community was able to provide a range of skilled workers, including metalsmiths, carpenters, weavers, and grass thatchers.

In any infrastructure project, once initial needs are assessed the role of the architects and engineers becomes critical.

distinction: the community must be at the center of the decision-making process, not merely an audience to it. We started in two settlements, Old and New Lalehun. Old Lalehun is the original village—generations old. An abandoned logging compound taken over in the 1980s by settlers displaced by war became New Lalehun. Both villages sit on the forest edge. The existing communities are directly affected by the construction of a national park; they will be living in close proximity to approximately 100 well-paid new park staffers, creating the potential for conflict. Thus, it was imperative that design strategies take the form of a dialogue. We believe that the process of negotiation does *not* render an architect any less productive or important. Nor does involving the community make the process any less creative or professional. In our experience it produces rich, multiparty participation, generating both surprises and new potential.

In projects such as the one for Gola, therefore, we abandoned heavy-handed design pedagogy and talks about construction techniques in favor of a series of transactions mediated through group work, plans, and models meant to help produce culturally appropriate design solutions. In this way, each community member not only has had a say in his or her future, but has been invited to mold that future into a sustainable community project once it is up and running. All of our projects are grounded in an understanding of what the community says it needs, including children's dreams. No one understands the most pressing needs of a community better than the community itself.

These participatory workshops, facilitated by our community-outreach officers, provided ample space to exchange knowledge, ambitions, and aspirations and also fears and complaints. The process acquainted the professional team with the residents' ideas while helping to establish a consensus among diverse groups of community members regarding priorities. Rather than looking inward at individual situations, the workshops

galvanized communities to think in terms of collective priorities and work as a team. During these balmy afternoons, we also quickly discovered that traditional gender roles influenced the process. Women were silent observers at the back of the room, while the men more than made up for their reticence. So, to make sure that we were able to capture the perspectives of the whole community, we divided the workshops into two groups by gender. As both groups mapped their world, examining perceptions about the local area and environment, it soon became clear that the men and women had widely disparate views of the layout of their village, symptomatic of the very different day-to-day roles they play. Men tended to produce geographically accurate maps, while women generated diagrams that were more qualitative, a perception of lived space. For example, their drawings mapped the need to find nearby water and codified social as well as geographic features. Our philosophy advocates active dialogue in which the people concerned in the project listen, participate, and compromise. In a conscious effort to unravel the fabric woven by years of colonialism and fluctuating aid cultures, this approach steers the designer away from classic practices that separate the donor from a passive clientele—people simply waiting for assistance—by putting the community members at the center of the process as responsible partners.

In addition to the mapping and assessment exercises, the groups were encouraged to prioritize needs by ranking them. We also ran day and seasonal mapping exercises so that the final building designs would suit the way in which they will be used year round. Finally, we needed to identify the skills available within the community, for these serve in the construction phase. For this we carried out a series of capacity and personal-resource surveys. As with all of the exercises, this one had the dual objective of assessing available skills and of making the professionals and the residents more aware of the community's collective capacities and talents. It also went a long way toward building community confidence and pride.

In any infrastructure project, once initial needs are assessed the role of the architects and engineers becomes critical. For example, at Gola the participatory workshops indicated that the most pressing issue for the existing communities in Old and New Lalehun was the lack of clean water. So our first act was to install clean-water pumps in the two villages. This provided a vital boost for all future activities. The original community now began to have the capacity to improve its health. Clean water heightens one's personal and collective sense of resilience and immediately encourages a community to be optimistic about the project—to feel that yes, this can work. A single, small intervention that addresses a pressing, immediate need helps us build a relationship based on trust and mutual cooperation, which tempers the otherwise disconcerting experience of change.

## BUILDING FOR SUSTAINABLE PEACE

Through such techniques as these we have been able to make fullest use of local resources and to involve the community in ways that will assist its members later to maintain and develop the project. Although this may extend the preparation and research time and work required before ground can be broken, it is well worth the effort. As architects, we have found that for every $1 donated to provide our services we gain $10 of value in the field. When the community is engaged from the earliest stage, designs became rooted in local knowledge and practice. This allows us to maximize the budget, keep the financial investment within the community, and develop flexible structures that can be modified according to local needs as the community gradually takes over the program. Thus, together with the provision of potable water we are also introducing integrated

environmental strategies for generating power, managing waste disposal, and distributing water—features that will add immeasurable value by creating opportunities for work and learning within the community. These are vital ingredients in any long-term peace-building process.

Once the information was gathered and collated from the respective workshops, a design started to emerge. At Gola access to water, the sanctity of local religious buildings, and fears about security were seen to be key factors in the program. The designers were also keenly aware that an influx of educated professionals (who would run the park), living near a comparatively disadvantaged community, risked creating discord. Decisions in design (spatial planning, access) can exacerbate or prevent exploitation of one community by another. We took steps to avoid allowing the new community to appear as an island of prosperity in a sea of poverty. We also wanted to prevent the existing community from exploiting the wealth of the new residents, a terrible situation in which everything from food to women becomes a medium of exchange. We addressed these concerns by including common facilities for education, social life, and trade in the design. Positive social transactions between the two communities can occur organically if they have open and neutral environments in which trust and knowledge can be fostered. Thus, both communities will share the benefits of a school, health clinic, and market.

The need to reconcile local wants and needs required particular attention. This is always a delicate part of the process. While it is true that a design developed in ignorance of local culture is a recipe for disaster, some of the suggestions the community put forth were also potentially a recipe for failure over the long term. For example, local interest in using concrete instead of timber as a primary construction material stemmed from a desire to imitate western styles, regardless of the fact that concrete is neither a climatically sound choice nor locally available, making it enormously expensive. It was necessary to address the general tendency of the community to distance itself from local materials by establishing a careful and sensitive conversation. After all, the construction of the buildings is only a part of a much broader process of peace building through local empowerment. Our work with the community revealed the specific cultural codes invested in particular architectural approaches. A timber building raised high from the ground on stilts may lend itself to sustainability, good ventilation, and security, but elders resented anything that smacked of colonialism. Architects engaged in the process of peace building must be versed not only in technical skills but in the aesthetic interpretations of design and in local history, as well as in the sociopolitical implications of space and structure. We pointed out the advantages of timber: that it uses less electricity, can be built quickly and on more difficult terrain (for far less money), and would help show the world that Sierra Leone is using sustainable practices. In addition, we promised that the new buildings would look nothing like those of the colonial era. Further, the headquarters, school, staff residence, and health clinic were designed to favor natural ventilation.

The design strategy also sought to ensure that construction would take place on sites accessible by existing paths, in order to disturb the rich biodiversity of the region as little as possible. We determined that sites should be used only if they had previously been farmed or logged—no valuable ancient woodland would be despoiled during the construction phase.

In tandem with cultural and social analyses, the planning process included a study of available material assets. Natural resources were scouted and harnessed as a top priority. Construction will be based on locally sourced materials wherever possible; there is a particular focus on efficient construction; easy, inexpensive maintenance; and flexible, multipurpose use. Nearby water sources were documented for a hydroelectric

power viability assessment and as a potential potable water supply. Boreholes and rainwater harvesting have been explored as water sources, and research is under way to determine how wastewater may be soaked away to prevent groundwater contamination. Household waste disposal is targeted; we plan to compost organic waste and reuse the nutrients in agriculture. The goal is to minimize energy consumption through smart design.

The original vision for the Gola Forest Programme highlighted the importance of preserving the integrity of the forest. Yet it is only by respecting the integrity of its residents that the forest can be preserved. Peace building must begin with people, and it is the people of Old and New Lalehun who, as the program grows in ambition and detail, have the opportunity to generate income and alleviate their poverty, thus reducing the risk that out of desperation they will use the forest's resources unsustainably. Initially, the local community will work on the construction, sell food to the construction crew, and cook meals. Eventually, these same people will have the opportunity to become park guides and rangers. As the school improves its offerings, administrative and managerial courses will be added. The process of building a solid, peace-driven community has no fixed endpoint, but rather, through good design, remains ongoing.

To accomplish its goals Article 25 is working with a master plan developed from the research and outreach we have conducted. At this writing it is a work in progress. Geographically, it proposes a progression from the center of village life in Old Lalehun through the gateway of New Lalehun to the new staff residences and village, and then into the forest itself, before it finally reaches the new Peace Park headquarters building. Individual buildings in the complex will reflect the lessons learned in the preparatory process. In a remarkable fusion that encompasses the aspirations of both designers and community members, the design of the headquarters building incorporates

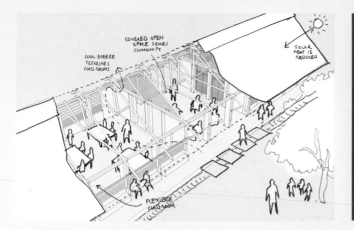

← The school has been designed to maximize its environmental performance and provide flexibility in how classes are conducted.

↙ In the headquarters building a dedicated space for community meetings (at right) is linked to the office facility by elevated walkways.

↙↙ View from the community space toward the office facility

↓ The design of the park headquarters building draws upon elements of the local vernacular, such as elevation on high stilts, as seen in this public building in Old Lalehun. Traditional buildings raise their food and asset stores on legs to deter thieves. The undercroft serves as a space to meet socially.

In this extraordinary African context Article 25 is seeking
to help reverse the classic trend of migration to urban centers by
harnessing the highest caliber of environmental conservation
and human development in a rural context.

elements of local vernacular architecture. Elevation removes the need for burglar bars and other security measures, which would otherwise have been required but would have conflicted with our desire to consciously reject a bunkerlike design. The elevated position allows the building to feel the benefit of natural breezes, as well as providing spectacular views of the forest canopy. Locally produced interlocking stabilized soil-cement blocks—evolved from traditional mud blocks—will be used in all one-story buildings. A small percentage of cement (we are testing cement-to-mud ratios at 1:20 and 1:12) is added so that the blocks will be durable enough to tolerate heavy tropical rains. These blocks can also be laid in an interlocking pattern, which requires less skill on the part of the bricklayers. In order to capitalize on the natural drama of the forest and avoid clearing trees, roads will be kept to a minimum.

There is a reason why the world's rain forests are the last habitats to be settled by humans: in spite of all our technological advances, we have yet to conquer the sense of impenetrable mystery and environmental hostility within them. The spirit of the master plan respects this. It is not intended to conquer but to harness the forest's natural riches and charm in a way that benefits both the ecology and the human residents.

## WHOSE URBANISM IS IT ANYWAY?

In this extraordinary African context Article 25 is seeking to help reverse the classic trend of migration to urban centers by harnessing the highest caliber of environmental conservation and human development in a rural context. But this development is not unchecked. No development is permitted within the forest boundaries beyond the master plan. Tourism is restricted to small parties, hosted by the government or the Gola partners, for professional, diplomatic, and educational purposes. The Gola Forest Programme is intended to steward natural resources and provide alternative livelihoods for local communities, who might otherwise devastate them. Today, when you enter the park, the temperature falls, the air quality improves, and the smells and sounds of the forest change. This ecosystem will be preserved intact.

We hope the Gola master plan will become a model for responsible development in remote villages, truly the embodiment of grassroots empowerment.[4] Such an approach may produce an interesting demographic transition. While the new park staff residents may experience a sense of return from city to rural living, the communities of Lalehun will see their rural home transformed by the presence of former city people. This is a form of urbanization, but one that defies traditional migratory patterns and processes that leave the countryside desolate. As we enter the second decade of the new millennium, we will witness the impact of climate change on migratory patterns, as a dramatically increased number of environmental refugees are forced to relocate. New configurations of urban and rural contexts need to be tested. In Sierra Leone these configurations favor a nationwide ecological strategy that facilitates opportunities for professionals who might otherwise leave the countryside. At the same time, the plan strengthens and densifies rural life ravaged by guerrilla actions during the war. Now Liberian staff have joined the team of park rangers. The Gola Peace Park offers an alternative rural model, without which the existing communities would remain untouched by progress and would stagnate economically. Prosperity and enlightened development are critical if the next generation is to avoid future conflicts.

To function well such an institution must be able to attract and retain highly trained staff. A challenge for the program will be to reconcile the new residents' urban expectations of high-quality buildings and services with their rural context. The existing residents also have high expectations; they are waiting for improved infrastructure, trade, health care, and schools. To preserve rural life means that this new urbanism must occur within the scope of what is feasible, determined by the site's geographical and ideological isolation and by the largely rural skills on which production and trade will be based. And yet there is exciting potential inherent in defining urban and rural life as fluid, shifting fields. In much of sub-Saharan Africa the generation who now live in cities can trace their roots back to a rural village in one to three generations. The lines of demarcation that separate urban from rural life are still porous, especially in war zones, where forced displacement has compromised tribal identity and livelihoods. As a result the sense of belonging that we take from these contexts remains open and flexible.

Cousteau asked, "Do we know how to act when confronted with peace?" The Gola Forest Programme offers an answer, one that we hope is holistic and resilient. Our design approach seeks to build beyond the buildings themselves, laying a foundation for the work of creating and maintaining civil society. It affirms the community's capacity to harness its creativity and resources for the purpose of making peace and fostering prosperity. Our task can be expressed in short and simple terms: to equip the community to progress and develop long after our role in the project ends. For Article 25 reducing the risk of future conflict in the Gola Forest region is not about conflict prevention. It expresses a belief in the potential of peace to thrive.

Notes

1 During the civil war that lasted from 1991 to 2002, tens of thousands were killed and 2 million Sierra Leone residents displaced—about one-third of the population. In neighboring Liberia the bloody civil war that erupted in 1989 took the lives of more than 200,000 people (1:17 Liberians); it was temporarily halted in 1996 only to break out again in 1999. The second war, which spread across the border into Sierra Leone and Guinea, lasted until 2003. See *CIA World Factbook*, at www.cia.gov/library/publications/the-world-factbook/geos/sl.html, accessed July 28, 2010; and *Frontline/World*, report of May 2005, Public Broadcasting System, at www.pbs.org/frontlineworld/stories/liberia/thestory.html, accessed July 28, 2010.

2 Government of Sierra Leone, Royal Society for the Protection of Birds, UK, and Conservation Society of Sierra Leone, *Gola Forest Reserves. The Proposed Gola Forest National Park Management Plan 2007–2012* (Freetown. Government of Sierra Leone, Forestry Division, Ministry of Agriculture, Forestry and Food Security, 2009), vii.

3 Article 25 partners for the Gola Forest Project are the Royal Society for the Protection of Birds (UK), the Conservation Society of Sierra Leone, the government of Sierra Leone Forestry Division, and the seven Lalehun chiefdoms. Consulting engineers are Price & Myers. Donors are the European Union, the Fonds Français pour l'Environnement Mondial, and the Global Conservation Fund of Conservation International.

4 This is Article 25's first such large project; others are planned. We are currently working with Outreach International, a US registered charity and humanitarian organization, and the Organisation for the Social Development of the Masses (ODSM), our local Haitian partner, on a large-scale school reconstruction program in Haiti. There, reconstructed, earthquake-resistant schools are designed as models of good methods and practice for future building.

"There is tremendous need for skilled, specialized, small teams to partner with the bigger organizations that can help scale up their good ideas and practices."

# HAITI 2010: REPORTS FROM THE FIELD

MARIE J. AQUILINO

On January 12, 2010, an earthquake measuring 7.0 Mw struck 10 miles (16 km) southwest of Port-au-Prince, Haiti. As many as 300,000 Haitians are believed to have died in it. One-third of the country's population has been displaced; 500,000 of these are children under the age of five. Five thousand schools, 188,383 houses, and 80 percent of the country's infrastructure were destroyed. Nearly 20 percent of federal employees were killed and 27 of the 28 federal buildings were leveled. Twelve months later 1 million people are still living in tents and under tarpaulins in 1,354 spontaneous settlements. Indeed, the number of campsites is growing, as Haitians who were not directly affected by the earthquake but are in desperate need of aid and support move out of their homes and into the over-stuffed camps.[1]

In June, when hurricane season started, only 226 camps, where nearly one-half million people were living, had been assessed for their vulnerability to landslides and flooding. A mere twenty-nine of these had undergone some sort of (unspecified) mitigation measures to protect families. So as winds and squalls whipped through, emergency supplies—90,000 extra tarps and 60,000 toolkits—were issued to weary Haitians slogging around in the mud, their plastic sheets already in tatters. Tarps, it was said, are better than tents, which are often of poor quality and take up too much space. Four families were living in the space where one tent would normally go. But tarps were never intended to be more than temporary coverings or to last longer than a few months; they certainly cannot substitute for shelters or homes. No one believed they would hold up in hurricane-force winds. Alerts were planned and lists of what to do in the event of (another) emergency were circulated, but in such circumstances it was nearly impossible to create an evacuation strategy should something go terribly wrong.

Fire remains a threat. Families are burning open-flame oil lamps and plastic is ubiquitous. Perhaps as few as 50 percent of displaced people are using the public toilets because the latrines are considered unsafe and unsanitary and do not appropriately separate men from women. Large parts of Port-au-Prince are at sea level, which means it is especially important that the latrines be emptied; otherwise heavy rains will wash raw sewage into the living areas. Recently, access to clean water in bottles is helping to reduce illness and disease, yet bottled water is an unsustainable means of supply. Rape and human trafficking in the camps are escalating, but continue to go largely unreported and ignored. Landowners are ramping up forced evictions by cutting off access to supplies, slashing tents, or offering residents small cash payments. At least 28,000 people have been forcibly removed from campsites. Meanwhile, tent villages sited too far from the capital sit empty in the middle of nowhere. Now, 171,304 cases of cholera have been confirmed; 3,651 people have died. The disease has spread to all of Haiti's ten departments.

At the same time 250,000 buildings have been assessed (most of them residences): 50 percent are considered habitable, so moving these people back into their homes should help decongest the camps—if residents are not too frightened or too financially insecure to return home. Another 27 percent can be restored, though how this is going to be carried out, in what time frame, and with whose assistance has not yet been announced. The rest will be demolished, which will add to the tons of debris currently clogging the city. To date, not even 10 percent of the rubble has been cleared—a daunting challenge that requires manual labor as well as heavy equipment. Cash-for-work programs are now almost exclusively organized around debris removal. In addition to the massive need for new homes, a solution for people who were renters (70 percent of Port-au-Prince residents) still has to be worked out.

So far 31,656 transitional shelters have been built. Tens of thousands more are said to be in the country or in the pipeline; most have been paid for. Underlying the slow pace of construction is the problem of land ownership: the government has been unwilling or unable to secure large parcels of land from a handful of landowning families for sites big enough to house the tens of thousands of stranded residents who need new homes. Thirteen such sites have been identified.[2]

## INTERPRET THE NUMBERS

The numbers are a stark reminder of the seamless, irrefutable relation between acute poverty and risk. It is especially difficult to respond effectively in a country where for decades failed policies have crippled government infrastructure, enfeebled civil society, and created endemic aid dependency—Haiti hosted 10,000 NGOs *before* the earthquake. It is easy to be stricken to immobility by the data. But this is hardly the time to act too hastily, we have learned that rushed, short-term solutions do not translate into cogent policy.

Yes, the situation remains dire. And the recovery process is painfully slow, despite the vast influx of donated funds. But it is worth remembering that one year after the 2005 earthquake in Pakistan few houses had been built, urban plans were not yet in place, and standards had not yet been set. Then the process started coming together: in less than four years 640,000 homes were standing. Despite the fact that the population remains greatly at risk, it is crucial that good decisions be made and good processes established for making those decisions—and this takes time. Undoubtedly, those working on the reconstruction efforts missed opportunities to implement daring, clever, efficient ideas that would have helped make camp life safer and decent. I fear that far too many people will still be living in the

(previous spread) A destroyed church in Port-au-Prince

↑ Before the earthquake the building culture in Haiti had been severely compromised by poor quality materials and a universal disregard for basic building standards.

A post-earthquake shop. Severe inequality, corrupt governance, poor planning, and environmental degradation have jeopardized lives and jobs in Haiti for decades.

precarious settlements when this book reaches the stores. But in a climate of urgency we must always have the courage to ask whether it is worth diverting long-term resources to alleviate short-term problems. And if the answer is yes, which of these should be tackled now? To inch forward constructively and without presumption, with the patience to achieve oversight, coordinated vision, and leadership, is the wiser course. As built-environment professionals we must keep our goal clear: to define and implement the principles that will sustain long-term development in Haiti.

## LEARN FROM THE PAST

Haiti can learn from Pakistan. The remarkable expertise and experience gained since the 2005 earthquake is now being marshaled to help the 20 million people displaced by the massive September 2010 floods there. Progress has been made on all fronts: financial-disbursement systems improved; technical standards in local construction materials and international best-practices shared; training curricula updated. There is good communication among the responsible sectors (both government and NGOs); urban recovery is now well understood; and water and sanitation policies have been integrated into the housing mandates. Pakistan's decision makers and technical professionals are together advocating for people-driven recovery that will allow individual households to take on the monumental responsibility of rebuilding their homes. Appropriate technical guidance based on extensive fieldwork will be available. Key principles are already in place, and the extraordinary individuals who played vital roles over the last few years are at the forefront of managing the recovery.[3]

Haiti can also learn from its neighbors. Cuba, 44 miles (70 km) away, has developed low-cost, energy-efficient building technologies and decentralized production of building materials. It has mastered affordable, safe housing through community consensus with the aid of the university-based Centro de Investigacion y Desarrollo de Estructuras y Materiales (CIDEM), a nonprofit organization that is now also assisting Nicaragua and Ecuador. The project is a model for disaster prevention and preparedness, as well as for the prospective actions of safe land use, environmental and community planning, resilient infrastructure, and sustainable building practices.

## DEVELOP DIALOGUE AND CONSENSUS

Technical professionals—engineers, architects, environmental and energy experts, housing and financial experts—must talk to one another if we are to optimize our knowledge and skills on the ground. We need to advise and act collectively. In Haiti at the moment even the most intelligent initiatives are going forward in isolation. This dilutes their potential. What's more, the capacity we help build should not be aimed solely at the beneficiary communities. We need to share knowledge and experience from profession to profession, and with government officials and municipalities. Together we can help train local organizations on a rolling basis, develop modules for university and polytechnic programs, and work with the local construction industry.

To build alliances and relationships is a precondition for success. Building structures is not enough; we must also know how to build discussion and understanding, vision and leadership, management skills, confidence, trust, optimism, and a sense of ownership and accountability. To do that, we must know how to stop and listen. A good intervention does not rush in. We must act like detectives: consolidate what others have to say, review and reinterpret what is known, then come forward with ingenuity and drive.

## PUSH FOR PERMANENCE

In Haiti we need permanent, livable homes that are climatically and culturally appropriate, employ a range of technically and culturally suitable materials, are inexpensive to maintain, sensitive to fragile environments, and able to withstand frequent storms and earthquakes. The need to focus on permanence is easily overwhelmed by day-to-day chaos and overshadowed by the idea of transitional shelters. Tens of thousands of additional lightweight, prefabricated transitional shelters are about to be rolled out as proof of our readiness, not because they are the best idea but because they have been bought and paid for and can show material progress.

Some argue that transitional shelters are the only defense against the irresolvable problem of land tenure in Haiti. But do we really believe that temporary settlements, housing as many as 50,000 people, can be relocated in three to five years? If not, then how will these homes be turned into permanent structures? What current agencies and NGOs will guarantee to return to ensure that supplies are available and additions and adaptations are made to good safety standards? What suppliers of transitional structures, fit for no longer than a few years, will provide the resources to prevent them from becoming the slums of tomorrow? The gains we make now in the name of urgent need will make little difference unless we make a commitment to permanence. The shelter groups that have flooded Haiti will be long gone before they are able to grasp how the full cycle of housing works. Permanence does not simply mean staying put; it means building for growth and change. To design for permanence requires architects and builders to understand that housing is a process: families manage incrementally, making a living and sorting out a home in stages, building what is most urgent first.

## SCALE UP

There is tremendous need for skilled, specialized, small teams, like many of those who appear in this book, to partner with the bigger organizations that can help scale up their good ideas and practices. Why aren't we leveraging their best results into the bigger programs? A quarter of a million people (more, if we count people returning from the countryside) will need new neighborhoods. How are these communities being envisioned? Are the guiding features sensitive to environmental demands, future growth, and long-term needs? Are urban plans being drawn up with the help and guidance of the people who will constitute these new communities? Are we calling upon collective expert input? Will these sites be models for decentralization and food security? Are planners and architects thinking about how to link the services and benefits of these new settlements to the communities on their margins, also in desperate need but not directly affected by the earthquake? Haiti's history of lack of equity across the population is the reason why people are leaving their homes for the risky campsites.

## EXPAND SKILLS

Technical expertise is not enough. The built-environment professionals who work in post-disaster situations must also be skilled diagnosticians and social anthropologists, gifted strategic planners, good communicators, and as attentive to household finances as they are to government priorities. For this, generosity and empathy are essential. Architectural culture has the appearance of being collaborative, but its teams usually comprise similar voices and agreed-upon roles. After a disaster teamwork is formed out of vast differences in expertise, opinions, and backgrounds. To be effective,

The need for space in Port-au-Prince is so great that residents elect to live on dangerous sites along unstable slopes. A hillside after the earthquake

architects need to privilege strategic contributions, compromise, and anonymity over control and authorship. Getting a good model into the mainstream or influencing an important decision may seem less rewarding than designing a signature model home, but it requires just as much creative effort and will reach far more people over time.

## LET PEOPLE CHOOSE

People overcoming a disaster need to be at the center of their own recovery. Yes, people need good, safe, appropriate building models that can become homes, markets, schools, clinics, libraries, offices, and sports centers. But we need to take care not to prioritize the physical signs of recovery, simply because they are the most visible, over the improvement of the deeper social and cultural infrastructure. This means putting resources in the hands of the community. The success of the Pakistan earthquake-resistant housing program is a case in point. Given the money, technical support, and a few basic controls, over 95 percent of the residents built houses to the required standards within four years. And they did so within a framework of other household decisions.

The survivors of a disaster are the best source of manpower that aid agencies and governments could hope to have. If people are given direct access to resources, they have more choices. And if some choose to pay off a debt or seek medical care with the money instead of rebuilding, we need to plan for this. Ask good questions. Ask people about their constraints and priorities, about what they are willing to put up with now and five years from now. People are creative; give them the money and materials, provide the technical support and information, and they will move forward toward a better life.

## JUST THE BEGINNING

For many of the contributors to this volume, work in Haiti is just getting under way. John Norton's organization, Development Workshop France (DWF), is working with Save the Children to establish safe building practices in a range of materials and site conditions. Robin Cross's Article 25 team is focused on schools, working with Outreach International and the Haitian Organization for Social Development of the Masses. The partners have completed a massive structural survey of thirty primary schools with secure land tenure. The three-year program will develop model building systems for sites in urban and rural settings to help the government replace the nearly 5,000 destroyed schools. Sergio Palleroni's BaSiC Initiative group has translated a self-build guide to confined masonry construction that is being taught in villages by teams from the Appropriate Infrastructure Development Group and Engineers Without Borders. They are also working with Swiss Cell on second-generation designs for houses that are simple and quick to put up, using factory-made panels. The partner architecture schools are currently running a design/build studio that will contribute to the DWF and Article 25 projects. Representing UN-Habitat, Maggie Stephenson is working with the World Bank on urban planning and recovery.

As I write, are there reasons for concern? Indeed. European nations are cutting funding for international development and aid that a few years ago would have been unthinkable. In times of economic pressure cuts are easier than strategic change. Using Haiti as its example, the European Commission is now stressing "greater efficiency" as a funding strategy; translated, this means that it is cheaper and easier to manage one grant, one contract, one audit (usually to a large organization) than to target and support smaller, highly innovative professional teams like many of those featured in this book. Local experience, international awards, outstanding records, low overhead, and the lasting benefits of cutting-edge best practices have little influence. Efficiency should mean getting excellent value for the money. Instead, some teams are struggling to maintain their presence in Haiti. Others have been told that they are so good that they will find funding elsewhere. This is distressing news.

Poor communities at risk face multiple problems, some emerging so quickly, at pace with rapidly changing weather patterns, that we cannot keep up with them. These communities deserve our best efforts, knowledge, and ingenuity.

They say catastrophic disaster is not inevitable; it is a failure of foresight. But that is not all. A catastrophe of the magnitude suffered by Haiti represents a failure to realize that we tend to value mercy more than dignity. The choice is a telling one. Mercy is neither just nor equitable.[4] Mercy favors emergencies. To ensure people's safety and foster their ability to prosper in the long term, dignity must be practiced as a human right. Haiti will be the measure of our success or failure to grasp the difference.

Notes
I thank all the contributors to this volume, but I am especially indebted to John Norton of Development Workshop France and Robin Cross of Article 25 for generously taking the time to help me better understand the current physical, institutional, and administrative challenges they face in Haiti, as their agencies help residents reconstruct their lives. I would also like to thank Maggie Stephenson of UN-Habitat, whom I count on to be honest and tough, for encouraging me to take the long view. It is easy to be overwhelmed or discouraged by the scale and number of challenges in Haiti. But we have powerful principles and excellent examples to guide built-environment professionals worldwide toward good decisions and better processes that include and will eventually be led by the Haitian people.

1   Estimates suggest that 661,000 people are living with host families, 604,000 in the countryside. Some villages and towns have grown by as much as one-third, putting a terrible strain on the existing infrastructure, water and sanitation capacities, and food supply, pushing some areas into extreme poverty. Nearly 162,000 people have moved to the northeast to Artibonite, itself a flood-prone region and where the current cholera outbreak first appeared. The government and strategists are hoping to encourage a substantial number of displaced people to stay in the countryside, but such decentralization will require tremendous economic and structural support.

2   At best, 31,656 transitional shelters can house 150,000 people, a fraction of those still in the camps.
In Port-au-Prince, for instance, proving land tenure, or ownership, is difficult because there are no longer any official records of who owns what. This question now rests on what sort of proof will be accepted as legal. Transitional settlement sites would require very large parcels. The government does not own enough such sites; the necessary land is privately owned, and there is no simple means of arranging for its temporary use. Land tenure issues in Haiti have long been problematic; they have been made that much worse by the earthquake.

3   The World Bank Global Facility for Disaster Reduction and Recovery (GFDRR) handbook *Safer Homes, Stronger Communities* has formalized tremendous progress in developing consensus among international financial institutions (IFI donors, such as the World Bank and International Monetary Fund), the United Nations, and major organizations involved in post-disaster reconstruction.

4   I owe an enormous debt to the philosophy of Mark Rowlands, who taught me the difference between mercy and dignity. For Rowlands the concept of dignity is essentially connected to that of flourishing. He observes that to respect the dignity of a being is to allow, and perhaps encourage, that being to flourish in the manner characteristic of the kind of being it is. He continues: "There are restrictions on the types of life in which a human can flourish, and there is a difference, an objective difference, between a human life that is flourishing and one that is not. Human flourishing is not simply a matter of alleviating suffering or augmenting pleasure, but of allowing humans to exercise their characteristic, perhaps distinctive, abilities. To respect human dignity, therefore, seems to involve the idea of putting people in a position not just to make choices but to make good ones. Typically, people are not in a position to make good choices when their very existence is under threat; and when the conditions in which these choices are made are seriously prejudicial, freedom counts for little. Good choices, choices that accurately and effectively allow us to bring our lives into line with our vision of how we would like them to be, can only be made from a position of safety; of bodily and emotional security." Mark Rowlands, "Human Dignity," 2010, courtesy of the author.

# AFTERWORD
# OPEN LETTER TO ARCHITECTS, ENGINEERS, AND URBANISTS

PATRICK COULOMBEL
DIRECTOR, ARCHITECTES
DE L'URGENCE, AMIENS, FRANCE

# I want to remind my colleagues of our ethical responsibilities.

It is the obligation of architects to provide dignified housing for the poorest communities, yet few architects have shown an interest in making such building the heart of their practice. In schools of architecture as well as in professional life, architects are trained to build all manner of lodgings—for those with the means to pay for their services. As a result the most beautiful, intelligent expressions of residential architecture are generally homes conceived for people of means at exorbitant cost. Ethically, it is appalling that architects remain uninterested in and *out of touch with* building for the most vulnerable and impoverished people. Entire countries, entire populations live precariously, day-to-day, in a perpetual state of emergency.

It is shocking that architects do not work to address the urgent needs of peoples touched by natural and humanitarian crises. We must find ways to house people after a disaster that are adapted to economic realities, local terrains and hazards, and available materials. We have the skills and expertise to do this. We should not forget that the foundation of our métier is to provide all people with a decent place to live.

Too few among us (and I am thinking particularly of the "star" architects who command the world's attention) have taken the time to consider the questions and challenges of emergency architecture. There are, of course, rare exceptions. Shigeru Ban has worked on projects that propose innovative solutions to the urgent problem of habitat. His paper-log do-it-yourself refugee shelters are beautiful and, in some contexts, effective, and provide an example of fresh, inventive thinking. Renzo Piano contributed to discussions of the rebuilding of historic Aquila, Italy, after the 2009 earthquake there.

Absurdly grandiose projects, designed and built by prominent architects, are splashed across the covers of architectural reviews and journals, but not a word is published about social-housing projects in the same countries. Media attention is typically given to such buildings only after a crisis, in the context of humanitarian action, and the narrative is often hijacked by particular political agendas.

At Architectes de l'Urgence (Emergency Architects) we realize that designing good housing for poor people is a highly technical practice—and very hard work. Architecture, construction, and urbanism are particularly complex technical domains that require deep professional knowledge. We must build functional homes and communities that are culturally pertinent, environmentally sound, affordable, and resistant to natural and created disasters, which affect poor communities disproportionately. Good solutions do exist, especially at the smaller scale. But these require careful analysis, research, development, and sound reasoning to become viable for mass production at an optimal cost. Who will step forward and do this work? Who has the expertise?

For more than thirty years generalists within humanitarian organizations have intervened to assist vulnerable populations, providing food, sanitation, water, and emergency shelters. Since professional architects, far from being preoccupied with humanitarian concerns, work mainly for the very rich, humanitarian organizations have been forced to carry out work that is complex and beyond their immediate competence, trying, with little means or funds, to provide people with shelter. With few expert technicians in the field, NGOs such as Doctors Without Borders and the Red Cross have done much of the work. They have done a remarkable job, considering that they are operating far outside of their areas of skill and training. But this is not enough.

Today, we architects must recognize our obligations and organize our strengths and talents to respond with professional expertise to the constant, urgent crises that confront people displaced by environmental hazards and conflict.

## RETHINKING ARCHITECTURAL TRAINING

Architecture schools are not unaware of the problem. Emergency shelter is a frequent subject for students. Typically, they take on a recent crisis or conflict that has been exploited in the media and generally they design something perfectly reasonable, architecturally. But they do so with little guidance or research, and so have absolutely no sense of how much their design would cost, especially when that cost is multiplied across the need. Nor do they take into account what the eventual costs in upkeep and maintenance would be for the people for whom their design is intended. For the most part their proposals would cost a fortune. These forays are only exercises in sentiment.

If students are not properly trained to make economics and other practical matters a part of their design practice, that failure continues after they are licensed. On the whole architects tend to work on prototypes completely dissociated from technical and economic realities. A simple statistic illustrates the point: the cost of an emergency shelter for a refugee family in Darfur is on the order of $250 and is expected to last about five years. Can an architect coming out of one of the world's excellent architecture schools create a good shelter on that budget? Will it be decent, culturally appropriate, durable, and safe? Will it be aesthetically pleasing, environmentally responsible, and ethically made?

Further, responding to a natural disaster is different from responding to conflict; it is easier to build an emergency shelter after a hurricane or earthquake than in a war zone. In war, problems of land use and land ownership are a constant preoccupation. Difficulties of transport, materials procurement, personal risk, and other variables affect all such projects. And good design on a tight budget and short construction schedule is hard—even harder when the design must be capable of being multiplied by the hundreds or thousands.[1]

Although it is necessary to be able to respond to an emergency with speed, short-term emergency shelter is not necessarily the best response. It is perhaps better to speak of *urgent reconstruction.* By this I mean rebuilding in a manner that is quick, durable, and permanent. In order to do this, humanitarian aid organizations need architects on staff and as consultants. And we need more NGOs, staffed by architects and engineers, whose primary role is to design and build shelter. Unlike most aid organizations, architectural NGOs have the technical know-how and the capacity to put long-term solutions in play, expanding the competence of the humanitarian groups with whom they partner. For example, an architect knows how to pass directly from the first emergency phase (tents, plastic sheeting) directly to semi-permanent or even permanent homes, without wasting time and money on interim shelters. At its best the process includes mitigating future risk while helping the affected local populations better understand their vulnerability.

After the 2007 earthquake in Jogjakarta, Indonesia, Architectes de l'Urgence demonstrated that it was perfectly realistic to reconstruct rapidly. We did so by engaging and training the local population to rebuild their own community with our guidance, assistance, and logistical skills. We followed two central principles: mitigate future risk and use local materials. We built fifty-three earthquake-resistant houses in two months.

## SUSTAINABLE DEVELOPMENT AND MASS EMERGENCIES

The architect has a responsibility not only to the residents who need new homes but also to the environment. Assessing the long-term implications of material procurement and selection is critical. A key protocol of emergency architecture is to make maximum use of local materials and building techniques that can be best adapted to the context, particularly since emergency projects may be on a very large scale. (But even small-scale projects should adhere to this rule!) Good architecture reduces the need for long-distance transport and thus environmental impact (as well as expense). Deforestation, as much as any tsunami or war, is a devastating emergency—one for which architects, builders, and emergency responders must take considerable responsibility. At Architectes de l'Urgence we try to integrate environmental priorities consis tently within the reconstruction program, from the outset; this includes producing local durable and sustainable resources for construction.

The scientific community is today unanimous that we are experiencing a significant change in the global climate. Among the effects of this are more powerful storms, rising sea levels, loss of indigenous plant and animal species, and accelerated desertification. All of these have architectural consequences. Already, enormous areas of land in Africa and Asia are undergoing desertification and there is a notable displacement of populations. As this problem increases, the greatest number of refugees will come from the poorest countries—those unable to provide solutions on their own.

Too few experts are working on assessing and preparing for the economic, social, and environmental impact that displaced populations will engender. Water is probably the resource that will be the most contested in coming years. To date, the question has been of little interest to architects and urbanists; they do not perceive themselves as having a role to play in prevention, mitigation, and response. This neglect is a death sentence for entire populations.

As ocean levels rise several meters by the end of the century, a direct consequence will be the ongoing displacement of coastal populations. Where are all these people going to live? What is going to become of Bangladesh? Of the Solomon Islands? Of the unique cultures of the great river deltas? How are we going to replace lost agricultural land?

The countries that will be the most affected by global climate change are those in the midst of development, with few resources. Rich countries will, however, feel the collateral effects of doing nothing, as they face the desperate thousands who will inevitably knock at their doors. Developing countries also suffer from the drain of educated and skilled workers, who leave for more secure careers in wealthier nations, depriving their homelands of their expertise.

In the west we are proud of these thinkers; we even boast of their role in advancing our progress. We are lifted on the shoulders of the most brilliant minds from the poorest nations. It is time, therefore, to put new partnerships in place. We cannot simply continue to attract the most promising students to our universities. On the contrary, we must send our most brilliant teachers to share their skills with countries in need. Just as universities need to develop architecture courses that teach students how to design for clients other than the wealthy, it is also necessary to create university courses for engineers, architects, and urbanists that teach them how to address the needs and cultures of developing countries.

## IN 2009 A BILLION PEOPLE WENT TO BED HUNGRY

Today, the earth is home to more than 6 billion people. For the past twenty years the number of people who could not feed themselves adequately was stable at around 800 million. Then in 2007 food prices began to soar, correlated to heavy speculation in the commodities markets, as well as increases in oil prices and droughts. By 2009 the number of people going hungry rose to above 1 billion, an increase of more than 20 percent in less than two years.[2] Worldwide food reserves are now diminished. In the event of a bad harvest rich countries will of course fare better than the poor, where starvation is already widespread.

At the same time, by 2050 the global population will have ballooned to nearly 10 billion people.[3] Today, we are incapable (given how we go about managing food production and distribution) of feeding 20 percent of the world's individuals. What are we planning to do when the population doubles? Climate change will reduce agricultural production along the oceans' coasts; how do we plan to compensate for this eventuality? And what, specifically, is the role of architects in this?

First, we must stop building on potentially productive agricultural lands. We need to urbanize in a different, denser, and more self-sustaining way. And it behooves us to develop many regional supply networks of sustainable, eco-friendly construction materials. Thus, architects and urbanists must stop being satisfied with serving narrowly self-interested private and corporate clients; policy makers in architecture, design, and construction must set standards and guidelines free from the short-term aims of politicians chained to election cycles. Let's demonstrate that we are capable of responsible design *today*, so that humanity will not judge us harshly in the coming decades.

## SAFEGUARDING BIODIVERSITY

Parallel with desertification and rising sea levels is the scourge of deforestation. The great forests are plundered day after day by individuals with few scruples; this is a catastrophe. The net loss of the world's forests is estimated at 32.1 million acres (13 million ha) per year.[4] We absolutely have to stop buying wood and materials harvested from the destruction of forests, which has become endemic, and stop building with exotic woods, which is entirely unnecessary.

Worse, when a primary forest has been destroyed, it becomes an enormous plantation for commercial agriculture—for products such as palm oil and soybeans. We cannot afford to increase agricultural lands by destroying forest ecosystems; we must, instead, reclaim and replant lands already cleared or wasted. Professional architects have a real role to play politically in helping to bring a logic and order to these responsibilities.

Supply networks for construction materials must be ecologically sound and must make the best use of available land, so that food production is not in competition with timber, clay, and stone production. We can assist farmers to develop networks of eco-construction materials. It is intolerable that simple solutions exist for shortages of eco-materials but are not employed. Every city on earth has waste ground—surfaces abandoned to arbitrary green space and poor-quality trees and shrubs. We need to retake leftover public spaces—for example, those along highways and train tracks, in empty lots and around industrial sites. In any given developed country of Europe, in every state of the US, there are thousands or tens of thousands of derelict, disused acres that could very well be put to good and productive use. Scrubland reclamation would not only provide materials close at hand, with a short supply chain, but would also contribute to and maintain biodiversity. Jaime Lerner, mayor of Curitiba, Brazil, and later governor of the state of Paraná, did just this. Trained as an architect, he developed a new master plan for the city, introducing efficient, inexpensive public transportation and incentives for recycling to combat waste problems, turning the downtown into a pedestrian mall and planting new parks. He did this in record time through "co-responsibility," in which everyone—unions, government, individual citizens—became involved. The project has become an example of enlightened urbanism.

Construction produces an immense volume of carbon emissions, but these can be reduced. Wherever possible we must build with materials that are sourced close to building sites;

a chain of well-organized local suppliers radically reduces the need to transport building materials over long distances.

For all this to work we cannot routinely impose western standards on the process without examining their validity and viability for the context we are addressing. In the west we tend to plan for safer-than-safe. That standard in many regions would be inappropriate, unnecessary, and prohibitive in cost. With advancing technologies in agriculture, energy, and construction it is possible to develop long-term and local solutions. But we architects and engineers will have to work assiduously to adapt these solutions to a wide range of contexts.

## DEMOGRAPHICS

Underpinning all the crises of climate change, natural disasters, armed conflict, and hunger, behind the bad policies and careless designs and inappropriate interventions lies a single, immense source of pressure: the constant and unmediated growth of the global population. The emergency that we face today is to feed and lodge the peoples of the world with dignity. When people are poorly fed and housed indecently they fall ill or into conflicts. Misery is crippling. It is our responsibility to take the necessary initiatives, to become the principal actors in the battle for the future.

Here are a few figures that underscore the gross imbalances with which we grapple. There are 1.2 million architects in the world, an enormous pool of competence that is underused and poorly distributed. In Chad, a country more than three times the size of California, there are only twenty architects; in France, with about half that land area, there are more than 50,000 professional architects.[5]

## URGENTIST ARCHITECTS

At Architectes de l'Urgence, in the course of responding to numerous natural catastrophes and wars, we have created the profession of *urgentist architect*. Initially, we just provided shelter in emergencies in whatever way seemed best at the time, but now, after years in the field, we are testing ways to respond to the needs and challenges of post-disaster reconstruction that are durable and lasting. And we have developed a list of core rules: to reconstruct for the long term with local materials; to introduce ideas of future mitigation into present projects; to work directly with affected populations; to use techniques that we—architects and engineers—ourselves are capable of putting in place. These are our first principles.

As I see it, the profession of architecture must be reinvented to embrace a commitment to solving these fundamental problems of civil life. This new profession is generated out of the combined forces of architects, manufacturers, logicians, construction workers, sociologists, historians, and so on—in a word, urgentists of all stripes. In effect this is a new approach to working, one that relies on real complementarity and collaboration among professions.

Ironically, in the west thousands of architects are having trouble finding work. I speak to you directly: you are more or less well trained and whether you know it or not, you have the competence to help countries move toward better development. I invite you all to contribute your talents and abilities to developing countries. The task is enormous and the context and conditions unfamiliar. But we have the means if we have the will. If we are to be truly useful as architects we will have to convey and practice different values. This is the challenge facing architects worldwide in the twenty-first century.

Notes

1   The scale can be vast: 630,000 homes were needed in the countryside of Kashmir after the 2005 earthquake there; in Haiti the 2 million people displaced by the 2010 earthquake will need 500,000 homes.

2   "The food price crisis of 2007–08 had several causes—rising demand for food, the change in the food equation through biofuels, climate change, high oil prices—but there is substantial evidence that the crisis was made worse by the malfunctioning of world grain markets." See Miguel Robles, Maximo Torero, and Joachim von Braun, *When Speculation Matters*, IFPRI Issue Brief 57 (Washington, DC: International Food Policy Research Institute, February 2009). See also press release, Food and Agricultural Organization of the United Nations, June 19, 2009, at www.fao.org/news/story/en/item/20568/icode/, accessed August 10, 2010; and BBC News website, "The Cost of Food: Facts and Figures," October 16, 2008, at http://news.bbc.co.uk/2/hi/in_depth/7284196.stm, accessed August 10, 2010.

3   US Census Bureau statistics at www.census.gov/ipc/www/idb/worldpopgraph. php, accessed August 10, 2010.

4   "Deforestation—mainly the conversion of tropical forests to agricultural land—shows signs of decreasing in several countries but continues at a high rate in others. Around 13 million hectares [32 million acres] of forest were converted to other uses or lost through natural causes each year in the last decade compared to 16 million hectares [39.5 million acres] per year in the 1990s." See *Key Findings: Global Forest Resources Assessment 2010* (Rome: Forestry Department, Food and Agricultural Organization of the United Nations, 2010), at http://foris.fao.org/static/data/fra2010/KeyFindings-en.pdf, accessed August 10, 2010.

5   Land-area data are from the *CIA World Factbook* at www.cia.gov/library/publications/the-world-factbook, accessed August 10, 2010; data on architects are from the Académie d'Architecture, Paris, and Entreprise Tchadienne d'Architecture et de Construction.

Haiti after the earthquake, 2010